BETTER PLAY

BETTER PLAY

Practical strategies for supporting play
for children of all ages in schools

Alison Woolf

Worth Publishing

First published 2016 by Worth Publishing Ltd
www.worthpublishing.com

Printed and bound in Great Britain by TJ International, Padstow, Cornwall

British Library Cataloguing in Publication Data
A catalogue record for this book is available from the British Library

ISBN   9781903269268

Text design by Anna Murphy

For my parents

Biography

Alison Woolf B.Ed., MA in Play Therapy, Full Member BAPT, is an educator and therapist, and has worked as a teacher and Play Therapist in a variety of school and education settings as well as working as a Filial Therapist in a Local Authority Post-Adoption Support team. She is a registered clinical supervisor with the British Association of Play Therapists and Co-director of a training and therapy company, and teaches at Glyndwr University on undergraduate and graduate programmes.

After many fulfilling years teaching and playing in Mainstream Nursery classes Alison re-trained as a Play Therapist and began work within the Alternative Learning Needs sector. As a therapist she worked in settings for pupils with different learning needs in both Primary and Secondary schools, before moving into tertiary education, where as a lecturer in Play and Creative Therapies, she teaches on both Counselling and Education programmes. In this role it is also possible to combine both her qualifications and to teach education students counselling skills for use in Education.

Outside of school work Alison trained and worked as a Filial Therapist, training parents in therapeutic play skills to support family cohesion, and in particular supporting fosterers and adopters to build relationships with their children. Since then she and her dog have also trained in Animal Assisted Play Therapy. This brings together all of her interests in the power of play, the impact of attachment relationships on our wellbeing and the role for animals in developing trust, confidence and self-esteem in humans of any age who may be at risk of exclusion.

Acknowledgements

To: My family - my love of playing grew from my own experience of growing up in a playful family.

The children I have had the privilege of working alongside and who brought to life everything I have learned about play in school settings.

Cris Ford, for showing me the sort of teacher I wanted to be.

The educators I have shared classrooms with, and who enriched the joy of playing at work. Rachel Edwards was an inspiration at work and the most fun, both in and out of school. Val Hall, Lisa Drayton, Denise Seddon and Rita Everitt each made a day at work a day at play. All the staff at Willow Grove School for everything I learned through working with them - and for being such playful companions. Without the support of Valda Pearson I would not have developed my therapy practice in school and would never have written this book.

Rise VanFleet who not only taught me the skills I needed to work with families and animals, but she has always given me the self-belief I needed to go on and use those skills in the workplace. And Chris Taylor who has supervised my play therapy practice with warmth and wisdom.

Thank you to Andrea Perry for reminding me to be playful in my writing and being the person that helped playing with the ideas in the book be both challenging and fun. And to Anna Murphy for translating the playfulness into print so beautifully.

Lastly to those I play out with; for all the laughter, cups of tea and friendship, Jane, Anne, Jane, Dee, Carol and my 'partner in crime'- Della Austin, and my partner in life - John Knox. You are all evidence that we never stop playing!

Throughout the book you will meet children and adolescents who help us to understand the world of their play. Sometimes I use vignettes to illustrate the ideas that we are thinking about. These are composite cases based on my experience in schools and at play. They are not actual events or children but they are, nonetheless, 'true' representations of play and play relationships.

> Ethnographic fiction (see Banks & Banks, 1998; Clough, 2002) is a narrative form in which fictional stories, which could be true, are told within an accurate cultural/social framework.
> **Wellington, J., Bathmaker, A., Hunt, C., McCulloch, G. & Sykes, P.** (Eds) 2005, *Succeeding with Your Doctorate*, London: SAGE Publications Ltd pp.157-8

Contents

Continues /...

SAFEGUARDING

In all our work and play in schools the National Guidance and the individual school policy on Safeguarding are our framework for keeping children safe. When children talk (or play) and we listen our responsibilities are clear. We are used to the ethical and legal complexities of sharing and withholding information in line with our responsibilities and the rights of children and families.

As our relationships develop through play or through the use of enhanced communication skills we can hold in mind the set of principles that ensure we adhere to policy and procedures, 'do right' by our children, and maintain our professional integrity:

● *Know the legal and organisational requirements relevant to child protection work*

● *Hold values consistent with the pursuit of social justice and equality*

● *Practice in ways that embody integrity and relational practice (duty of care, respect and justice)*

Embrace personal reflection and reflexivity to assist in the practitioner's development and organisational learning.

Lonne, B., Harries, M., Featherstone, B., & Gray, M. (2015)
Working Ethically in Child Protection London: Routledge

Introduction

"There might as well be no colour if you can't play!"

The thoughts of a child *in* Kapasi & Gleave 2009, p.18

Yes - that is so very, very right! I could never have explained play this well: thank you, you wise and poetic child. My case for the importance of play is now already made, thanks to the ability of one who really knows to wrap up a complicated and philosophical argument in 11 words. But I do have a lot more to share with you about play and how it colours our lives and our world.

Play is amazing!

I don't want to contemplate life in a world with no colour, and I'm sure that the thought sends shivers through you too. What would anyone choose if there were a choice to be made? A Technicolor play-full world? Or a play-less monochrome existence? Luckily we mostly have play in our lives; so this book is more about reflecting on the types of play we offer our children, and about the time and the space we give over to play in homes and streets, and particularly what we can offer in our schools.

Players are doing amazing things!

Increasing time for play and getting better at supporting play means we can offer opportunities for pupils to learn what no-one else can teach them. *Better play* develops better relationships, leads to better communication and creates better communities. When we have a better understanding of -

➡   the nature of the behaviour we call play

➡   the role of free play in child development

➡   the impact of our adult interventions on play

- we *notice* more and are inclined to *do* less.

People who know about play are amazed by it!

This book brings together a lot of current thought about play and makes links between new knowledge about play and how we in schools can create richer play experiences for our pupils. Following the theory come some ideas for our practice. One reason for this book is to bring ideas from other professions into our schools, so we can know more about *why play matters* and have new ideas about how to respond when play happens.

Throughout the text, whether looking at theory or workplace practice, as well as considering the question *"Why play?"*, I will introduce you to experts who answer the question: *"What if we don't play?"* A lot of the understanding we now have about the role of play in our lives comes from experts in the field of animal studies.

A few amazing play facts

For bears, meerkats, horses and hyenas, plentiful play experiences increase brain size and improve the chances of survival into adulthood and beyond. In rats and primates, play increases social integration and relieves anxiety and stress in social groups. In the animal kingdom, better outcomes for individuals and for groups are directly linked to play. Many researchers on animal behaviours don't believe that mammals play because they are young; instead, they believe that mammals have an extended period of immaturity in order to give them more opportunities and time for play. Play is *that* important to success and wellbeing in animals that live in social groupings. And that means social animals like us.

In schools we are in the business of brain development and social integration. So while we nurture our young during their extended period of immaturity, let's give play the chance to do some of our hard work for us.

Playing better: *What's in it for me?*

Reading this book I hope you will learn why play is the child's natural medium for finding out what the world can offer them, and what they can offer the world. And why this makes snatched moments of playfulness or hours devoted to play, time well spent in the education of our children.

The research and knowledge we have gained over the last decade about play and the brain, play and social inclusion, and play and emotional wellbeing in animals, both use the term 'play' to mean activities freely entered into, with no externally set goals or outcomes. But in education terminology, the word play refers to both *adult planned and directed activities*, and *adult supervised child-led activities* alike. This broad and generalised use of the term has made it more difficult for practitioners to know which particular benefits 'play' is providing to children in our schools.

As the text takes you through sections devoted to different areas of play and to specific skills that we use when we provide for it, you will see examples from the last decade where politicians, educationalists, medical professionals and academics have all acknowledged the importance of play, both for individuals and for society.

You will also hear how policy makers, practitioners and social commentators acknowledge the current deficiency of the right play opportunities. Their comments on the what, who and where of how to meet the play needs of our children and communities are sometimes less clear and harder to find.

My aim is that *Better Play* will be a guide for everyone working with children in schools who wants to understand more about play and how to provide better play experiences for the pupils in their care. I'll be introducing you to current research that explains how play can improve outcomes for everyone and I'll be presenting practical knowledge and skills that we can all use to develop better play opportunities across the school day.

So now, as the creator of Winnie the Pooh might say:

… perhaps the best thing to do is to stop writing Introductions and get on with the book.

From the introduction to: Milne, A. (1938) *Winnie the Pooh*

(Twentieth Edition) London: Methuen & Co Ltd

Better play

SECTION 1 : WHAT IS PLAY?

Chapter 1

Better play for all

I have been lucky enough to work at play and to play at work all my professional life. As a child I played at being a teacher, with teddies and dolls arranged on the staircase; then, as an adult, I played *as* a teacher with children who were not so ready to sit still and listen!

Later on my understanding of how I could provide play in a different way developed through training to be a play therapist. I had thought I had 'arrived' in terms of play expertise, but I was lucky to find out that there are many more facets to the simply named phenomenon of 'play' than my education training had taught me. My journey of discovery continues as I work and play and read and hear more and continue to listen to pupils and clients who are younger and wiser than I am.

In writing this book I am drawing together the threads of my knowledge, the colours of my experience and the texture of my play life, in order to create a picture of the joy and the power of play. This picture is not a one-dimensional canvas to be looked at, but more an invitation to join in; and like the child at play, to colour over, glue together and create a vibrant collage. A living work of art with spilling-over edges, and a definite air of unfinished-ness!

We will begin the journey by thinking about what we know and believe about play.

THE QUESTIONS TO CONSIDER ARE:

WHAT IS PLAY?

What do we mean when we say the word 'play'?

PLAY IS …

How do play writers and researchers define and describe their understanding of play?

PLAYTIME IS …

When we talk about playtime, we often mean the bits between lessons in school, or 'recess', as American schools call it. But can any time be playtime when you know what you're looking for?

LETTING THE CHILD DECIDE

One way to know when action is play and when time is playtime is when a child has decided that 'This time is my time, and I am going to play!'

Does a child's belief about whether or not they are playing make a difference to their enjoyment and their learning?

Let's start the outline of our picture with the obvious question:

WHAT IS PLAY?

"I like playing with my brother - pushing him around in the laundry basket, that's my favourite game. I don't know what it's called; just the 'pushing my brother around in the laundry basket' game."

Six-year-old boy, IPA Scotland 2011, p.2

And what a game that must be! It feels like an innovative game, unique to these two brothers; while at the same time being a timeless activity handed down across generations. The only resource needed, the laundry basket, just standing around waiting to be discovered as a transporter of children. Just like the empty box that the toys came in: just add kids - stand back - and let the magic begin.

I'd agree that the opposite of play is depression (Sutton-Smith, 2001; Brown, 2009). But the joy of playing does not mean a player is not sad, angry, frustrated or disappointed. Play is ambiguous and contradictory.

Play: energises

develops understanding

sets us free

And it: soothes

creates uncertainty

encourages participants to keep the rules

Play is fun and it is serious in turns or in tandem. The nature of play may be paradoxical but it is irrefutable that play is *vital*. Vital (The Free Dictionary 2013) means:

of, relating to, or characteristic of life

necessary to the continuation of life; life-sustaining

full of life; animated

imparting life or animation; invigorating

necessary to continued existence or effectiveness; essential

No ambiguity there: play is most certainly vital. It's vital to each individual, any organisation, and every community. It's vital to the *quality* of life and increasingly recognised as contributing to the *quantity* of life - we are learning that playful adults *feel* better and *are* healthier.

Some studies indicate that playfulness is a positive contributor to healthy ageing (Yarnal & Qian, 2011; Proyer, 2013). Other research suggests that people living in Britain, have 'shorter - and more unhealthy - lives than residents of most other European countries' (Boseley, 2013). Boseley offers ten ways for ageing Brits to 'buck the trend'. These include the usual advice on eating healthily, drinking in moderation, not smoking and taking plenty of exercise. But she also advises us to, 'move to Japan'; 'stay out of hospital'; 'don't get stressed' and 'live in the south of England, not the North'. 'Be playful' might be a less drastic and more achievable maxim! To qualify as play, an activity should be:

SPONTANEOUS
fluid and without a predetermined goal
unpredictable
OPEN TO CHANGE OR DIVERSION
responsive to the moment
FREE TO BE STOPPED OR WITHDRAWN FROM AT ANY TIME

see Hughes 2012, p.78 & Lester & Russell 2008, p.42

The laundry basket game has all of these elements, as well as the social play skills of cooperation and collaboration. The game also sounds as though it could be a bit risky (another of Hughes' essential qualities of play), and above all, fun. Not that play has to be fun in order to be play, but we will return to that misconception later.

Am I playing?

Do you and I still play or act playfully, despite our age or desire to be taken seriously? When did you last doodle? Affectionately tease? Try on a dress or a tie you were *never* going to buy or to wear? How often do you sing or dance when you know no-one is looking? Balance on kerbs or jump over cracks in the pavement, just because you feel like it? I know I both sing and dance when I'm dusting or hoovering and I skip and I hop because the sun is shining and I just have to celebrate.

So ... am I playing? Mark Twain coined one of the probably best known definitions of play (1992, p.14):

> *Work consists of whatever a body is obliged to do, and ...*
> *play consists of whatever a body is not obliged to do.*

I guess this is certainly *one* answer to the question - *'What is play?'* What else are people saying play is? Let's consider some other ideas about its nature. Within our school context in the UK, I believe that Early Years Education has clouded many of our ideas about play. The Montessori notion that 'the child becomes a person through work' has led educators to plan for the play of children in school *as if* play were work. But Elkind (2007), among many others, insists 'play is not work, nor is work play' and that prominent educators such as Montessori, are wrong to say 'play is the child's work'. Brooker (2011, p.162) feels that it is:

> ... time to acknowledge that we need a new term to describe the activities-
> based, adult-inspired and 'potentially instructive' tasks which practitioners
> so diligently and creatively organise for the children in their classrooms.
> We could then return 'play' to its original status as an activity which is
> voluntary, goal-less, [and] spontaneous.

Elkind (2007) also suggests that play is a 'healthy counterpoise' to work. Later I'll be exploring whether play and work are opposing activities, interdependent activities, or are threads that intertwine through all our actions and thoughts, particularly in Chapters 8, 11 and 12.

PLAY IS:

Tina Bruce (2005, p.261) named 12 features of play she believes are essential for the play to be termed as 'free flow'. The first three, about what '*it*' is, are listed below;

- *It is an active process without a product*
- *It is intrinsically motivated*
- *It exerts no external pressure to conform to rules, pressures, goals, tasks or definite directions*

Driven by unconscious thoughts or feelings, play emerges or erupts. As an idea takes shape, it is clear to anyone watching that the child or children are carrying out 'a job that 'needs doing' (Brooker 2011, p.160). How often do we ask a child or young person *"Why did you do that?"* *"Dunno"* may be the most frequent answer; and rightly so: the reason for a sudden playful moment, or hours of apparently 'fruitless' activity', is *"... because it had to be done."* *"What made you do that?"* is another question we often ask. Not every child is aware of their 'intrinsic' motivation; or able to express such a difficult thing to work out or understand.

When Frank, aged 11, was asked the question *"How do you choose what to play?"* he answered in his own words: that he chooses in response to *"...something what tells me to go over there."* (Woolf 2009, p.10). Presumable the 'what' he describes is his inner voice, his internal drive, his innate wisdom that the chosen play will meet some momentary or long-term need. In Chapter 16 we will look at how replacing our questions to children with new ways of waiting and noticing what happens can develop the child's language and processing skills, and often also improve our relationship with them.

Another of Bruce's (2005, p.261) features of free flow play is that 'it is about possible, alternative worlds'. Play is *'What if…?'*, or *'As if…'*. Children sometimes feel the need to reassure adults that they are 'just pretending'. *"I'm not really a lion - I'm just pretending."* All that roaring and growling is Jess, acting *'as if'* she were a lion protecting her cubs. Animals also signal that they want to enter a play world, in other words, to pretend. The play bow of a dog is saying 'what follows is play' (Bekoff & Allen, 1997), *'let's pretend to fight'*. *'Let's pretend…'* is a frequent invitation to play between peers. *'Let's pretend'* is the doorway to an 'alternative world', a world of possibilities, the only place where anything truly is possible.

> The first person he met was Rabbit.
> *"Hallo Rabbit,"* [Pooh] said *"is that you?"*
> *"Let's pretend it isn't,"* said Rabbit, *"and see what happens."*
>
> A.A. Milne (1938, p.110)

Play is exploration. Play is a way of finding out. Finding out *'what if…?'* The unique thing about pretend or imaginative play is that, if Rabbit does not like pretending to not be Rabbit, he can reveal himself to Pooh with a flourish of triumph: *"Ta Da! Fooled you! I am Rabbit!"* and the game can be over. Or the drama may go off in another direction when Pooh counter-claims *"But I am not Pooh!"* Possibly Rabbit may find out in this game of *'what if'* that he rather likes being somebody else. Then he might try being different again, and maybe get used to being a bit more like Tigger or Piglet sometimes.

The amazing thing about play is that you may discover something you didn't know was there to be discovered. What other activity affords such potential for changing our understanding of the world or of ourselves? Early Years Educator Pat Broadhead describes a child's play as: 'their self-actualization, a holistic exploration of who and what they are and know and of who and what they might become' (2004, pp.122-3). Anne Cattanach (1993, p.47) agrees that 'play is a journey of self-discovery for the child … a way of making sense of the past, present and future'.

So when do we get these opportunities for discovery and development? What makes time for play different to other times?

PLAYTIME IS:

Playtime generally is safe time during which transgressions are accepted by others especially when one player is a youngster.

Bekoff & Allen 2002, p.435

Playtime is a place for animals where errors do not cost lives. The misjudged play bite does not usually lead to play fights becoming real fights. Animals make allowances. Mistakes are survived and learned from. We all make mistakes and playtimes are the best place to make them (there is much more to come in Chapter 3 about the benefits of play-fighting and of the unique advantage of having a chance to 'get it wrong' in rough play). 'Play is a process of trial and error in which the error is as valuable to learning as is the success' (Hughes 2012, p.281). Just as the scientist undertakes a process of *'What if's?'* and has far more 'failures' than 'successes' on the road to his groundbreaking discovery, so the player alters, adapts, repeats and refines until meaning becomes clear or the tower is built. I'll consider play as scientific exploration and science as playful imagining of possibilities in more depth in Chapter 11.

The time for play can be fleeting or extensive so our 'journey' can be as short or as long as time allows or as the fancy takes us. It is like the city tour guide bus: hop on, hop off, there will be another chance to rejoin the trip later. Children hopping on and off the play-bus may not be evident to us, or indeed in the conscious awareness of the child.

Because a time is called 'playtime' it does not mean all, or any, of the time is spent at play. Also playtime can happen during non-playtime, and in our school language of differentiated timetables and daily structures and routines, some activities may not be 'playing', even though they are happening during time-tabled 'playtime'!

Playing when you should be playing?

The Oxford online dictionary has two definitions of play: to 'engage in activity for enjoyment and recreation rather than a serious or practical purpose'; and: to 'take part in (a sport)' and to 'perform on (a musical instrument)'. Hughes (2012) believes that 'if the activity is bounded by adult rules, if it is stiff, formalised and dominated by the need to score points and flatter one's ego, that is not play, it is something else' (p.325), while according to developmental psychologist, Jerome Bruner, play is an approach rather than an activity. It's not what you do, it's the way that you do it that makes an action 'playing'. Football might not be playing when you are a David Beckham. Tennis may not be playing when you are a Serena Williams; but it is certainly playing when I kick or bat a ball round the garden with my dog. So the one word 'playing' has to describe and give meaning to two very different actions or ideas.

So when does football as play, become football as work? When you get paid a small, or rather large, fortune every week to do it? Or when you train until it hurts? When you *have* to play, *have* to win, *have* to behave a certain way and *have* to do as you are told? Can 'have to' ever be words associated with play? Back to Mark Twain again; play is anything 'you don't have to do'. Play as a process is not concerned with goals, aims, rules and boundaries of time and space, unless the player decides that it is (*see* p.45).

The very essence of what play is … the self-evolving movement into somewhere we do not know in advance.   Hae-Ryung Yeu 2011, p.129

Not possible if you cannot go over the lines, outside the area or, a typical play strategy, change sides half-way through the game! But my ability to 'play' while not playing, or to play while 'playing' by the rules or playing to the music, offers opportunities for the ambiguity and paradox of play that Brian Sutton-Smith (2001) writes about.

The notion of playing in both of its meanings is illustrated in an iconic sketch from the *Morecambe and Wise Show* (BBC 1971). Eric Morecambe, much loved British comedian, is trying to play Grieg's piano concerto. The accomplished and award-winning musician, André Previn, is conducting him.

Previn   *You're playing all the wrong notes.*

Morecambe   *No. I'm playing all the right notes. But not necessarily in the right order.*

The two are 'playing' with the word playing!

Play is comprised of sequences in which players switch rapidly between well-controlled movements similar to those used in 'serious' behavior and movements that result in temporary loss of control.

Bekoff, *in* Huffington Post Blog 2011

If we agree with Mark Bekoff, then 'playing' Grieg's concerto is not play, unless the 'player' allows him or herself to go in un-anticipated and novel directions. That's probably something which isn't going to happen if an audience has paid to attend a night of the Proms in the Royal Albert Hall. Yehudi Menuhin, one of the greatest ever violinists, acknowledged the tension between playing and playing: *"I would hate to think I am not an amateur. An amateur is one who loves what he is doing"* (undated, en.wikiquote.org). A professional has external pressure to perform. An amateur plays because they want to.

Even the most consummate professional may have started off playing playfully. Playing golf is a different thing to playing *with* golf. Tiger Woods (2013) reminisced how he used to 'throw golf balls in the trees and try and somehow make par from them'. Novel, presumably spontaneous and intrinsically motivated - in other words - play. Woods had a goal, but he made up his own game, the *getting the ball in the hole from up in a tree in a certain number of shots* game. This challenge reflects another of the attributes of play;

> … children who play are constructing an edifice of constraints which, in making play more difficult, makes it more worthwhile.
>
> Brooker 2011, p.156

Defining play in terms of activity does not allow for personal preferences, attitudes beliefs and abilities. For example, I can play for hours in my house because I like cleaning, I like cooking and I *love* rearranging the furniture. I live in a life-size doll's house, my own 3D SimCity. Others find housework a completely play-free zone, where cooking is a chore, cleaning is a duty and wherever the removal men put the sofa down is fine by them. The time and the place turn play into work and chores into play. Getting paid to bake and decorate a wedding cake by Friday is one thing: looking in the cupboard, picking out whatever catches your eye and creating a new sort of cupcake, just because you can, is another.

LETTING THE CHILD DECIDE

Play can be conceptualised as activities that are chosen by the child, that are identified by the child as play and the child engages in them playfully.

Sturgess 2009, p.22

Maybe the best way to define play is to let the child decide whether it feels like play or not? Certainly a child's perception of school activities as play can have a big impact on their success at school and their enjoyment of school. In one study of young school children's attitudes about play, the children who called almost everything they did 'play' were found at the end of adolescence to be more successful and happier at school than those who called almost everything they did 'work' (Kemp et al 2013). This finding was confirmed in 2013 by Howard & McInnes, who found that children who undertook an activity that they recognised as 'like play' scored higher on a measurement of emotional wellbeing than those children who undertook the same activity when they identified it as 'not like play'. This is hugely significant and exciting for those of us who are passionate about the value of play. It affirms our belief that children not only want, or rather, *need* to play but also that play re-frames things for them and makes them more 'vital'.

· ·

and so ...

And remember that if the behaviour is not play, 'any benefits that are said to come from playing, will not apply'   (Hughes 2012, p.78).

KEY POINTS

> *Play is anything we don't have to do*
>
> *Play is unpredictable, surprising and follows its own path*
>
> *Play cannot be planned, directed by an external adult, or have a pre-determined outcome or be right or wrong*
>
> *Play is the way we explore and discover*
>
> *Play is the answer to uncertainty. It is the way to answer the questions 'What if ... ?'*

What is play? *Where do we go from here?*

In order for changes in practice to take place in line with the position statement of the Play England *Play in Schools and Integrated Settings* (2008), the following developments need to take place in government policy. The position statement recommends:

Government provides guidance to local authorities and all primary and secondary schools on minimum standards to provide for children's free play needs before, after and during the school day, including a minimum allocation of time for break-times and lunchtimes.

Playwork training, qualifications and an understanding of playwork principles should be available to all adults who interact with children and young people in the non-curriculum part of the school day.

Government encourages schools to use a whole school approach to develop and implement successful play policies as suggested in the National Union of Teachers (NUT) play policy, *Time to Play* (NUT 2007).

Government encourages schools and integrated children's settings to nominate a senior manager to promote and secure quality play opportunities and develop playwork skills of staff.

from Play England, 2008, *Play in Schools and Integrated Settings: A position statement* London: NCB

The play-full school would -

☺   Have a member of the Senior Leadership Team responsible
    for play in school

☺   Have at least one member of staff who is a trained Playworker

☺   Have annual whole school training in the evolving understanding
    of the nature of play

☺   Have a whole school play policy covering indoor and outdoor
    provision, and curricular and extra-curricular opportunities for play

☺   Dedicated play time for school staff, and why not school governors too!

If you want to know more, try reading

Sutton-Smith B. (2001) *The Ambiguity of Play* Cambridge, Mass: Harvard University Press

Woolf, A. (2009) Providing Therapeutic Play for the Whole School: An undertaking of 'EPIC' proportions. *British Journal of Play Therapy*, Vol. 5 pp.4-22 BAPT

If you want to understand more, try reading

Ravin Lodding, L. (Author) & Beaky, S.(Illustrator), (2011) *The Busy Life of Ernestine Buckmeister* New York: Flashlight Press

If you want a 15 minute group or individual training, try watching

Stuart Brown's 2008 TED talk *'Play is more than just fun'*

Ted talks can be found on the TED (Technology, Entertainment and Design) website ted.com/talks or on youtube.com

Chapter 2

Why play?

"If children don't play it makes them yuk and boring".

So reported an observant member of a focus group of children aged between seven and 14 in Kapasi & Gleave's 2009 *Because It's Freedom* report (p.18). Can I just add, *"... if we adults don't play, we get to be yuk and boring too"*! So why do humans and animals play? What does play do for us and for children in particular? And what happens if we don't play?

Having thought a bit about what play is, and what the word means, in this chapter we'll be looking at what the act of playing might be doing for the child. I think if we naturally give lots of time and energy to play, especially when we're young and our bodies are growing and our brains are learning the most, then it shows that the hours and calories given over to play must be doing something for us, and I'll explore this. And if there isn't enough time for play, might we be missing out - on not only immediate benefits, but long-term gains as well?

I agree that a person without play would be boring (and probably bored as well). I think I play for many, many reasons: to wake myself up and to calm myself down; to fill time and to extend time; to find out new things and to remember old things. And I also feel that if I had a day without play I would be bored as well as boring!

In this chapter we will think about the reasons for play.

THE QUESTIONS TO CONSIDER ARE:

WHY DO WE PLAY?
WHAT ARE THE PAY-OFFS OF TIME SPENT PLAYING?
WHAT DOES PLAY DO FOR US?

Looking in more detail, how does play develop health and wellbeing in the following seven areas? (there are others too, and I expect you will feel I've missed some that you would include!):

Building resilience   Adaptability for survival

Emotional regulation   Developing social skills

Being able to communicate   Building better bodies

Play as social lubricant or 'ice-breaker'

After thinking about some of the important - no - rather essential - reasons we play, it will be time to think about -

WHAT HAPPENS IF WE DON'T PLAY?

If play is doing so much for our all-round development, what might happen if play opportunities are missing? How are our feelings and behaviours impacted when we just don't get enough of all the good things that time spent playing can give us?

WHY DO WE PLAY?

Do you feel better if you play? Or maybe you sometimes feel surprised when you notice that you've been playing? Is play something you recognise as a necessity for us adults? Or do you regard it as a 'guilty pleasure'?

Experts in animal behaviour are amongst those grappling with the questions *"What is play?"* and then *"Why do we do it?"* Some researchers suggest there is no immediate benefit, but that looking over time, benefits may be easier to see.

Neuroscientists looking at the brains of animals and humans identify which parts are involved in play. In both areas of study, social bonding is linked to play (*and see below*, p.45). Stuart Brown (2009), amongst many others, believes that animals, including humans, play because it firstly increases chances of survival, and secondly, improves quality of life. Both these reasons for play apply to the individual and to the group. Play has benefits for physical, cognitive, emotional and social development. Play also develops group cohesion.

As adults charged with the care and education of our children, we are bound to be interested in why children play. As educators, we need to know what knowledge and skills are developed by playing and why play is a powerful medium for learning. As carers, we need to understand why health and happiness are supported by play and why play is a protective factor for emotional wellbeing. So in this chapter, I'm going to consider the underpinning evidence we draw on as advocates and ambassadors for play.

Play has important rewards for individuals and communities.

People who play develop many atributes and capacities:

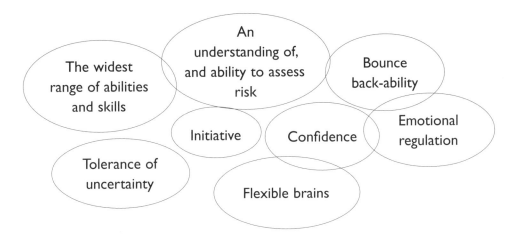

Play develops resilience and good mental health. Or, in other words, people who play become 'rounded, educated individuals'.

The characteristics above look like ideal personal attributes to include in a job application. Or the things I might look for in a friend. Certainly the list would persuade me to enrol my child in a school with these as part of a mission statement for the entire school community. My guess is that if you think of outcomes of schooling you'd want for your child, or personal attributes you might look for in a friend, that the things that first spring to your mind are also outcomes of play. So let's look at some of them in more detail.

WHAT DOES PLAY DO FOR US?

The opposite of play ... is vacillation, or worse, it is depression.

Sutton-Smith, 2001, p.198

The Mental Health Foundation (1999, p.6) identifies 'unsupervised' play as an important activity for supporting good mental health. The Foundation reports that play allows the child to experience risk-taking and decision-making, thereby increasing resilience and confidence. The report acknowledges the value to human wellbeing of the ability to 'initiate, develop and sustain mutually satisfying personal relationships'. Brown (2009) and Bekoff (2002) talk of animal 'play cues' as invitation to relate through play; while DeBenedet & Cohen (2010, p.16) explain how 'during play, animals and humans need to constantly communicate with each other. Verbal and non-verbal play cues convey the message *"Don't get upset with me if I mess up; this is still play"* (this is a special attribute of playtime as I described in Chapter 1, and I'll return to it in Chapter 3). Attuning to others through play builds realistic relationships that tolerate and survive the accidental knocks of close contact; both physical and emotional. Cohen (2001) not only recognises the role of play in strengthening and maintaining relationships; he also believes that play is the best way to repair relationships. When a friend says sorry and you graciously accept, the initial repair is in place; but the connection is restored when you feel safe enough to tease each other, deliberately bump and jostle each other or trade affectionate insults that say *"You know and I know, this is play; and we can do this now because we trust each other again"*.

The ability of play to repair relationships leads to resilient relationships that can, and have, survived fall-outs and misunderstandings. Knowing that repair is possible, and that bad and difficult things can be turned around or resolved, increases our resilience to knocks and emotional bruises.

Building resilience

Resilience is the basis for good mental health, or indeed, for robust communities.

> Resilience is the process of adapting well in the face of adversity, trauma, tragedy, threats, or even significant sources of stress - such as family and relationship problems, serious health problems, or workplace and financial stressors. It means 'bouncing back' from difficult experiences.
>
> American Psychological Association, 2014 (www.apa.org)

Resilient people and resilient communities can recover from knockbacks, weather the highs and lows of life, roll with the punches and have an underlying stability that keeps them going when the going gets tough. Resilient people face life with a sense of optimism and equilibrium. They have 'poise' as Stuart Brown (2009) explains, a sense of balance in life. The equilibrium which can come from play experiences of conquering fears and beating the odds gives us the ability to meet the unexpected with a calm sense of hope. Poise and a sense of balance in life - what a great aim for educating the whole person to become a happy, healthy, successful member of society! It is by becoming used to, and tolerant of uncertainty and surprise through play that we become resilient to experiences, and grow into assured adults who together create stable communities.

Adapt or die

Flexibility leads to longevity; in animals those most able to respond to a myriad of scenarios will live longest. Societies and species that can adapt to change and who have the ability to move into different environments will survive when others decline or disintegrate. Play is an expedition into the unknown. Because of this quality, it is often a time and place for the child to face uncertainty and to imagine fearful places, dreadful characters and threatening experiences. From *Grimm's Fairy Tales* such as *Snow White* and *Hansel and Gretel*, to modern classics like *Where the Wild Things Are* (Sendak 2000) and *We're Going on a Bear Hunt* (Rosen 1997), children's stories reflect their play worlds. Children enter into other worlds, set off on epic journeys or conquer fear and danger, gaining in stature and collecting 'notches on the belt'.

Whether you roared at the threatening monsters, and then stayed around to rule the world of Wild Things; or whether you ran all the way back through the long grass and squelched all the way back through the mud, away from the danger lurking in the dark cave, back to the safety of home, you had an amazing adventure. Both endings are necessary and right. Sometimes it is right to stay and sometimes it is right to go. Play is about having choices, making decisions and not being eaten, or lost forever, or maybe turning into a despotic megalomaniac. Whether you run or rule in play you take a risk, become an adventurer: but most of all, survive. And you increase your repertoire of possible behaviours.

Children who engage in emotionally arousing play scenarios develop a variety of viable responses they can keep in their emotional repertoire for later use.   Russ & Niec 2011, pp.31-2

Only by living through threat and facing up to danger, or experiencing success and the heady heights of being amazing in playtime, can humans and animals learn to 'meet with Triumph and Disaster, and treat those two impostors just the same' (Kipling 1939, p.112). The ability to cope with strong feelings; to manage pleasure and pain, without 'acting out' those feelings to the detriment of self or of others, may be taught in schools: but we can make it part of who we are through play.

Emotional regulation

Self-regulation: the process of maintaining balance between pleasant and unpleasant emotions (Lester & Maudsley 2007, p.46). Sounds simple? This is actually a high order skill, and like many other complex and mature behaviours we see it in a child's play before we see it in other areas of their life. This 'complex business' of self-regulation includes 'regulation of intensity, ... windows of tolerance, recovery process, access to conciousness, and external expression' (Siegel 1999, p.244). This means:

- ➡ regulation of the intensity of an experience (being in control of making experiences harder or easier, more or less painful and so on)
- ➡ staying within your personal 'window of tolerance' (pushing yourself, but also knowing when to give yourself a break)
- ➡ allowing time and space for the recovery process
- ➡ having the ability to listen to yourself and communicate your feelings to others

The ability to tolerate loneliness, boredom, frustration and unhappiness may seem vital to the emotional wellbeing of us all, but the ability to tolerate excitement, joy and success are equally important for our emotional, physical and social wellbeing. Real play offers opportunities for experiencing the highs and lows of life in a safe place, where the child has control and can sense when they need to stop or move away.

Children themselves seem to recognise that they experience a variety of feelings through self-chosen play. In one school where children all had weekly, classroom-based, half-hour free play sessions (Woolf 2011; Woolf 2013), one ten year old boy summed up his experience in general to me by describing sessions as; easy, challenging, difficult, safe, dangerous, fun and frustrating. One session he recalled feeling: better and worse; confident and unsure, happy and sad. Most of the children I asked about their feelings during or after play sessions described play with similar 'contradictory' words. Apparently children have no difficulty in recognising and tolerating the paradox or ambiguity of play.

Play experience of life's ups and downs prepare the child for emotional maturity. As adults we are 'programmed' to protect and to care for our young. Watching a child at play who is struggling or suddenly defeated often stirs a need in me to intervene and make it better. As I observe a youngster lie, trick and dominate another, I can feel an impulse to correct or deflect the play rising to my lips. Listening to the teenager whose play appears arrogant, implausible or unkind may press my 'button' that says 'teach: guide: enforce'.

As professionals we are regarded as referees, sorter-outers and purveyors of justice and fair-play. *"Miss - Terri just stole my spaceship - tell her she has to give it me back"*; *"Sir you're not allowed to cheat, tell Jezza he can't pick up the ball"*. The pleas that trigger our internal protective, corrective drive and the external pressure to directly teach, make it hard to 'stand back' and believe in the safe space of play and the abilities of children at play. Sometimes I have to keep everyone safe, other times I can wait just a little bit longer and watch as the players sort it out for themselves.

The impact on, and expectations of the adult provider of play may mean children are 'rescued': or it may be that play is disrupted if we as adults are unsure of our role. In my rush to protect, or possibly my need to not feel helpless, I have re-directed play that I assumed could be emotionally harmful. Glad to be included or deferred to, I have taken over play that belonged to the children. In Chapter 9 I am going to look at the literature around why teachers are drawn to the job and how that might mean we have some ways of being that we are just unaware of. And how the ways I am and the things I say and do sometimes change play experiences and make them less powerful and not so much fun. And then in Chapters 14 and 15 we'll take on board just how important each of us is to our pupils, and think about ways we can make that importance work for children, through us grown-ups becoming more playful.

Hughes (2012, pp.160-186) warns us that children need a balance of experiences; some of which elicit positive feelings, others of which elicit negative feelings. My role is not to 'edit' play, in order that pleasure is experienced but that any pain is excluded. In Chapter 1 I said we would return to the idea that play does not have to be fun - which is a really important piece of information that was news to me, but quickly made absolute sense when I watched children play with that thought in my mind. Mental wellbeing means knowing bad feelings will not overwhelm you, that feeling sadness and anger are part of feeling alive. It also means not feeling guilty to be happy, or feeling scared to be content. In the play stories of adventure, of loss, of success and of the seemingly banal, the child 'chooses' what it is he needs to find out about (remember Frank on p.22 - who chooses without realising why the choice had been made). This play can be the training to meet with 'triumph and disaster,' and the experience of finding a balance by managing them both. An adult's acceptance of the different emotional outcomes of play gives the message that *"It's OK to feel that way"; "I have faith you can tolerate this"; and "Whether you are sad or happy - I like you just the same".*

> I don't actually think there is anything called happiness that doesn't include the capacity to tolerate sadness, unhappiness, loneliness, confusion, doubt; otherwise the happiness is entirely synthetic.
>
> Susie Orbach 2013, *in a* BBC Radio 4 interview

Developing social skills

> You need to play so you don't turn into a hermit.
>
> Kapasi & Gleave 2009, p.18

Building relationships and feeling a sense of belonging are both consequences of play; and vital to emotional wellbeing. 'Social play encourages children to focus on the rules that underlie the play episode and makes them aware that certain rules underlie all social interactions' (Hughes 1999, p.193). Play involves many social skills: the ability to communicate, empathise, take turns, trust, have an understanding of logical consequences, know who to include and who to exclude, and the skill of being able to do both in acceptable ways; as well as having the grace to be accepted or rejected but still daring to ask to play next time. As well as skills we actively foster through the school curriculum and ethos, other skills are evident in play which we may not dare to acknowledge as useful. The school leaver who has not developed a range of skills, some less 'socially acceptable' than others, and the resilience to withstand these strategies when they are used against him or her by others, may be ill-equipped to face the real world outside the school gates (*we'll think more about this in* Chapter 3).

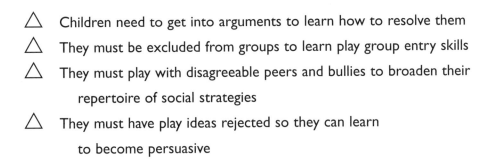

△   Children need to get into arguments to learn how to resolve them

△   They must be excluded from groups to learn play group entry skills

△   They must play with disagreeable peers and bullies to broaden their
     repertoire of social strategies

△   They must have play ideas rejected so they can learn
     to become persuasive

When we as adults intervene too quickly in conflict, these opportunities are lost (Trawick-Smith 1998, p.246). How to judge what 'too quickly' means will not always be easy. Balancing the needs of a group of peers means that one child's experience will often be compromised for the 'good' of the group. Working with children is a privilege and a constant source of delight and of angst. We all grapple with the daily decisions we must make, choices we have to negotiate, and the edicts we enforce, and only then realise there was another way! More awareness of potentials and possibility adds another consideration to the responses we need to deliberate over, but learning that struggle in play strengthens the child is important stuff for us all to recognise and consider. The impact on the adult of watching children struggle with the difficulties of 'real life' in the arena of play, and how responses from grown-ups can enhance or deny learning experiences, will be the subject of a later chapter.

Luckily for both the adult observer, and for the child at play, playing fairly appears to have a pay-off, certainly for animals (Bekoff & Allen, 2002). Turn-taking, not only turn to play but also turn to win or turn to choose the game, is a skill that is developed through play. It's necessary to social play and it increases players' acceptability to other playmates. Pellis (2002) calls it the '50:50' rule. In observations on animal play, where no external arbiter exists, players who are too dominant eventually get excluded from play.

Anyone who wants to engage in social play will also learn the skills of cooperation and collaboration in order to be included in the game. I have seen children hold back on their physical superiority of strength or of skill in games where they perceive inclusion is more likely if they don't always win. I am sure you have seen children employ the 'adult' strategy of 'not seeing' a pair in a game of Snap, because their pile of cards is so much higher than their play partners' and they don't want to win too quickly, too decisively or too often.

Being able to communicate

In order for joint fantasy play to work, children must emotionally commit to one another, and pay attention to what the other is doing. They have to articulate what's in their mind's eye - and negotiate some scenario that allows both their visions to come alive. When one kid just announced the beginning of a ninja battle, but the other wants to be a cowboy, they have to figure out how to still ride off into the sunset together.

Bronson & Merryman 2009, p.129

One of the most magical elements of play is the social interaction. How do we know what our fellow players intend? How do we 'negotiate' roles, outcomes and who gets to wear the fireman's hat? Play both needs no words, and, at the same time, develops language beyond the current ability of the child in their everyday life (Vygotsky 1978, p.102) - another of the paradoxes of play. Watching children at play we see the silent solitary player, the lone player talking to himself or to imaginary playmates or inanimate objects, as well as the rowdy group shouting, arguing, giving orders and counter-orders while another group busily and wordlessly create a joint venture. The communication in play can be as effective when it is physical cues and the unwritten language of turn-taking and collaboration, as when it is conversational or instructional and quite audibly vocal.

Observing children in middle childhood you often see one child silently place an object in an unusual, unconventional or random situation, and their play partner laughs at the private joke. No explanations are needed. There is an attuned communication, bonding participants through a shared experience and mutual understanding. The unspoken conversation goes something like this:

Player A	*I find this funny.*
Player B	*Yes, I do too.*
In unison	*We two have much in common!*

These playful interactions can happen in a moment, in passing, in the midst of concentrated work; or in play times when the children can start up an extended conversation. Player B then might put another object into a different, unexpected position, and Player A confirms with a snort that he finds that idea funny too.

Invitations to play seem to be learned without being taught. Glances, winks, nudges; did anyone ever teach us that these mean: *"Shall we ..?"*, *"The next thing I say will be teasing ..."*: *"I dare you..."*? Like most of our learning at play, these communications are 'caught', rather than taught, mostly through family interactions from our earliest age. During play a frown is enough for another player to retrace their deviation from the game and to follow the 'rules'. We know that from birth humans are seekers of meaning in the faces of others. During formal learning and when we're using explicit language we don't always pay attention to the face of the speaker, relying instead on our ability to follow language. But in play we want to really connect and are alert to subtle signals as well as ritualised play structures and unspoken play rules. 'Animals ... have evolved clear and unambiguous signals to solicit and maintain play' (Bekoff & Allen 1997). And we are not so different!

Our desire to connect is evident in the fascination babies and toddlers have for a stranger of their like. When we watch a baby or toddler as another small child comes into their view, we see their eyes widen, their gaze focus and very soon their arms start to stretch out toward the object of their interest, the other little person. Have you ever wondered at the way children make new friends on holiday within hours of arriving in a country where another language is spoken? The human need to relate requires a medium through which a connection can be made. Play is that medium.

Play as social lubricant or 'ice-breaker'

TALES FROM OZ 🐾
New pup on the block

Oz, a five-year-old lurcher, spends odd days at Doggie Day-care. He isn't a regular and this means he often meets new dogs who have enrolled since he was last there. I notice when I pick Oz up at the end of the day that he is usually being tailed by a dog I haven't met before. When I visit in the morning, or call early in the afternoon, Oz is usually out in the garden chasing around with the pack, or up on the sofa chewing gently at the ears of a fellow day-care canine. Oz shows new dogs they are welcome, not by offering to show the newcomer around, but by offering to play with them.

Oz is playful; and on meeting new dogs his opening gambit is an invitation to play. The move from never having met, to chasing, rolling, chewing and pouncing, happens in just moments. The amount of play two dogs engage in often decreases as they become more familiar to each other, but in order to establish a new relationship, play starts at full physical pelt.

Oz is always one of the social day-care 'in crowd', not because he is clever, good-looking, kind or controlling. Oz is popular because he plays.

At the moment, in the area of animal behaviours, it is the social benefits of play that are being most studied by experts. Their findings unanimously extol the benefits of 'rough-and-tumble' play for bonding between individuals and for creating and maintaining group cohesion. It is also through social play that we find or forge our place within the social group. Pellis (2002) describes two main roles of rough-and-tumble play: social bonding and social testing. Rough-and-tumble, or physical play, is so important for wellbeing that you will find it appearing again, and not exclusively, in the next chapter.

Being part of a group and finding your place in a group have been essential for physical survival in the past and are now being recognised as important for emotional survival. The physical pay-offs of our social wellbeing are also becoming increasingly apparent. In terms of longevity in humans, as I already mentioned, the benefits of social relationships are the same as the benefits of not smoking, and more beneficial than exercise or avoiding obesity (Holt-Lunstead, Smith & Layton 2010). Being able to have positive relationships with others is of real importance to us all. Play has been demonstrated to be an important medium for meeting, and becoming part of, social groups. This has implications for all of us in education, since our schools are social groups, as are our classrooms, choirs, football teams and, oh yes, our staffrooms! Bringing play into all of those activities and spaces will lead to improved social relationships and cohesion.

So play is important in building and maintaining social relationships; and social relationships are important for physical health and emotional wellbeing. Let's look at how play supports social success for individuals and how play increases social cohesion for society.

When someone joins our group unexpectedly we may ask, *"Do I know you?"* If we want to find out who someone is, I hope by now you have guessed the best way to do it! One piece of research (*Stranger to Familiar*, Antonacci et al 2011) describes how some potential sources of social tension around meeting unfamiliar members of a group can be reduced. The findings suggest that play:

➡ develops more fluid and democratic groups which are
   more open to incomers

➡ reduces tension and uncertainty in specific social situations,
   such as groups who only meet occasionally

➡ inhibits and regulates aggression

➡ helps to establish or re-establish a sufficient level of familiarity

➡ limits xenophobia by inviting newcomers in, and by reminding
   established members of the group that they belong

➡ enhances friendly interactions in the critical process that
   upgrades a stranger to a familiar individual

So scientific research and animal studies are evidencing what children instinctively know:

It stops more fights if you get more play … *from* Kapasi & Gleave 2009, p.15

Meeting new people can be inherently stressful; in the animal kingdom, it is often more of a direct threat to survival. Antonacci et al's work (2010) on play and xenophobia found that play was an effective ice-breaker and a way to integrate new members into social groups. The team monitored groups in the lemur and bushbaby family of animals, and observed new and unfamiliar animals meeting with established groups. As might be expected, there were aggressive behaviours between established males and male newcomers. However after play, conflicts between unfamiliar males decreased to the levels that existed between familiar males.

Developing social relationships sometimes needs no words, like at Doggie Day-care where Oz may take the chance of a few misunderstandings or misjudgements in early interactions with newcomer dogs. But he is investing in the end-game of a happy and relaxed time with his 'pack'. Remembering how new kids in my class might be asked *"Where are you from?"*, *"What do you like?"*, *"Will you be my friend?"*, I wondered what strategies Oz could employ to find out about the new puppy in the pack. Without rough-and-tumble play it is hard to imagine how dogs could find out about each other. Children and dogs alike though can ask new potential friends *"Would you like to play?"* The answer tells both human and animal player a lot about the new 'other'. And if the answer to the invitation is *"Yes"*, what follows tells both players more than words ever could. Plato has been quoted as saying *"You can discover more about a person in an hour of play than in a year of conversation"*. So the play conversation helps us to know and to understand the 'stranger' who then quickly becomes 'familiar'.

Thus play has social benefits for the individual, and this increased social health *in* individuals and *between* individuals has huge benefits for healthy societies. These benefits are not the only good things play does for the health of us all.

Physical benefits

The physical benefits of play are not just improved motor skills, a reduction in obesity and improved cardio-vascular fitness: nor are the benefits simply improved chances of a longer, healthier life. The physical benefits of play are, most importantly, changes in the brain. It is physical play, rough-and-tumble play, play-fighting and interpersonal play that have many vital consequences for our optimal brain development. These kinds of play:

➡   rewire neural networks (Panksepp 1998)

➡   lead to organisational changes in the brain (Pellis & Pellis 2009)

➡   make new connections between different parts of the brain, such as
        thought and feeling centres (Brown 2009)

➡   'are essential for competent emotive behaviour patterns'
        (Panksepp 1998, p.295)

➡   stimulate neuron growth within the cortex and hippocampus regions
        of the brain, responsible for memory, learning, language, and logic
        (Debenedet & Cohen 2010)

And some chemicals which encourage positive feelings and are known to 'fertilise' the brain are released into the brain by physical play:

➡   Opioids, anti-stress & anti-aggression chemicals, which make us feel
        "I don't want to fight" (Sunderland 2009)

➡   brain-derived neurotrophic factor (BDNF) - 'fertilizer' for the brain
        (Debenedet & Cohen 2010)

➡   dopamine and adrenaline, equivalent to low doses of Ritalin
        (Sunderland 2009)

The physical manipulation skills required in play also create maps in the brain for manipulating things. As we develop as children, our brains become able to 'play' with these neural networks without using actual blocks or beads: we become capable of solving spatial problems in the inner spaces of our minds. Children manipulate the world through interaction with external objects: older children, adolescents and adults manipulate ideas in our heads.

Piaget called this change in abilities a move from 'concrete' operations to 'formal' operations. In America the National Aeronautics and Space Administration (NASA) has a policy for the employment of recruits in Research and Development. They look for candidates who have experience of manual problem-solving; from Meccano or Lego, to car mechanics or electrical wiring. NASA believes that better abstract problem-solving skills are developed through playing with concrete resources. More importantly, physical skills developed through play are developing more complex patterns in the brain.

And in fact play grows bigger, better brains (Brown 2009). It also develops strong bones and muscles, keeps joints flexible and exercises the heart and lungs. So do structured exercise programmes and sports skills sessions. But the less structured and predictable physical play is, the more it adds to the flexibility and adaptability of our brains, while it builds the strength and stamina of our bodies.

AND WHAT HAPPENS IF WE DON'T PLAY?

"If they are playing, then they are happy, but if they are not allowed,
then they become more naughty because they are not able to go out
and play off their naughtiness."

Children on children, *in* Kapasi & Gleave 2009, p.19

Having dogs, I subscribe to the 'lack of play = naughtiness' theory in canines. By 'naughtiness', I mean a restless need for challenge, action, stimulation and a need for 'something to happen'. I wonder if this is what we often describe as naughtiness in schools - actually the biological need for stimulation or play (*and see the section below for further discussion about the 'need' for play*). Some children seek *sensory* stimulation, while others look for *social* stimulation.

For dogs it is often the need for physical play or for problem-solving play. Oz shows the same effects from physical play, running, jumping and chasing, as he does from problem-solving play, 'find the biscuit', hide-and-seek and open-the-parcel. Both physical play and problem-solving play lead to relaxation and sleep. Not enough play means Oz will be looking around as if wondering to himself, *"What mischief can I get up to now?"* Play 'marks a positive state of arousal and alertness to the possibility for producing uncertainty, a desire to disturb things, and to inject surprise into the mundane practicalities of everyday experiences' (Lester 2010). Naughty and playful behaviours can be affectionately responded to or impatiently reacted to. 'There is a time and a place' might be the most commonly applied axiom. The appropriate time and place for play and playfulness will be considered further on.

Mum - I'm bored!

While it is a highly valuable skill to be able to tolerate boredom, boredom is about not knowing what to do, not wanting to do anything, everything being wrong, feeling that life is dull and that nothing is there for us. Boredom comes from inside: when you are free to act, free to move, free to change, but somehow feeling without the energy or impulse to do so. Frustration arises when you know you need something but the world conspires to deny it to you. The frustration of 'needing' but not getting is something akin to a hunger. When we need to feed a hunger, no other activity or solution will work. And we all need play. When I need to play, only play will feed me. I might though manage, if I can have a quick play 'snack' pro-tem - or if I know that a bigger play 'meal' is coming, if I can just hang on.

Play Wales (2003) looked at the research evidence into the effects of play deprivation. Their summary concluded that:

➡   Not having enough play experiences, children are more likely to be
      aggressive, anti-social: extreme deprivation leads to violence and
      depression

➡   Lack of play impairs the development of social skills and appropriate or
      healthy emotional expression

➡   Play deprivation adversely affects brain growth

I just can't get enough

Play Wales also links the studies on human play with studies on animals deprived of
play opportunities:

> When other species are deprived of play they show highly aggressive and
> bizarre behaviour and appear to completely lose touch with the social
> norms and accepted behavioural protocols of that species.   *ibid*, p.3

Animals suffer other difficulties when deprived of play experiences. Hughes (1999)
describes these as:

> A difficulty becoming successfully aggressive as adults (in human terms,
> they don't know how and when to be assertive)
> A difficulty in assessing the intentions of others. Either they perceive a
> threat when there is none, or they fail to see a threat that is real (in other
> words, poor risk assessment skills)   p.30

Panksepp (1998) recognises play as a need; a biological drive. Animals and human
animals need sleep or we become tired; food or we become hungry; play or we
become ... it seems there is no word that describes play deprivation in terms of its

outcome. How can we express our need if there is no word that conveys its meaning - *"I feel tired": "I feel hungry": "I feel ... "*? The child expert may call the feeling 'yuk' (Kapasi & Gleave 2009, p.18) or we may say the child is being 'naughty' (*ibid* p.19), but whatever we call it, Panksepp tells us there is such a state. It may be a feeling you recognise, but hadn't ever thought about the need to have for a name for it. I have never used a name for it either, but now I am asking myself to think about what I might call my feeling when I'm empty of play. I think 'empty' is just the word I would use. Empty and 'flat'. In need of 'a breath of fresh air'!

In schools, children struggle to thrive when they often feel hungry or tired. Indeed we all recognise that their brains can't physically be optimally receptive to learning until their basic needs are met. Yet many of us still don't consider whether children in a state of play deprivation have the physical brain capacity to learn.

I wonder why this conversation has not been as widely engaged in as the argument for breakfast clubs and the Government's initiative for free school lunches (DfE 2014a)? The cynic in me wonders about the power and the money behind food producers in contrast to the fact that play can be free, and not necessarily a product or a branded commodity. Or possibly it is because play is like breathing - it just happens and we all take it for granted, never considering what might happen if for some reason play is not possible. Or, alternatively, perhaps it is because the question is so big, with no (relatively) easy answer like 'a piece of toast' or 'a plate of hot food' (as for breakfast clubs and school lunches), that we have not addressed the need for a sufficiency of play as a pre-requisite for optimal learning.

If we do start to take seriously the brain's need for play in order to be primed and ready to work, then the good news from Panksepp is that: after enough play, the need is satisfied.

· ·

and so ...

Play matters. It has physical, cognitive and emotional benefits for the player. There are many reasons why we play. There are immediate, short-term benefits and cumulative long-term consequences. Some things can only be learned through play: critically, missed opportunities for play mean that children can't learn the things which just can't be taught. Lack of play also means children can't access things which can only be taught to brains that are ready and able to learn. Play gets us ready, keeps us steady, and makes the social world go round.

KEY POINTS

Play is the way we learn what no-one can teach us

Play builds relationships

Play releases chemicals which build the brain, induce relaxation and encourage cooperation

Play is a communication in itself and also aids communication per se

Play keeps us physically, mentally and emotionally flexible and fit

Play builds resilience, helps us to cope and gives us 'bounce-back-ability'

Why play matters: *Where do we go from here?*

In order for changes in practice to take place, the Play England *Play in Schools and Integrated Settings* Group (2008) believe that the following developments need to take place in government policy. The position statement recommends:

> Knowledge and understanding about play and its importance to children's development should be included as a requirement in both the Qualified Teacher Status (QTS) and head teacher professional standards.
>
> *from*, Play England, (2008), *Play in Schools and Integrated Settings*:
> *A position statement* London: NCB

The play-full school would -

☺   Ensure staff have opportunities to attend CPD on play whatever their area of responsibility

☺   Have annual whole school training in the evolving understanding of the role of play in development

If you want to know more, try reading

Brown, S. (2009) *Play: how it shapes the brain, opens the imagination and invigorates the soul* New York: Avery.

Antonacci D; Norscia I. & Palagi E. (2010) *Stranger to Familiar: Wild strepsirhines manage xenophobia by playing. PLoS ONE* Vol. 5:10 (online) plosone.org/article/fetchObject. action?uri=info%3Adoi%2F10.13 71%2Fjournal.ne.0013218& representation=PDF

If you want to understand more, try reading

Williams, M. (2004) *The Velveteen Rabbit* London: Egmont Books Ltd

If you want a 15 minute group or individual training, try watching

Mark Bekoff's talk on play for Play Wales at playwales.org.uk/ eng/ipa2011videos

Chapter 3

Play nicely or don't play at all

> "*From now on, you must take good care of your toys, because if you don't,*
> *we'll find out, Sid! We toys can see EVERYTHING! So play nice!*"
>
> Woody, Toy Story (Disney 1995)

If children won't 'play nicely' for parents or school staff - maybe they will for their toys. The 'play nicely' approach is so widely agreed on that we even employ Disney to help us control the play of our children!

In this chapter we will think about how we sometimes expect all children to be 'sugar and spice and all things nice' and the possibility that if rules in play demand only nice behaviour, we might just be limiting our children's experiences unnecessarily.

THE QUESTIONS TO CONSIDER ARE:

PLAY NICELY!
If play is an education for life, what lessons are our nicely playing children missing out on?

THE VALUE OF PLAYING ON
How might letting children sort it out for themselves build resilience and independence?

PHYSICAL PLAY - FROM ROUGH-AND-TUMBLE TO PLAY-FIGHTING

Why is one of the types of play we adults find most discomforting actually the play we are most programmed by our biology to need and to relish?

SOCIAL PLAY - POWER IN RELATIONSHIPS AND ITS USE AND MISUSE

Someone's got to be the boss! One of our children will be our future Prime Minister, many of them will manage big businesses, captain sports teams, lead social justice movements or command in the forces. How do children work out (through playing out) how to be powerful but fair and kind too?

PERSONAL PLAY: SHOULD I? COULD I? WOULD I?

Can play chosen by the child help to integrate and make sense of who they were or might have been? Who they are or can be, and who they might become?

SUBVERSIVE PLAY - FINDING OUT ABOUT PRIVATE THOUGHTS AND FEELINGS

Play is in some ways no different to life, but because it takes place in a parallel universe, it means anything is possible. Could breaking rules and being 'bad' in play actually help make good people?

PLAY NICELY!

'Some children are seen to know how to 'play properly' whilst the play of others is rejected as 'unsuitable'' (Olusoga 2009, p.57). The 'play nicely approach' (Lester, Jones & Russell 2011) has a massive impact on the way that children are free to play. Where adults draw the line can often be more about our needs than the needs of the child. We adults also stop play, not because the play is dangerous or unpleasant; but more because of our worries over 'where it might lead'. Play is 'shut down' before it has been observed long enough to 'ascertain the spirit of the play or the motives of the players' (Olusoga 2009, p.60). But children choose play that is important to them. Stopping children playing is probably rather like stopping adults talking. If, like me,

you talk a lot, it's easy to imagine how frustrating that must be! Play, like talking, is a way of working through how we think or feel about things. Both are ways of telling others what we need. Instilling in children that some things are 'bad' and not to be seen in play could well be limiting for their development and wellbeing.

I believe there are several consequences of the 'play nicely' approach when it is implemented as policy. I imagine we've all felt uncomfortable or unsure of our responses when witnessing children including challenging experiences and feelings in their play stories. There are some topics of conversation that are difficult for adults to address: betrayal, failure, fear and death being just some of them. Van Dyck (2012) for example, acknowledges our natural human fear of dying. But she feels our lack of ability to talk about it is more due to us not having 'the words, the framework, the familiarity with the topic that helps us find a natural segue to start'.

Where can we find these foundation blocks of understanding? Through play. When we witness a child being denied opportunities for play which includes the big themes of life and death we may be watching one of the reasons we perpetuate our struggle to accept and live more easily with the 'not nice' but inevitable parts of our world. Other themes or behaviours can also cause us to devise rules that exclude certain types of play. Our natural concern for safety and our beliefs around 'nice' ways of being and relating to others may mean that one group's interests are particularly discouraged. It is likely for example that 'zero tolerance policies disproportionately affect boys' (Olusoga 2009, p.60).

Western society in general and the workplace in particular, seems to be shifting away from an appreciation for such traditionally male characteristics as physical prowess, dominance, and quick decision-making and toward an emphasis on traditionally female traits of self-control and strong communication skills. Carlson 2011, p.11

Observation in classrooms quickly tells the story; boys being stopped and told to play nicely, when all they want to do is play at being hunters, providers, rescuers and protectors. Male brains got to be how they are because of the roles they traditionally filled. Even in Early Years classrooms,

> 'cognitive' tasks are frequently privileged over rough-and-tumble; and boys' self-initiated play is more likely to be frowned upon than that of girls'.
>
> Brooker 2011, p.156

In current society we seem to find boisterous play very uncomfortable. I know, even though I rejoice when I see it, I also speculate about how it might end, and wonder *"Is everyone enjoying that - or just the bigger or stronger one?"* - I imagine you might have concerns like that too?

If children know that wild behaviour in play is pretend, then why do adults struggle so much to accept this? Acceptance and permissiveness around play allow children to accept and allow for the more negative, 'not nice', parts of themselves. In *Killing Monsters*, a book about the vital role of aggressive, superhero play, Gerard Jones recalls how his parents' acceptance of his play and the needs it expressed was enough to make him feel better about himself.

> We still didn't talk openly about my angers and frustrations, but at least we talked about my fantasies of being powerful and destructive. I felt that the darker side of myself was being seen and accepted for the first time.
>
> Jones 2002, p.16

We often make assumptions about aggressive, wild, 'not nice' play leading to the same behaviours and attitudes in non-play activities. The research doesn't support a 'causal link' (Olusoga 2009, p.59). There is conflicting research around this important issue, and much more work needs to be done on whether there is a connection between role-play and the real behaviours of children. Some research suggests that 'aggressive' play *reduces* a need for real aggression; while other research suggests it encourages it. This uncertainty between experts does not help us when we struggle with our feelings about certain sorts of play. My reticence to let it go on and my hesitance to call a halt to aggressive play mirrors the lack of decisiveness in the research findings. *"To stop or not to stop?"* That is often the question: and *"Help!"* is also often my internal plea to those better informed than I am on the subject. But as the jury is still out on this question, there is no universally agreed recommendation for practice.

And because we are emotional and relational beings, when we stop children playing, we're often not considering scientific evidence; we are acting on our own assumptions, feelings and beliefs.

> Although the play may be stopped, the underlying motivations of children
> engaging in war, weapon and superhero play continue to exist. In fact they are
> so powerful that children tend to continue to subvert play and play resources
> in order to continue exploring these themes.   Olusoga 2009, p.60

THE VALUE OF PLAYING ON

We know that the brain and body produce chemicals that create conditions in the brain that influence our behaviours. The brain uses electrical pulses to communicate across different parts of itself and to tell the body what it needs to be doing. Stopping play that is exciting, scary, energetic and dynamic means that the chemicals and electricity are left with nowhere to go (although *my* chemical arousal will be lowered immediately - *"Phew, I'm back in charge"*; *"Wow - that could have got nasty - I feel better now that I put a stop to that play, it might have got out of hand"*).

When allowed to play on, children's feelings and actions will often be 'played out', and the chemicals and electrical impulses will be used up or altered in a natural process of emotional regulation. *Without* following through on play, children do not experience this cycle. When our bodies are used to the fact that feelings subside and change, it stops big feelings seeming so scary or overwhelming. Getting to know our brains and bodies and finding out 'what works' in terms of appropriate and safe discharge of energy and impulses will give us life-long strategies for coping.

So what are the areas of play that we adults might see as 'bad'? I think most people would agree they include:

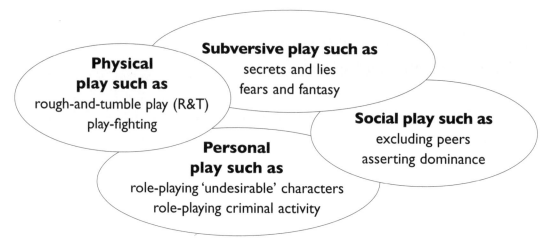

Physical play such as
rough-and-tumble play (R&T)
play-fighting

Subversive play such as
secrets and lies
fears and fantasy

Social play such as
excluding peers
asserting dominance

Personal play such as
role-playing 'undesirable' characters
role-playing criminal activity

Let's look at the different ways that each of these play types may naturally challenge us as providers of play, and how the duty to provide environments that are safe and happy, as well as experiences that develop abilities and resilience, create ongoing dilemmas for us all the time. Later we will explore the need to balance our different responsibilities and also start to think about how we can develop our own tolerance of times when not everyone plays 'nicely'.

PHYSICAL PLAY:
from rough-and-tumble to play-fighting

Do we smile indulgently at the dad who throws their still very young son or daughter up above his head before expertly catching him or her? Or do we shake our head at the folly of any adult exposing their child to such danger or fear? Does the toddler asking for a pony ride on Grandma's knee want to very gently trot along or do they want to gallop like the wind? When we watch families in the park rolling down slopes and chasing round trees, it may look like the most natural thing in the world for adults to engage in physical play with their children. This physical play in families has important functions. The benefits of rough-and-tumble play (R&T play) and play-fighting are two-fold:

➡   physical benefits to the brain through physical and social contact

➡   social benefits to the individual through making and maintaining
          relationship bonds

Drawing together a large body of research on rough & tumble play, Jarvis & George (2009, pp.258-9) identified many benefits of R&T and also the skills children need to gain these benefits. The children they observed across a large number of programmes were mainly boys, and were between the ages of three and ten years old. The researchers point to the fact that the competent player's interpersonal, social and physical play skills usually develop because the successful child had R&T experience with family, and in particular with a father figure, in early infancy. The benefits identified amongst the skilful players include:

➡   Increased popularity with peers

➡   An ability to differentiate between playful and aggressive approaches

➡   Better social problem-solving skills

➡   Reduced aggression

➡   Better sociocognitive skills (understanding of social hierarchies).

Fergus Hughes (1999, p.198) agrees with Jarvis & George that early R&T play with parents, in particular with fathers or father figures, increases social wellbeing later on. It even has a significant impact on how school staff think about pupils; children rated as popular by their teachers are the most likely to have parents, and particularly fathers, who engage in a good deal of physical play with them. Hughes feels that parent-child physical play is an activity that develops self-control and the ability to 'decode' how others are feeling. In physical play, players notice and adjust to the facial expressions of other players in order to keep the game going. Whitebread (2012, p.19), reporting on a study by Mellen in 2002, also notes a strong correlation between early physical play at home and later social skills. He describes R&T play as:

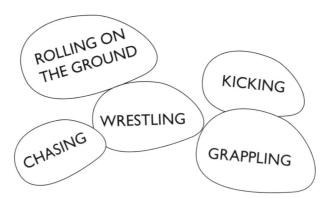

We can mostly recognise the play when we observe it. Often we know it because many of us played that way ourselves. Some of the play Whitebread names may feel less challenging to us than others. Chasing games and rolling play can conjure up images of sunny days and laughter, while kicking and wrestling play may immediately press our alarm buttons and lead to us issuing a list of rules that reduce our anxiety (remember our chemically alert brain?) but which alter the play beyond recognition: while other times we go straight in at the level of a total ban. I wonder if you can remember times when you wrestled as a child with a sibling or peer? I know that I can - and I can still feel how it could be challenging and empowering to wrestle in play, and I also remember that sometimes it hurt! I must have had physical play experiences that were safe enough, but still risky and fun, and with real physical consequences that my body learned to predict and my brain learned to manage.

> Most adults can remember running, wrestling, rolling, and roughhousing as
> children with their friends and siblings, and loving to play this way.
>
> Carlson 2011, p.11

R&T play always involves 'reciprocal behaviour' (Jarvis & George 2009, p.176), the innate play custom of turn-taking; like the unspoken understanding - *"I'll win this go, then you can win after"*. This role reversal in physical play forms the foundation of give-and-take behaviours, a physical forerunner of communication skills of speaking and listening. It is the keystone for all turn-taking across interpersonal interactions.

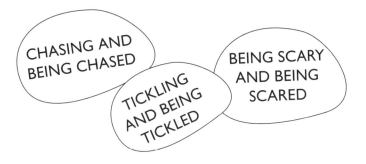

No matter what height, weight, age, or skill differential in the opponents, turn-taking and role reversal are always present. If they aren't, it isn't rough-and-tumble play.

For play-fighting to remain playful, it needs to follow the 50:50 rule (Pellis 2002), and that may help us as adults to gauge whether what we are witnessing is playful enough to allow; and also to believe that if we *do* permit the play to continue, it will be of value to each of the participants and not just to the one who appears to be on top from the start.

Remember earlier we considered why 'playing on' was important for participants for their individual process to be completed? Playing on is also important for social play, so that each player gets a turn at feeling good about him or herself. If this is not happening, despite time being allowed, then the 50:50 rule is not in place (*at last - a guideline that helps me to know my role, what a relief!*) and we need to step in to model how play means turns for all. Give-and-take physical play must also feel like play to both, or all, participants. Otherwise for some it won't be play. *Only when it feels like play for everyone can it be an activity that creates and maintains relationships.*

> Like most types of play, it continues to be enjoyed, usually between family members and close friends, right into adulthood. It is easily distinguishable from actual aggression by the evident enjoyment of the participants, and appears to be wholly beneficial. *ibid*

The beneficial nature of 'good old-fashioned horseplay' play is that:

Roughhousing makes kids smart
Roughhousing builds emotional intelligence
Roughhousing makes kids more likeable
Roughhousing makes children ethical and moral
Roughhousing makes kids physically fit
Roughhousing brings joy   DeBenedet & Cohen 2010, pp.13-23

'For a variety of reasons, however, this rowdy, vigorous style of play is not valued much today' (Carlson 2011, p.11). DeBenedet & Cohen, along with Carlson, are fulsome in their advocacy of horseplay for healthy human development. Other advocates for the benefits of play-fighting are more commonly researchers and writers who study animal behaviour. Cozolino (2013) recounts how he understood the role of physical play best through observing the relational play behaviours of a wolf. I too have learned much from the 'wolf' in my living room!

TALES FROM OZ 🐾

Knowing and not knowing how to play

My own experience as an observer of animal behaviour has hugely informed my knowledge and understanding of the role of play-fighting. As an owner of rescue dogs I have two dogs who could not be more different in their attitude to play. Oz, who I introduced you to earlier, is confident (mostly), quick on the uptake (always!) and amazingly co-ordinated and agile. Joe, a terrier of uncertain origins, is anxious and seems to lack the flexibility (brain plasticity I guess) to adapt or to change despite lots of consistent experiences. Joe appears not to know how to play; Oz plays as part of all his human and animal relationships. The question of whether Joe lacks confidence because he can't play, or whether Oz plays because he feels safe, matters to those of us who advocate for play. For me it is more about how the nature of my dogs and the nurture I provide for them interact. My interest in the inter-relationship between personality and play in my pets has led me to read a lot of things that I otherwise might not have found out about. Like the play life of rats!

Don't get ratty with me!

Pellis (2002) researches play behaviours of rats. He explains that the function of play-fighting in juveniles is hard to discover. Just why very young rats play fight is still not understood. But the role of play-fighting in the relationships of adolescent and adult rats is clearer. For these older animals, play-fighting is a way of social bonding and social testing. Pellis demonstrates that more complex brains have a larger repertoire of behaviours, giving them more choices. In this hierarchy of brain size and complexity the rat outstrips the humble mouse.

A mouse meeting another new mouse has two options; to fight or to ignore the newcomer. Rats have a third option. Rats can fight, or they can ignore the possible friend or foe. But they can also find out more about the stranger by play-fighting him. Pellis thinks the rats use play-fighting to work out whether the new rat will dominate or submit to the established one. Where will the stranger 'fit' in the scheme of the rat pack? Rather than find out in a real fight, and get hurt in the process, rats can find out through the safe medium of play.

Human brains are more complex than those of the mouse or rat, and play in humans provides additional benefits. We can use the rough-and-tumble of words and verbal sparring skills to assert rank, or to turn a stranger into a friend (and we will look more in later chapters at how playful communication can have the same properties and outcomes as other more physical play).

Interestingly, within already established hierarchies of rats, weaker, less dominant rats often play-fight with stronger, more dominant group members. Pellis sees this as their way of maintaining 'friendly relationships'. In Antonacci et al's (2010) study with animals of the lemur family, the use of play-fighting 'upgraded' a stranger to a friend; and maintained already established relationships. The research supports Pellis' findings that play-fighting is an important and safe way to:

➡ Reduce tension
➡ Create group cohesion
➡ Assess relationships

And it is fun! But that does not mean that:

➡ players never get accidently hurt
➡ play-fighting never turns into real fighting

In physical play, there is undoubtedly a chance someone will get hurt. This is not only an issue relevant to personal tolerance of danger or risk but also an issue of organisational attitude and of society's policies; there will be much more exploration of these considerations in the following chapter. In Chapter 17 we will return to this important issue with some ideas about how to give limits in ways that feel as gentle as possible while still being firm and non-negotiable in your role as the safety officer or the keeper of the peace.

In pretend fighting there's a chance it will become real (so no wonder we're instinctively uncomfortable, or have a heightened attention, when play-fighting erupts). Research evidence can show the probability of someone coming to harm as a result of play-fighting. The other side of the coin is harder to measure: the risk that *not* engaging in physical contact play with others will detract from cognitive, emotional and social development. Throughout our exploration of play this question appears - *what if we don't?* And a lot of the evidence is telling us that children will be the poorer for it, and our wise young player at the opening of the introduction tells us life will be less colourful for the lack of it. A further risk in *not* having safe play-fighting experience early on is that it could increase the probability of exclusion from groups and of *unsafe* play-fighting experiences later on, when the player is bigger, stronger and more dangerous.

So lots for us to think about in relation to physical play, with perhaps no easy answer or firm drawing of guidelines (apart from the wonderfully simple 50:50 rule): but hopefully we can start to think about why rough-and-tumble matters and how we might use an understanding of its benefits to inform our provision of play opportunities.

SOCIAL PLAY:
Power in relationships and its use and misuse

Watching young children play can make us feel uncomfortable; whether it is the use of 'toilet humour' or the 'unkind' treatment of peers.

> *Can I play?*
> *No, you can't*
> *Please can I?*
> *No, go away, we don't like you.*

The exclusion of peers is a powerful strategy for keeping control of ideas, stories and the lead role in the play. It is also a way in which a child can feel in charge of a life that is mostly under the control of others. Without the possibility of excluding someone or being excluded, many opportunities are lost:

△   If a child is never allowed to refuse entry to their play they are never
    able to *choose* to include others

△   If a child never experiences being excluded by peers they never learn
    strategies to manage the feelings that creates; or the strategies to
    get themselves included or set up a competing play where they can
    include or exclude themselves:

Finlay	*Can I play?*
Callum	*No, you can't*
Finlay	*I could be a runaway lion and you could catch me and put me in jail and everyone will clap*
Callum	*OK then - you be a lion, and I'll catch you and make you into my pet.*

Jodie	*Can I play?*
Sarah	*No, you can't*
Jodie	*Please can I?*
Sarah	*No, go away we don't like you.*
Jodie	*Hey, Stella do you want to play? Let's make a castle and play George and the Dragon.*

The child who is rejected but finds a way to manage those feelings feels good about himself or herself in a way they would not if an adult had sorted the 'problem'. The 'play nicely' rule and the 'be kind' directive make children obey rather than play. *Rules* about inclusion may not change *attitudes* towards inclusion. Others being kind is not a universal truth of relationships. Children need to be able to manage their feelings when others are unkind and to have strategies for how to move forward when things feel hard.

> Play in all its various benevolent and malevolent forms appears to encompass not only preferred skills such as cooperation, sharing, taking turns, following rules, but also survival skills such as harassment, deception, teasing and trickery which are certainly not encouraged in classrooms by any teachers but which are inherent in successfully navigating the world and human relationships.   Gupta 2011, p.88

The child's need to play with notions around power, social relationships and the rights and wrongs of always being kind are also apparent in personal play and subversive play. Maybe the reason we like stories about children becoming the powerful ones is because we still root for the child we remember being in a world where the adults got to have all the power and to 'keep us in our place'. The humour in films like *Big* (20th Century Fox 1988), where a 12 year-old who feels thwarted by the rules of the adult world wishes he was 'big' and wakes up next day fast-forwarded into adulthood, relies on our identifying with the child who suddenly gets the power they wished for. Stories like Hansel and Gretel (Morpurgo 2008), where the wronged children rescue themselves from danger by their own guile and wisdom, also appeal because the listening children hear about other children who are brave, independent and self-reliant.

PERSONAL PLAY: Should I? Could I? Would I?

This book is like play: it threads and weaves ideas, thoughts and feelings together in an attempt to make sense of life, or the life of play, or the play in our lives. Looking at our fears around 'not nice' play, our discomfort around whether it is play or not, our anxieties about whether it is safe or not, our lack of knowledge about what play is doing for the player; means making connections between the chapters on risk, what play is, why it matters and so on, as well as thinking about our own experience as children, and even as adults. Our responses to play will be based on our training and knowledge but also very much on our feelings and beliefs. Acknowledging my personal feelings about the play I am witnessing can help me to consider the response I initially want to make, and balance that with how I might make a different choice that is still good for me and is perhaps better for the players. I may think about taking a deep breath, looking for actual signs that a child is not happy with the way the play is going, rather than assuming that because I wouldn't like it - no one else would either.

A child's personal search for certain play experiences can be motivated by a variety of needs.

△   the child is trying to make sense of experience

△   the child is trying to find out about him or herself

△   the child wonders *"What if ... ?"*

The need of the child could be about -

△   **the past**   *I might need to replay events until I can manage my feelings or change how it was and how I felt until it is manageable*

△   **the present**   *Am I? Can I? Should I?*

△   **the future**   *I wish something would happen; or I fear something could happen but if I play it through now I will be better prepared if it does happen.*

In the classroom we often stop any play that:

△   seems scary   *although children like to feel scared in a safe play space*

△   seems unruly   *although children who stick to the rules in reality love transgressing them in play*

△   seems antisocial   *although children learn about life through exploring extremes, reflecting on antisocial activity helps children make informed choices about being pro-social*

In day-to-day life, children see and hear things that frighten, worry, excite and puzzle them. Remember the answer to uncertainty from the Key Points at the end of Chapter 1? It is, of course, play. Children play because they are confused, uncertain or almost sure, but not quite definite. They play in order to 'work it out'.

Elizabeth Wood (2012, pp.4-5) offered some case studies to a course being created by Early Years specialists for training school staff in the use of play. One of the case studies of an Early Years group was from a planned theme of Pirates.

> *The children were engaged in dynamic imaginative play themes, which involved kidnapping, killing, robbing and handing out punishments such as walking the plank and being tied to a tree. Objections to this case study were raised, on the grounds that the children's play was 'aggressive' and 'anti-social', and should not be encouraged. This case study was duly removed.*

This example raises two issues:

- ➡ The sanitising of play by adults, denying the true nature of play and of childhood
- ➡ The 'play nicely' approach actually inhibits us from training staff to deal with the 'not nice' play that matters so very much to our children

Denying children opportunities to be pirates stops them making sense of the contradictory things they know about pirates; whether from the Caribbean (*Pirates of the Caribbean*, Walt Disney 2003) and to be admired and loved; or from the Arabian Sea, and to be feared. Denying trainee school staff opportunities to reflect on play that is challenging to adults leaves them ill-prepared for the reality of the classroom.

Denying the complicated reality of life, the opposing view of different groups on what is OK and what is not, the messiness that is being human, means no-one gets to 'work it out'.

> Dramatic playing with narratives allows people to try out different
> 'possible selves.'   Edmiston 2011, p.53

Children play being pirates, or anti-heroes, or robbers. Does it mean they will grow up to be such people? No. Does it mean they wonder how it feels to be 'bad'? Yes. Should we have a problem with that? Children also play being doctors, teachers, or firmen. Does it mean they will grow up to be one? Sometimes. But mostly not. They just want to feel powerful, important, clever and strong.

Children arrive in school with a rich variety of early experiences. Cultural, economic and social differences mix together for maybe the first time. Politics, religion, socio-economic factors and family culture inform moral, ethical, practical and pragmatic family practices. Banning some ways of playing gives strong messages to children about the acceptability of those practices.

"We don't play with guns here" (Holland 2003) is the battle-cry of many an Early Years practitioner. I was one myself. Having taught for many years, in many schools, in several areas I have had children in class who will be familiar with guns. Some families will have illegal guns held for reasons that are criminal. Other families have guns legally held for sport, while others still in rural communities have guns as part of their job or lifestyle. 'Guns are not nice' is a message that can make children feel ashamed, proud, embarrassed or rebellious. Working out how guns fit in the world is a personal exploration as well as a social responsibility. Personal beliefs are 'up for grabs' in play. In my view, all that 'zero tolerance' probably does is 'avoid dealing both with children's needs and the bigger social issues underpinning them' (Holland

2003, p.99). So play with guns is most often symbolic play - it is about the child's need to feel powerful - a reversion of role in play for the least powerful members of society.

> Perhaps most important of all, he can find temporary relief and refuge from being small, inexperienced and without any real power, by creating in his imaginative play a world where he is king, where his deepest wishes are fulfilled, and where it is he who makes and breaks the rules.
>
> Kellmer Pringle 2000, p.45

Telling children 'no guns', 'no swords', no symbol of power or protection, tells them - don't think you can be king - you are little, weak and helpless - even in play. We adults are powerful and must use that power with caution. Holland (2003, p.100) warns that blocking children's fantasy play could encourage children to compulsively resist or over-comply with authority without thinking. We benefit when we reflect on the demands and expectations of our workplaces and work cultures, and children can gain from opportunities for choice and reflection too.

Attempts to ban guns in one Nursery I worked in led children, no longer allowed to wield 'guns' made of Lego, to use pan-handles instead. Pans, handles pointing outwards, became the new model of firearm. When pans were removed, cutlery became a weapon, duly put off limits. As the home corner became more and more depleted it was clear the children would play guns in spite of our embargo - possibly more encouraged by the illicitness of it all! Finally, the dolls were pointed at players, to the accompaniment of machine gun sounds and riotous laughter (and yes, the adults laughed too!).

> … children play to violate rules as the existence of rules or taboos itself stimulates children to take risks and transgress boundaries.
>
> Hae-Ryung Yeu 2011, p.133

SUBVERSIVE PLAY:
Finding out about private thoughts and feelings

For children of this age, pretence is a dominant and powerful discourse that they can draw upon to maintain their play, providing the potential for excluding and resisting adult agendas.   Ailwood 2011, p.27

Subversion, the act of undermining the regime, is often a part of being young. It is part of the way to become separate. The child in an Early Years setting is finding out that he or she can have a life that is not completely controlled by adults, and can even be unknown to adults. Whispering and passing notes behind the teacher's back is a subversive act as old as the hills. Something inside each of us drives us to 'get away' with 'pulling the wool' over the eyes of authority figures; whether that is parents or teachers; or the referee missing a sneaky hand-ball at the crucial moment of a football match while none of the players own up, and the instructor turning her back on us while we take a quick breather in the middle of our exercise class! Subversive play develops:

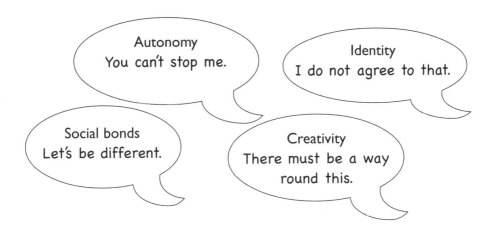

I guess we don't know when we might need any given skill from our repertoire of behaviours, but maybe we can all think of times when a little dissembling or a quick sleight of hand got us out of a tricky situation or maybe helped out a friend in a moment of need. As an adult I know it is easy for me to employ the double standard of: accepting that I and most other adults engage sometimes in subterfuge, but not accepting that children (or trainee, apprentice adults) should be allowed opportunities to do so - even in play!

And as a society we can't know how one person's difference, creativity and ability to not follow unthinkingly the fact that *"That's just how it's always been"* or *"That's just how we do it round her*e*"* will provide innovation and change that improves lives and practices. But most of us may agree that difference should be valued and creativity must be fostered. You probably guess by now that I'm going to say - *play is the way that we do that!*

I don't remember being particularly defiant or disobedient as a child in school or at home, but I do remember 'playing tricks', cheating at games, waiting till no-one was looking and weighing up the possibilities around 'being found out' before breaking a rule or not following a request. I imagine that subversive play is part of developing a questioning attitude and also a belief maybe that 'anything is possible' and that 'where there's a will there's a way'.

> Let us … praise the perpetual subversiveness of the tyke and the scamp.
>
> Kane 2005, p.147

'Scamps' find the cracks in our spaces, rules and logic and then play there. 'Tykes' squeeze between the rails, run over the boundaries and jump the walls we put in their way, and when they get where they are going, they play. Hae-Ryung Yeu (2011) knows children well enough to recognise that they break rules for the sake of it;

play in ways they know we adults don't like and are 'egged on' by the very things we do to try and limit their experiences. Researchers seem to agree that 'children in particular are like Houdini: they escape and contest the definitions, boundaries, rules and policies that adults impose on play' (Wood 2012, p.4). And thank goodness they do. As Kane says - let's praise the ingenuity and determination of children to play.

and so ... ?

If we don't allow 'not nice' play, children cannot choose to 'play nicely'. Imposing rules limits the players' options for creating their own rules. Without 'baddies' there can be no 'goodies' in the drama.

> In the fairy tales, side by side with the terrible figures, we find the immemorial comforters and protectors, the radiant ones; and the terrible figures are not merely terrible, but sublime.   C. S. Lewis 1982

Like everything in life, balance is key in our approach to play and in our belief of how 'nice' children have to be. We can find ways to provide play time when our rules are in place and also some time when children get to play in ways that they choose. Children then get to develop strategies for managing feelings and situations that are 'not nice'. Playing children learn from opportunities for feeling good about the choices they willingly make to include others: to compromise their own wishes for the good of the group: and to deny themselves pleasure in order to spare others' pain.

KEY POINTS

Children need time to work things out for themselves in play

Life skills include coping strategies for difficult 'not nice' experiences and children need play opportunities to learn them

Superhero play includes saving the world, as well as destroying it, giving children the time and space to explore the dark and the light

Symbolism is one of play's most important and useful components: stabbing, shouting and shooting in play may mean anger, frustration, jealousy and fear can be worked through

Pretence and fantasy are not the same as actions in reality

Play nicely or don't play at all: *Where do we go from here?*

In order for changes in practice to take place, the Play, Schools and Integrated Children's Settings Group (2008) believe that the following developments need to take place in government policy. It recommends:

> Play is a principal and recognised part of Healthy School status. All Healthy School coordinators need to promote the importance of play in children's health and wellbeing.   Play England, 2008, *Play in Schools and Integrated Settings: A position statement* London: NCB

The play-full school would -

☺ Include a member of staff with Playworker qualification in their PSHE team

☺ Provide free play opportunities within their PSHE provision

If you want to know more, try reading

Jones, G. (2002) *Killing Monsters: Why children need fantasy, super-heroes, and make believe violence* NY: Basic Books

Olusoga, Y. (2009) We Don't Play Like That Here: Social, cultural and gender perspectives on play *in* Brock, A; Dodds, S; Jarvis, P. & Olusoga, Y. *Perspectives on Play: learning for life.* Harlow Essex: Pearson Education

If you want to understand more, try reading

Sendak, M. (2000) *Where The Wild Things Are* London: Red Fox

If you want a 15 minute group or individual training try watching

This might be your worst fear - Toy Story clip 3 'Rough Play' on youtube.com: youtube.com/watch?v=GrwcycSgmPU

But this is the reality - Rough Play the Renegade Way - from *It's OK Not to Share* youtube.com/watch?v=0nqcjrDi8dc

Chapter 4

Play is a risky business

"Adults don't really care about you playing - they are too worried you will hurt yourself."   Eight-year-old girl, IPA Scotland 2011, p.5

Is this the message we are giving our children? Can we know everything that we do about the role of play in brain development, emotional wellbeing, resilience and social belonging, and still seem to value child's play so little? Is it that sometimes, as busy parents and carers, we can't always make the time to let the children play? Or are we naturally and rightly anxious about what could happen to children while they play in our care, and so sometimes become unable to also hold in our minds their absolute need for this play?

When I see a small child, I find I often wish they could be protected from the challenges and difficulties of life. And yet I recognise that I too have experienced pride, exhilaration, a sense of achievement and personal strength when the going got tough but I managed to 'hang on in there'. Bob Hughes (2012) tells us that 'Play, like life, is not safe, and if it is, it is not play' (p.207). While most of us might not agree with the idea that play *has to be* 'not safe' in order to be called play, I imagine more of us can agree that play prepares us for life: and that the truth is that neither play nor life can be safe for all of us all of the time.

In this chapter we will think about how we balance our play provisions to offer both risk and safety, and to meet the needs of the players and the providers, ourselves and the places we work.

THE QUESTIONS TO CONSIDER ARE:

RISK - THE CHANCE OR PROBABILITY 'SOMETHING' MIGHT HAPPEN

Do we understand the difference between chance and probability, and what do we make of all the statistics?

ELIMINATING RISK (AND THE RISKS IF WE DO SO)

Ensuring physical safety is the responsibility of parents and professionals: if we get it wrong by being consistently over-cautious, do other important things get lost along the way?

GETTING THE BALANCE RIGHT

How do we keep children safe enough to explore and test out their world?

EMOTIONAL RISK TAKING

Sticks and stones may break your bones and words can surely hurt you: how are life's painful lessons diluted in play?

TAKING PHYSICAL RISKS IN ORDER TO INDUCE, THEN MANAGE, FEAR

What does the physical risk-taker learn about him or herself and is it about more than just what the body can bear?

BUT WHAT IF WE DON'T ALLOW ANY RISKS?

Quite rightly, sometimes we absolutely won't allow or tolerate risk. But what happens if we never do?

RISK

Life is uncertain; it is full of risk. 'Danger is everywhere and always' (Blastland & Spiegelhalter 2013, pp.4-5). 'Be prepared' - for life and its inherent riskiness - may be the best we can achieve. Safe play provision is essential, and it's important that we learn how to recognise and avoid hazards. But learning to take risks that are within our capabilities is important as well.

> To understand caution, to compute risk, to respect the built and natural environments from the perspective of the risks they contain, but not to be afraid of them, is essential to personal survival and a happy life. It is need-to-know material ...
> Hughes 2012, p.113

We seem to live in a time when 'risk' can only be bad and is always associated with danger. If there's a risk it could rain, it just means you need to take an umbrella or 'risk' getting wet. *"Try it - but there's a risk you might like it"* can apply to the 'danger' of finding you actually love broccoli after years of believing you would hate it; or the possibility you could find out you become hooked on stamp collecting after telling your friend he is wasting his time filling albums with little sticky squares of patterned paper! The 'danger' of making a new friendship, with someone utterly different to the rest of your mates, might just be the risk you take that reminds you of forgotten parts of yourself - that you then enjoy re-aquainting yourself with (and I bet brings out new ways to be playful too!).

Trying new things always involves a degree of risk, in that we are entering into uncertainty - our brain has no history to draw on to predict the outcome of our new behaviour. That is probably why facing a new experience we often become extremely polite with an *"After you";* or a *"No really - you go first";* or in other words, *"I can learn by your experience and that will give me additional information about how to approach this"*. *"I will if you will"* means - *"If I am going to make a fool of myself, it will feel better if I am not the only one."* The inherent risk in trying something new can be that: I may look silly; I might fail; I could hurt myself; or I might possibly discover I need to change my beliefs about myself or my world.

Risk contains two elements: 'chance' and 'probability' (Blastland & Spiegelhalter 2013, p.291). The *chance* it could rain in Britain always exists! The *probability* it will rain on any given day is a topic of many a conversation. Risk exists, so does danger, but the *perception* of risk may influence the choices of individuals, institutions and societies, and impact on each of us in ways that we have yet to understand. The chance something *could* happen is not the same as the likelihood something *will* happen. The risk of something happening is a reality we need to have a means of thinking about. If there are lots of things I want to try, I will need to recognise that some of these actions may have consequences that I may not enjoy or that may hurt me. So I need to have an 'internal set of scales' in my brain that can *weigh up* losses versus gains, and pain versus pleasure. I need to have an 'in-built ruler' for *measuring* little risks and big risks.

> *I was attending a conference one Saturday at some distance from where I live, and I was booking my train ticket in advance. I found I had two choices; a train that gave me just 30 minutes to cross London after the conference was scheduled to end, or a later train that meant me waiting over an hour at the station, even if the conference finished a little late and the journey back to my station took longer than it should. I was able to consider the facts:*
>
> i   *I wanted to be home as early as possible*
>
> ii   *I did not want to have a frustrating wait at the station*
>
> iii   *I might miss the earlier train and then have to pay for another ticket*

My 'scales' weighed up the potential for pleasure versus the possibility
of pain, and my 'ruler' measured the acceptability of the consequence of
a financial cost if an additional ticket had to be purchased. I booked the
early train, and when I caught it and sat back as it drew out of the station
I experienced a smug satisfaction. If I had missed it I think (but can't
know) I would have accepted that the risk had still been worth the cost.

The ability to weigh up and measure are part of having 'common sense'. They are part of being wise. They are not skills we are born with, but they can be developed with practice and experience.

As a child, like most people, I took risks that worked out and ones that didn't. I was not unusual in sporting almost constant grazed knees; frequent sticking plasters, and occasional tiny black stitches. But apart from one particularly ill-judged gymnastic display in an old concrete coal-bunker, most things worked out OK in the end! I think I learned to juggle my desire to fit in with my sense of my own capabilities; balancing my wish to look cool with my own beliefs around being kind. Without knowingly thinking back to times I took risks in play, I have a store of information to unconsciously refer to, and bruising memories are likely to be retained as experiences to be learned from.

More difficult to stick with were play times when I had to wait and trust the game and myself and my peers. Pastimes such as hide-and-seek (or, more often, you-hide-while-I-peek) stretched my patience, my tolerance of isolation and my sense of 'it will be alright in the end'. But I did find my hidden friends, or my friends got fed up with waiting to be found and gave up. *And* I was found and welcomed back, not lost forever or left abandoned while the seekers went home for tea. When the waiting to be found felt uncomfortable or lonely I learned ways of 'cheating' that passed for humour, and even more helpfully, I learned not to hide too well if I didn't like waiting ages to be found. Risk management for littlies - learning on the job.

Eliminating risk

The body most frequently blamed when activities are banned, games are prohibited and fun is outlawed warns:

> Don't use health and safety law as a convenient scapegoat or we will challenge you. The creeping culture of risk-aversion and fear of litigation ... puts at risk our children's education and preparation for adult life.
>
> Judith Hackitt - Chair of the UK Health and Safety Executive
>
> *quoted in* Blastland & Spiegelhalter 2013, p.61

We may soon find that the biggest risk we are taking, in avoiding any possible hurt bodies or hurt feelings, is that we are creating a generation who cannot assess potential for danger in the environment, or their own potential for coping. Somewhere, somehow, we are getting it wrong. And our children know it. They see the flaws in our arguments over safety and risk. In one school next to a recreation ground (Kapasi & Gleave 2009, p.23), children noted that:

> *"We play at the recreation ground in school time. When we go over there, we are not allowed to play on the play equipment and it's unfair, but we are allowed after school, and it's 'perfectly safe' then!"*

Other children are picking up on the anxieties of us adults. Only 35% of the children in a Scottish survey feel happy and safe playing in their street (IPA Scotland 2011, p.29). Children are aware of the reasons parents worry about safety. They know parents worry about their child:

Getting into, or being hurt by gangs

Getting lost ✗ Being followed ✗ Being taken

Encountering violence

Other surveys however, show that parents and children are not averse to risk - it is the professionals who have responsibility for providing play and play spaces who avoid any possibility for blame or guilt for accidents during play.

> Although the children's mothers and Early Childhood practitioners believed risky play was an important aspect of learning and development and encouraged this type of play, observations of children's play at a local playground and their Early Childhood centre revealed that these contexts provided limited opportunities for risky play. Regulatory factors and requirements for playground safety were identified as having a detrimental impact on the quality of play in these settings creating tension between adult beliefs about the benefits of risky play and its provision.
>
> Little, Wyver & Gibson 2011, p.113

Parents and professionals may feel they can accept or tolerate some risk. But fear of litigation, or of being the only ones brave enough to follow their gut instinct on what is right, means local service providers have become far more conservative. Wheway (2011) found relatively consistent results to consultations on playground provision.

Among parents,

> about 21% thought playgrounds were too safe
> about 73% thought they were about right
> about 6% thought they were too dangerous

He also found that '... whenever I do consultations, many children and parents ask for equipment that is 'bigger', 'faster', 'higher' etc.' (p.7). Whether it is parents or professionals sanitising play experiences, latterly there have been many pressures that impact on play provision. This in turn impacts on the opportunities for children to learn to manage risk.

Tim Gill, the author of *No Fear: Growing up in a risk averse society* (2007, p.20) gives two reasons he regularly hears for the rise of our current 'risk averse society': regulatory bureaucracy (the Nanny State), and so-called 'compensation culture'. Gill also argues that it may be political or organisational targets for easily-measured outcomes that contribute to the creation of risk-averse play provision. Staying safe by creating a 'tick box' measure ignores or avoids the harder-to-quantify consequences of experiences and opportunities, and is at odds with the complexity of life. Quantity is so much easier to measure than quality.

While we aim to reduce accidents, increase exam results or spend a certain number of hours studying subjects at desks, we are not concentrating on what experiences children miss through the things they are no longer exposed to. Measuring a child's ability to assess risk is harder than measuring the number of hours they spend doing literacy. Quantifying the 'bounce-back-ability' or resilience to set-backs and knocks is so much harder than numbering accidents in the playground over any given week. In target-led times, the things that are most important in life may take second place to the things it is easier to measure or to prove.

GETTING THE BALANCE RIGHT

"You need to be protected but not that much that you can't learn anything."
11-year-old girl, IPA Scotland 2011, p.5

The news is full of the dangers in our communities, but the perception of the risk we are exposed to by these dangers may have nothing to do with the numbers; the 'chance' or the 'probability'. By and large, childhood is actually a relatively safe stage of life in the West. After the first few weeks of life, risk of death is the least it will be until we hit 50 (Blastland & Spiegelhalter 2013).

> Babies don't do much, but they do live dangerously, briefly, compared with others. As soon as they become young children, they get up to allsorts, safer from death than anyone.   p.23

Numerically, that is just how it is. Children in many countries now live safer lives, they have fewer accidents. Here in the UK we have done a great job of protecting our children from accidents.

> The good news is that the number of accidental deaths has been declining steadily. In England and Wales in 1979, almost 1,100 children were killed in accidents, compared with 139 in 2012.   Miskin Group 2014

Is all the news about recent changes in children's lives good? Do children have happier lives? Does their adult-enforced protection from harm in childhood lead to continued benefits from harm later on in their lives? I'm not sure we know the answers to those questions yet.

While death and disability from accidents in childhood has decreased dramatically, mental health issues seem to have substantially increased. Young Minds (youngminds.org.uk) figures in 2014 tell us that:

- 1 in 10 children and young people aged 5-16 suffer from a diagnosable mental health disorder - that is, around 3 children in every class

- 290,000 children and young people have an anxiety disorder

- Nearly 80,000 children and young people suffer from severe depression

- Over 8,000 children aged under 10-years-old suffer from severe depression

- The number of young people aged 15-16 with depression nearly doubled between the 1980's and the 2000's

Another study found significant increases in reports of emotional problems, including depression and anxiety, in children between 1979 and 1996 (Harvard Medical School 2013). If depression *is* lack of play (Sutton-Smith 2001) then maybe changing how, when and where children play might be having unintended consequences we have yet to understand. It's possible that ensuring children's safety in the short-term by regulation and adult-enforced risk management could be leading to detrimental long-term implications for children's emotional health, the other side of the risk-benefit equation of providing 'safe enough' risk in children's play provision.

Kathy Caprino, whose interest is in developing leaders, writes about the '*7 Crippling Parenting Behaviours*' that stifle our children's development (2014). She recognises arrogance and low self-esteem as two significant outcomes of not letting our children experience risk. *Arrogance* is bound to be contrary to realistic judgement, and probably contributes to poor perception and management of risk. *Low self-esteem* brings with it other kinds of dangers for the future safety of our kids. Not only may low self-esteem mean we don't trust our own judgements and then too readily rely on the choices and directions of others, but it also detracts from emotional wellbeing. Little & Wyver (2008) agree that taking away opportunities for play that can involve risk leads to children lacking confidence in themselves.

In most areas we encourage our children, and we credit them with the ability to make choices and take responsibility. We want them to have greater self-esteem and self-belief. But our perceptions of danger where our children are concerned are always influenced by emotional irrationality. Human risk analysis is an emotional process. Following the World Trade Centre attacks in 2001 one statistical study showed that over one thousand additional deaths occurred on US roads in the following three months. People afraid to fly chose to drive instead, presumably some despite their knowledge of the vastly increased risk of harm involved in choosing this mode of transport (Ropeik 2010, p.66). Fear overrides rational thought. It makes us look at the benefits of our choices and ignore the potential downsides.

Children now have only a small chance of having an accident; but the *fear of things happening* may be stopping us from allowing children to develop independent risk assessment skills that will offer them protection in later life. Recovering from scrapes, scratches and sprains may be physically painful and temporarily knock a child's confidence and desire for independence: but never experiencing the bumps and knocks of physical play may do more to damage resilience in the long term.

'Cotton wool' children are growing up without having been given the opportunity to learn how to assess risks. Children have to have bumps and scrapes to teach them what's safe and what's not.

Dr Amanda Gummer, *in* Gill 2011, p.10

The Play Safety Forum brings together experts on play and specialists in safety in order to shape the most appropriate policy on safety in play provision. This 'risk analysis' is a model for how the pros and cons of activities should be assessed. The Forum considers:

➡   the likelihood of coming to harm
➡   the severity of that harm
➡   the benefits, rewards or outcomes of the activity

Play experts can argue for the benefits of play, the importance of risks in play, and the value of independence and choice in play from their perspective. This is balanced by the experts in accident prevention offering their perspective on risk. This weighing up of the possible harm versus the established benefit leads to an informed decision on how to proceed. If schools have no Play Policy, no Play Leader, no informed advocate for the benefits of play or a play expert who understands the potential harm to the child of living in 'A School Without Play', an uninformed or catch-all approach to policy on Health and Safety will win every time.

The latest government advice for Health and Safety in schools makes it clear to schools that they are an important element in the child's development of ability to manage risk:

●   *Children should be able to experience a wide range of activities. Health and safety measures should help them to do this safely, not stop them.*

●   *It is important that children learn to understand and manage the risks that are a normal part of life.*

●   *Common sense should be used in assessing and managing the risks of any activity*

- *Health and safety procedures should always be proportionate to the risks of an activity.*
- *Staff should be given the training they need so they can keep themselves and children safe and manage risks effectively.*

DfE 2013a, p.4

The addition of two final points of guidance:

△   Informed consideration of the *benefits* of activities must always
    be included in every assessment
△   Evidence of any *detriment* from not experiencing the activity
    must also be considered

… would be better still.

> Children need and want to take risks when they play. Play provision aims to respond to these needs and wishes by offering children stimulating, challenging environments for exploring and developing their abilities. In doing this, play provision aims to manage the level of risk so that children are not exposed to unacceptable risks of death or serious injury.
>
> Play Safety Forum 2008

Providing children with 'stimulating, challenging environments for exploring and developing their abilities' changes outdoor play provision. The thought of it may add to our anxiety levels as staff, but the reality may improve behaviour and increase social cohesion while also making children safer. Investing in, and improvement of, play provision can pay off in terms of measurable increases in physical and emotional safety during outside playtimes. For example, one study by the Forestry Commission and a Glasgow primary school (Groves & McNish 2011) which enriched outdoor play opportunities, led to a 'demonstrable' increase in resilience (p.iv) and to a 'dramatic' decrease in accidents. Playground 'incidents' (physical squabbles) also fell significantly, as did children reporting problems. Children and adults recognised this was due to better provision increasing enjoyment and minimising problems.

A new play ethos, improved play spaces, and play training for all of us working with children in schools might support a change in our feelings and confidence, which in turn will probably nurture our ability to allow more 'scope for children to risk assess and take decisions for themselves' (Groves & McNish 2011, p.iv).

I know that sometimes my response to the question of how to keep children safe has been to limit their play opportunities, and by doing so, risk squashing their exuberance. Improving play spaces and providing better staff training is a far better answer (*see* Chapter 17, on limit setting).

TAKING EMOTIONAL RISKS

'Risky play' is thrilling and exciting forms of play that involve a risk of physical injury' (Sandseter 2011, p258). Sandseter makes a distinct subset of play that is 'risky play', unlike Hughes at the beginning of this chapter who believes all play involves risk. For different children, at different ages and stages, the severity of risk changes. This is true for most activities, with maturation. For example, the twenty-five year old (hopefully) has a greater capacity for empathy than we might expect from a five-year-old. Often the longer a worker has been employed, the higher the level of responsibility.

The adolescent's need for risk taking is far greater than that of a two-year-old. When a two-year-old learns through trial and error, through bumps and bruises, just what his body can do, his brain is developing risk-assessment skills. It is vital that the risk balancing and measuring tools (the ones that we rely on so often in navigating our world, *see above*) have been learned through smaller, safer, more manageable, age-appropriate risks at two, rather than in adolescence by a teenager who is unable to make decisions based on previous experience.

Most skills we build up in our children over time: from giving a toddler the right change to hand over the counter, to helping them select from a handful of coins, to giving them pocket money and encouraging some budgeting skills before the young adult finds himself out in the workplace or running a home. Weaning is another example: the new-born's liquid diet is usually moved through puréed then mashed food before chewing and biting. The 2001 UNICEF report, *Child Deaths by Injury in Rich Nations* notes that,

> … children's judgement of potential dangers and of their own physical ability is developed through pushing the boundaries of their experience, developing their own sense of risk and danger, and taking progressive responsibility for their own lives.   2001a, endnote 2

As well as developing resilience through physically testing play, I would also say that many play experiences are emotionally risky: and that doing things that may involve a risk of emotional injury or hurt pride is also important for developing emotional resilience. I would argue that risky play also includes play that is thrilling because it involves a risk of social or emotional injury, rather than necessarily a physical one. By concentrating solely on the risk of physical injury, and understandably attempting to eliminate risk to the body, we may have failed to consider the human need for emotional and social risk-taking.

Imaginative play, role-play or social play, all involve the risk of rejection, derision, 'failure' and pain. An adult unable to 'compute' these risks will expose him or herself to danger or damage that could have social or emotional consequences. In my view, the life or love-limiting impact of *not* taking emotional risks is as damaging as the total avoidance of any situation with the risk of physical injury.

> ... what the evidence seems to point to, across both natural ... (neuroscience and social (ethnography) science perspectives, is that children deliberately seek out uncertainty (both physical and emotional) in their play.
>
> Lester & Russell 2008, p.11

The research and writing on risk and physical play also applies to play that has social, emotional or cognitive risks. Uncertainty, fear, anxiety, joy, disappointment, pride and surprise are all outcomes of every type of play. All play offers opportunities for failure and for success. Learning involves challenge and the potential for emotional hurt. But the difference with emotional risk and challenge in play is that in play it can be a safer risk.

In the long run of play, 'He who dares, wins'

Control over action and outcomes in play can help a child to explore a situation that is scary and unclear:

Sudi	*You be the brother and I'll be the Dad.*
Billy	*Ok - I'll be the brother who is leaving home.*
Sudi	*No - you be the brother who is sick. You lie there and be really ill.*
Billy	*Ow, ow it hurts, it really hurts.*
Sudi	*NO, not like that, very quiet and crying.*
Billy	*Sob, sob, sob.*
Sudi	*Don't cry my boy, Daddy is here.*

Sudi	*Doctor, doctor, we need a doctor.*
Nan	*Knock, knock, Doctor Haddad is here.*
Sudi	*Doctor can you make my son better? He needs special medicine*
Nan	*Yes he must have a BIG needle right now.*
Sudi	*No - you say he has to go to hospital.*
Nan	*Put your son in the ambulance.*
Sudi	*Ah - I think he's better now - come on Billy let's do the car-wash game.*

Control over how far to take an idea in play gives the player a safety not available in the real situation, and gives opportunities for managing feelings and increasing emotional tolerance. Sudi had a narrative firmly in mind and let his fellow players know it! But abruptly, after seeming to be taking the play in a certain direction he could end the story and move away to a new, less anxiety provoking activity.

This scenario reminds us that play will not always be fun or make the player feel happy, as we discovered in Chapter 1. It also shows us that a child can often stop the play for himself when it becomes uncomfortable for him, and he won't always need us to make those decisions. If I had been watching Sudi and was aware that his brother was actually very poorly and that Sudi had been really upset about it earlier in the day, I might have moved in to try and alter the play in some way - which actually might have prevented Sudi from feeling a sense of control over a scary reality, or developing an understanding of his feelings or the feelings and behaviours of others in his life. Letting the play unfold might have given Sudi these possibilities.

I hope the last chapter helped you to reflect on some ways we act around the play of our children, and how 'trusting the process' - believing in play as the way children regulate their feelings and find out what they think - means adults can sometimes watch and wait while children work through the thing they are looking at through the lens of their play. And don't forget that in Chapter 16 we will think more about what to say and how to say it when we are alongside a child at play.

Dramatic play offers opportunities for being in social relationships, and for observing the playing out of social roles, often in extreme representations. *Cinderella* is a children's classic (Perrault 2002). The quiet child playing out being an Ugly Sister gets to have a 'best friend' in a gang of two; gets to be mean to someone and gets to lose out to the quiet child, Cinders. When being Cinderella, she gets to believe that the Ugly Sisters are really horrid and nobody likes them really and they don't get their man in the end. All of this social commentary can be acceptable and often enjoyable because it is play.

Social play offers challenge but hopefully it is a safer risk, as children are more tolerant and more forgiving to peers in play than at other times. Play itself can make children more cooperative. Play is rewarding to children and they invest in making it work, even if that means compromising with others and 'putting up with' peers they don't usually get along with.

> In play the roles and rules of the world can be experienced and explored by the child in a safe environment, free from the consequences possible in the real world.   Olusoga 2009, p.47

You know the risks

So as well as providing hazard-free spaces for physical play, children need safe places and times to explore thoughts and feelings too, as much as or possibly even more than their physical exploration of the world. 'Some experience of physical and psychological pain and pleasure is essential to making informed and balanced life judgements' (Hughes 2012, p.158). 'One valuable approach to risk management in play provision is to make the risks as apparent as possible to children' (Ball, Gill & Siegel 2008, p.116). While this is clearly relevant to physical play it is also relevant to cognitive risk-taking and involved in risk-taking in social and dramatic play.

If children know the things that *could* go wrong, the way that they *may* be embarrassed, they will feel safe enough to take risks and to learn to balance the harm versus reward risk in play. A fifteen year old boy dressing up as a banana may feel safe in his class with peers and a teacher who he judges will support his play. Risking the Headteacher coming in might be something that needs further consideration (*benefits* of the fun versus *risk* of being embarrassed): while knowing that an older class will pass the windows during the lesson would be essential information for informing his choice. Control of choices is essential for activities to be play. Control of risk and levels of difficulty ensure that playing is a dynamic process, where the player manages his own tolerance of uncertainty.

We need to gradually relinquish control of the risk level in play to the child at a pace appropriate to their unique capacities. Through play, children learn about the outside world of danger, pleasure, harm, reward and reality. They also discover their internal ability to cope with fear, disappointment, pain, pride and joy.

TAKING PHYSICAL RISKS IN ORDER TO INDUCE, THEN MANAGE, FEAR

play at great heights

play at high speed   ✗   play with dangerous tools

play near dangerous elements   ✗   rough-and-tumble play

play where children can disappear/get lost

Anyone who knows children will recognise each of these play types, some of them often appearing together.

➡   It is the "*Higher!*" and "*Faster!*" of the toddler on the swing

➡   It is the "*I'll fight you for it!*", "*Give that here!*", "*You'll have to make me*" of the middle childhood argy-bargy

➡   It is the "*Bet I can*", "*Bet you can't*" of the teenage rope-swing river crossing and it is from the 'peep-bo' games of babies, to the "*Let's run away from home*" of the adolescents who only come back when the hours without food mean that the pangs of hunger takes over from the thrill of the adventure

Any new play, any stretching of the experience of established play, will involve risk - the uncertainty of how it will go and the understanding that the consequences will be greater than previous play challenges that have already been overcome and added to a '*done that*' list. The rewarding feeling of the thrill will be heightened, the painful feeling of the failure, disappointment or shame will be magnified. So why do we all do it? Push ourselves to develop or expose ourselves to risk? I think I play at the boundaries of my previous experiences and at the edge of my comfort zone because I want to know what I am capable of. I also recognise times when I play with ideas, reactions and possibilities to lessen the impact of things that I anticipate may happen. *"How would I cope if ...?'* is a thought I am familiar with and asking myself *"What's the worst that could happen?"* is a technique I have learned. Both are playful ways of looking at anticipated problems.

> Sandseter and others (2011) provide compelling evidence that taking risks in play is a natural coping mechanism, which helps to reduce fears and tackle phobias. In this sense, risk-taking in play mirrors many aspects of cognitive behavioural therapy; by thinking less negatively about anxieties it can help to reduce anxious behaviour. Over-protection can cause children to become more anxious and develop behaviours associated with anxiety throughout their lives. The report suggests that risk-taking in play can reduce anxiety problems in children.
>
> Gleave & Cole-Hamilton 2012, p.11

Gray (2011, pp.455-456) agrees that when playing, players 'seem to be dosing themselves with moderate degrees of fear, as if deliberately learning how to deal with both the physical and emotional challenges of the moderately dangerous conditions they generate'. Although I'm not a fan of horror movies I love reading thrillers and 'who dunnit' novels. Why do I love the feeling of turning the page, knowing I'm going to find another shock that will tingle my spine or make my hair stand on end? I think it's because I can laugh at myself and say *"It's not real, it's not my life."* But it may also be so that if ever 'it' did happen, my previous vicarious exposure would at least give me some sense of familiarity. Children themselves recognise the ambivalent feelings they experience when taking risks in play. They know, just as we adults once did, the dread and excitement, the thrill and the apprehension, of the rollercoaster ride. They understand that 'the goal of risky play is balancing on the edge between intense exhilaration and pure fear' (Sandseter 2011, p.3).

> *"It's very fun and very scary and all sorts of things ... and then I feel both excited and really scared at the same time!"*   Five-year-old boy, *ibid*

When I 'dose' myself (Gray 2011) with little bite-size chunks of the seemingly intolerable, I am learning how much fear I can tolerate and how much challenge I feel comfortable with.

> If too little fear is induced, the activity is boring; if too much is induced, it becomes no longer play but terror. Nobody but the child himself or herself knows the right dose, which is why all such play must be self-directed and self-controlled.   Gray 2011, p.456

These benefits of play as mastery over experience, play as de-sensitising exposure, play as practice for future fearful times, and play as recovery from past fearful experiences are some of the elements of play that make playing therapeutic as well as fun.

BUT WHAT IF WE DON'T?

Back to our old friend - the *"What if we don't provide play?"* question. Lots and lots of play, including play that involves risk and challenge makes us able to face future threats and difficulties with a *'can do'*, *'there's got to be a way'* attitude. No play, or not enough of play that gets us used to our feelings of fear and our ability to problem-solve and overcome, makes us see others and the world in general as a very unsafe place.

> For the well-versed player, life in all its challenges can be experienced as a complex playground. For the play-deprived, life is too often seen as a battleground.
>
> Stuart Brown, *in his introduction to* Crenshaw & Stewart 2015, p.xii

We have all seen children willingly choose to take a risk in their play. Hughes (2012, p.207) acknowledges that play chosen by children will include elements of physical or emotional risk. He believes that risk is 'essential'. Without risk-takers there would be no problem-solvers. But if risk-takers don't have good enough risk-assessment skills they won't be around long enough to solve many problems! Taking risks in play is the way we learn to be safe risk-takers. Not developing risk management skills in childhood could lead to not only risk-averse populations, but more damaging still - 'risk-naïve' adults (Hackitt, *in* Gill 2011, p.10).

We all want the very best for our children; and natural instinct helps us to protect our young from dangers in order that they survive. We may be well on the way to minimising the number of childhood accidents and increasing infant survival in our Western economies: now is the time to enable our young to flourish and to become independent, risk-savvy, resilient grown-ups. It is up to us to create spaces where children have the safety they need in order 'to explore, experiment, try things out and to take risks' (Tovey 2007, p.102). And the way to do that is to play.

and so ...

KEY POINTS

Through experience children learn that new challenges often carry a risk to wellbeing

Children need to understand that some risks are worth taking - others are not

With overcoming risk comes satisfaction and new skills, new friends, new understanding and so on

Experience teaches that with failure comes feelings of disappointment, embarrassment, pain, and so on - but these pass, and you survive

Managing risks develops resilience and feelings of being strong

There are 'safe' risks that feed the hunger for challenge, peer recognition and chemical thrills

Taking no risks is dangerous too!

Play is a risky business: *Where do we go from here?*

In play provision we will always follow National Government guidance and our own school's policies and procedures on safety and risk assessment.

But we need to all know what the Health and Safety Executive are saying about play provision (and not, as I have done in the past, guess, assume and listen to media misrepresentations!). Their 2012 'Children's Play and Leisure - Promoting a Balanced Approach' advises:

Striking the right balance *does* mean:

✓ Weighing up risks and benefits when designing and providing play opportunities and activities

✓ Focussing on and controlling the most serious risks, and those that are not beneficial to the play activity or foreseeable by the user

✓ Recognising that the introduction of risk might form part of play opportunities and activity

✓ Understanding that the purpose of risk control is not the elimination of all risk, and so accepting that the possibility of even serious or life-threatening injuries cannot be eliminated, though it should be managed

✓ Ensuring that the benefits of play are experienced to the full

Striking the right balance *does not* mean:

✗ All risks must be eliminated or continually reduced

✗ Every aspect of play provision must be set out in copious paperwork as part of a misguided security blanket

✗ Detailed assessments aimed at high-risk play activities are used for low-risk activities

✗   Ignoring risks that are not beneficial or integral to the play activity, such as those introduced through poor maintenance of equipment

✗   Mistakes and accidents will not happen

The play-full school would -

☺   Have its own 'Play Safety Forum' and gather pupils' views on play and risk in their school across all provision

☺   Include an analysis of *lost benefits* when considering risk

☺   Monitor unintended consequences of *lost opportunities* or changes in practice

☺   Ensure all staff have copies of

Ball, D., Gill, T. & Spiegel, B. (2013) *Managing Risk in Play Provision: Implementation Guide* (second edition) London: National Children's Bureau

Managing Risk in Play Provision: A Position Statement Play Safety Forum (2008) London: Play England/National children's Bureau

If you want to know more, try reading

Blastland, M. & Spiegelhalter, D. (2013) *The Norm Chronicles. Stories and numbers about danger* London: Profile Books Ltd

Caprino, K. (2014) *Crippling Parenting Behaviors that Keep Children from Growing into Leaders.* Available at: forbes.com/sites/kathycaprino/2014/01/16/7-crippling-parenting-behaviors-that-keep-children-from-growing-into-leaders/

Department for Education (DfE) (2013a) Health and safety: Advice on legal duties and powers for local authorities, school leaders, school staff and governing bodies. London: DfE

Groves, L. & McNish, H. (2011) *Natural Play: Making a difference to children's learning and wellbeing. A longitudinal study of the Forestry Commission - Merrylee Primary School - Glasgow City Council partnership 2008-2011.* Available at: edubuzz.org/equallywell/files/2011/11/Natural-Play-Study_Forestry-Commission_1008111.pdf

Little, H. & Wyver, S. (2008). Outdoor play - Does avoiding the risks reduce the benefits? *Australian Journal of Early Childhood.* Vol. 33:2 pp.33-40.

Little, H., Wyver, S. & Gibson, F. (2011) The Influence of Play Context and Adult Attitudes on Young Children's Physical Risk-taking During Outdoor Play. *European Early Childhood Education Research Journal.* Vol. 19 pp.113–131.

UNICEF (2001a) *Child Deaths by Injury in Rich Nations.* Available at: unicef-irc.org/publications/pdf/repcard2e.pdf

If you want to understand more, try reading

Rankin, J. (1998) *Scaredy Cat* London: Red Fox

If you want a 15 minute group or individual training, try watching

Christopher Barnes' 2013 TEDx Talk on 'The Merits of Risk'

Available from Tedx on their website tedxtalks.ted.com or on youtube.com

Chapter 5

Play and the X-box factor

Confusing reporting suggests that time spent playing on or with technology can improve the lives of children, or, harm the developing child and take time away from other vital play activities. Never has a saying been more relevant: 'It's not what you do, it's the way that you do it' (I will come back to this saying in Chapter 15 when we think about our role in the lives and play of children and how we can make such a difference to both). Gill (2011, p.4) acknowledges that there are pros and cons to having the new play media available to young people. He feels that there used to be more freedom in children's play life, but it was also 'less glitzy'! I think young children are often drawn towards bright colours and fascinated by fast movement. Hand-held devices offer access to a 'glitzy' fantasy world, that can be at once more realistic than other toys, but also more dream-like or nightmarish. A tablet or phone offers instant access to Hollywood or Disneyworld. We can be on a spaceflight or on a front-line whenever we want and wherever we are.

Having considered in earlier chapters what we think the word 'play' means, can we apply that meaning to online activity? Now we know something of what play is doing for players, particularly children, how can we know if technological and digital 'toys' are providing those same - or different - benefits?

Let's take some time to think about computer games and online social spaces and compare those activities with what we know about play. We may be making assumptions about what screen time is likely doing *to* our children or not doing *for* our children. These beliefs may not actually represent what the research is finding. I know I have had to change my ideas around this subject as I have read more about the chip-driven activities younger generations enjoy.

In this chapter we will look at the various ways children and young people 'play' in a digital world.

THE QUESTIONS TO CONSIDER ARE:

GROWING UP WITH TECHNOLOGY

There are lots of new opportunities for children to interact with the world through a screen. Do we understand any implications this new experience may have on their development?

It wasn't like that in my day! Or was it? Have things changed as much as we imagine they have?

SOCIAL INTERACTION AND NETWORKING ONLINE

How social is social networking? What are the possible outcomes of hanging out in cyberspace, and the implications of our physical separation from others on our ability to relate?

YOU ARE WHAT YOU EAT
DOES THAT MEAN YOU BECOME WHAT YOU WATCH?

What does research say about the effects of play on screens and devices? Are there losses and gains for the child of today?

WHERE CAN IT ALL GO WRONG?

Some people are more at risk from the 'dangers' of certain types of play. How can that information inform our choices when supervising time spent with technology and in cyber space?

WHERE CAN IT ALL GO RIGHT?
WHAT ARE THE POSITIVES OF ONLINE AND ONSCREEN PLAY TIME?

Any good diet needs variety - a play diet does as well. When we know a bit more and have had time to think, can we provide the balanced play diet our children need to support healthy lives?

A balanced diet is all that most people need to stay healthy. Do we recognise when some children need a bit more of this or a bit less of that? Or when intolerance or adverse reaction means some things have to be eliminated from the diet or supplements added to counteract the effects?

GROWING UP WITH TECHNOLOGY

The connections our children may make online and the images they might view online mean that the use of technology is a concern to many of us in homes and schools across the world. The amount of time spent watching television, playing on gadgets or socialising online is an issue concerning health and educational professionals alike. The developing way in which electronic communication is used across the world, particularly in established and burgeoning wealthy economies, is a revolution in terms of the experience of growing up in the 21st Century.

Students today live digitally every day. They use the Internet, text messaging, social networking, and multimedia fluidly in their lives outside of school and they expect a parallel level of technology opportunity in their academic lives. There is a disconnect between the way students live and the way they learn, and student engagement ultimately suffers. Closing this gap is a challenge for our current school systems.

Blackboard 2008, p.5

Blackboard (*ibid* p.8) advocates that school staff model the 'effective, productive use of technology'. When staff relate confidently and enthusiastically with the media of the digital generation, the pay-off for staff-pupil relationships is that children feel adults are able and willing to 'engage in their world.' There is, as yet, very little long-term research on the effects of considerable amounts of leisure time being spent in front of screens - it is quite simply too new a phenomenon. And research on the far-reaching implications of the loss of this time to other more physical, social, imaginative, creative and personal play is, as yet, years away.

It wasn't like that in my day! (and even now, even for younger staff, things can change so fast that any one of us can feel left behind very quickly by the ways the next generations communicate with each other and fill their leisure time). A recent survey (Gill 2011, p12) illustrates how times are changing:

36% of children said they only played with friends once every two weeks or less outside school: 80% of their parents reported seeing their friends a few times a week or more.

Compared with 'my day' then, this is a big turn-around. Opportunities for play today are different. Children do not spend as many hours playing out; children are not seeing friends as much in their spare time. But that does not necessarily mean that children themselves are changing. Children probably want and need the same things as children always have. But there are new opportunities presented that compete for their time, their interest, and of course their money (or the money of their parents!).

What choices children make are influenced by many external factors, including us (remember in the previous chapter on risk? - "*I think it might be safer if William stays home alone and plays on the computer, rather than go out with friends to goodness knows where*"). My assumption, that children will always choose their digital game device over playing out with friends, is also influenced by advertising, media reports and simplistic stereotyping.

So what if the things children get to do might not be the things that they want to be doing? Are our children really 'living on junk food and sugary drinks, entertained exclusively by television, DVDs, computer games and the internet'? (Voce 2007, p.xi). No, almost certainly not. A Playday survey in 2006 found that:

> 86% of children prefer outdoor activities, including playing out with their friends, building dens and getting muddy, to playing computer games and the like. 82% said that their favourite places to play were natural spaces, such as gardens, parks and local fields. *ibid*

Until the numbers are in, or until our experience confirms our 'worst fears' about screen time, we really are living in uncertain times and navigating unchartered waters. Society as a whole is playing; playing with the way we spend our time: playing with the way we socialise and conduct our relationships: and playing with the ways in which we play. My generation's suspicion of new technologies, or at least of the amount of time and enthusiasm we seem to think children have for them, is perhaps an age-old experience of fear of the unknown, rejection of the new and a desire to stick with what you know.

It is hard being an adult whose child knows more than you do. It is worrying to feel left behind by competent primary school technology users. It is frustrating to be unable to enter the secret lives of teenagers (forgetting it was always this way - even without the new teen language and contact media!). Is my generation's resistance to being 'dragged' into the future, actually an adult, or political, desire to retain power and status? 'The bias against the dot-com generation is partly an attempt by print literate élites to defend the cultural basis of their authority against rising new literacies' (Kane 2005, p.164). For sure the power base changes when information and technology become more widely accessible. Children from as young as two are more computer literate than some of their grandparents. Teenagers converse in their own texting language, excluding adults from their gadget conversations. The wide-spread use of new 'literacies' is a reality. And it is mostly a feature of youth.

It is difficult to advocate and argue for the uncertainty of play, and then to protest about the novel ways we now communicate with each other, and the way children enter into other worlds through gadgets and the cybernet community. Exploring is play; the internet allows exploration in a way that is not bounded by geography of place, history of time or science of reality. Play is creating virtual spaces and alternative realities; the childhood drive to play is a perfect fit for the nature of the internet, as a limitless (cyber) space to play in. Perhaps the only thing we can say is that times they are a-changing, but things in many ways still remain the same!

But are there inherent dangers in watching rather than doing and in messaging rather than conversing? Let's take a look at the evidence.

SOCIAL INTERACTION AND NETWORKING ONLINE

"If they (my children) are communicating solely online then you are not going to get the face-to-face interaction and get a feeling for how the other person is, because I think there is very little emotion

transmitted. If you are sitting in that person's company then you understand so much more."   A dad from Scotland, *in* Gill 2011, p.14

The first of our concerns about virtual play spaces is often about the lack of interaction with others - or with others who are there in the same place as we are. Babies' and toddlers' brains develop in optimum ways through face recognition, physical contact and using all their senses to appreciate their world. Throughout life, touch remains hugely important for physical and emotional wellbeing. So *being with* matters a lot to most of us. All the non-verbal cues of 'in the same room' relationships add to our ability to bond, to empathise and to communicate. Play both requires us to feel safe, and helps us to feel safe. We control our engagement in play; opting in or opting out as we choose, (just like Sudi did in Chapter 4) pretending to be who or what we want to be. The anonymity and an 'otherworld' quality of social media spaces may create the illusion that we are safe, that we are in control: that we are at play. And sometimes online play is safe and sometimes it isn't - like life.

TALES FROM OZ 🐾

There is something different about seeing and believing at an unreachable distance. I grew up watching quite a bit of TV and never question that I sit and stare at a square box with moving pictures. But when I was on my first Animal Assisted Play Therapy training (risevanfleet.com/aapt/), the 'Playful Pooch' programme, we were all highly amused when one of the training dogs, a collie picked for her intelligence and aptitude for learning, stared at a video projected on the wall. Her intense interest made us smile and the way her head moved from side to side as she followed the action was just so funny.

But why? No different to my behaviours and frequently chosen activity. I think of myself as 'playing' when I watch a film or a comedy show. And learning when I watch the news or documentaries. I know dogs play and I know dogs learn, so why find this human-like behaviour in this dog so amusing?

I believe that it was because Meg thought she was watching reality. Her 'window' opened onto the world outside and the dogs she was watching could fly through that opening at any moment, so she better keep an eye on them and be ready. This same amusement occurs when babies and toddlers reach out for things on screens that we know are not there. Given enough exposure to screen time, Meg might learn that these virtual dogs are not real in her world, and then quickly lose interest. Because for an active, intelligent, vital, non-human animal, only reality and touchable, catchable and physically playable things matter! Or she might relax as she realises they are no threat or opportunity for her, but still watch because she cannot help being drawn into the lights and movements that are naturally fascinating to hunters and chasers.

Either way my reactions to dogs watching films is interesting. I sort of wanted to make sure Meg knew it was not real - a feeling I often get when I am not sure a child can separate screen life from real life. I also questioned that hypnotic effect of movement. Do I want my children to spend hours being fascinated (in the true sense of the word - enthralled, transfixed, captivated) by watching actions rather than doing things? I am not sure, because I don't know what hours of being mesmerised by rapid movement might be doing to their brains. This might be something you're thinking about as well, from what you've noticed.

In face-to-face play we tell others that we are playing by the look on our face, the movement of our body and the tone, pitch and accent, of our voice. Online, all this is missing. Even online video links can be grainy, patchy, jerky and out of synch. A touch on the arm accompanying an insult; a nudge alongside a lie and a ruffle of the hair together with a threat are social cues denied to online players. Touch can soothe and cool, or can energise: it can reassure and connect. It is a vital part of human interactions. Physical cues and clues help us keep one foot in reality: we are aware of who we are with and how close we are in physical space. Crucially, this helps humans to judge closeness in psychological and personal space too. In cyberspace, personal space is impossible to measure or to judge.

> We need to ask whether online social networking, which is particularly popular with teenagers, is the same as real live interaction, or whether it might be denying the developing teenage brain of important real life interactions. There is as yet no research on this important question
>
> Blakemore 2010, p.746

'Social', from its Latin root, means companionship, suggesting company, or being together in one place. Internet companions are together in one space - a space not physically accessible. Our brains are physical readers, not mind-readers; they are not cloud dwellers, or out-of-body dwellers. Brains put together information about social interactions from our senses: sight, sound, touch and smell. What information humans gather about the intentions and meanings of others from pheromones is a whole other unexplored area! But the sight of a human face has emotional effects on human brains, the sound of human voices has emotional effects on human brains and physical human touch releases chemicals into blood streams and brains.

Divorcing social relationships from physical closeness is not new; letters, phone calls, emails and then texts; people have 'met', developed long-distance relationships and married in the past. But the illusion created by instant messaging and video-linking that friends 'spend time together', when not in the same physical place, is a new complication to navigate in the way humans build safe, sustainable and sustaining relationships.

YOU ARE WHAT YOU EAT.
Does that mean you become what you watch?

Another of our adult concerns around what children are doing in 'screen time' is about them watching and playing things that are violent, or that seem to 'glorify' fighting and aggression.

Different research findings offer varying evidence on the possible link between video gaming and violence. Even summaries of the findings on violent video games and corresponding violent behaviour offer conflicting results. We want to do the right thing by our children, and we look to the experts to guide us through this recently laid mine-field. But they don't make it easy for us! A recent report gathering together the findings of other studies (Greitemeyer & Mügge 2014) found that who does the research seems to consistently impact on the outcomes.

While one researcher may always find a positive correlation between watching violence and aggression, another may always produce results that counter this. I'm sure this is true in many fields of research but when I just want to know *"Should I stop Marika watching Star Wars?"* or *"Is it best not to let Lois play Angry Birds?"* I don't know where to turn for an answer. So the answer seems to be that there is no simple rule, but a judgement to be made by each of us about what is right for the particular child.

So be sure when you step.

Step with care and great tact.

And remember that Life's a Great Balancing Act   Dr Suess 2003, p.40

Following Dr Suess' advice, in order to succeed in our judgements we will remember that regulating technology play, like life, is a great balancing act (and after thinking so much about balancing risk against benefit in Chapter 4 we might be getting quite good at doing this!). The 'individual' approach to balance with regard to video gaming is supported by Greitemeyer & Mügge (2014) who list other factors in the exposure to violent media that may have influence on outcomes for children. These influencing factors include:

whether games are played alone or in teams

whether games include pro-social elements as well as violence or aggression

and, possibly most significantly, the amount of time spent playing or watching violence   (pp.585-586).

SO WHERE CAN IT ALL GO WRONG?

"Parents don't understand video games, they think they melt your brain'
Glenn, Knight, Holt & Spence 2012, p.11

Most experts agree that game playing and watching violent media is one risk factor that, when associated with other experiences in a child's life, can become toxic. So as we balance our act and consider individuals it is important to think about a child or young person's wider context - their strengths and their struggles and most of all their temperament. By that, in this context, I mean the ways we know they tend to behave, to respond to situations, to react towards others and their ability to manage their feelings, and seek support or comfort from others. James Garbarino (2000) for example explains that when it comes to watching violence and gaming, 'the most psychologically vulnerable among our children are the ones most likely to show the effects' (p.108). He explored why some boys are more vulnerable to developing violent tendencies from watching or playing violent material.   His findings demonstrate a link rather than a cause.

Gerard Jones (2002), often an advocate for physically engaging imaginative play and the safe playing out of 'violent' fantasy as a means to regulate and safely manage feelings, also sees violence in TV and video games as a risk factor for those already vulnerable to their influence: 'Either children connect with a fantasy at the profoundest emotional levels or they quickly toss it aside' (p.57). So to these researchers, the effects of watching/playing violent screen media are different depending upon the child's experiences, interests, needs and already existing resilience or vulnerability. These findings underline that we need to take stock when thinking about what would be most helpful for a particular child we know. In his book *Why Kids Kill: Inside the minds of school shooters*, Langman (2010) insists that 'these are not ordinary kids who played too many video games … these are simply not ordinary kids. These are kids with serious psychological problems' (p.15).

In *Ghosts From the Nursery: Tracing the roots of violence*, Karr-Morse & Wiley (1997) discuss how our earliest relationships and experiences shape who we become. In their list of risk factors for the development of violent behaviour, watching/playing violent media is one of six environmental factors, and one of over thirty factors altogether. They identify factors before and around the time of birth and family and relational factors as the major determinants of violent behaviour. I think it is easy to understand why children who grow up without the affection and care that they need, in chaotic homes, or in fear of physical harm, will be more vulnerable to another 'layer' of risk through violent programmes and games on-screen.

However, Greitemeyer & Mügge (2014) are convinced that 'findings clearly demonstrate that violent video games increase aggression' (p.585). No qualification

- no ifs and no buts. They cite a 2010 summary of research (Anderson et al) which included results from over 130,000 participants. The findings of this summary conclude that playing violent video games:

- increases aggressive thoughts
- increases aggressive feelings
- increases aggressive behaviour
- decreases empathy
- decreases helping behaviour

Greitemeyer & Mügge are not surprised by this finding as they see it as 'in line with almost all theories of human aggression' (2014, p.585). If we 'learn' aggression, become used to violence, see them as 'normal', they become part of our repertoire of behaviours. The final summary of their findings across all the recent relevant research is that 'in our view, violent video game play should be regarded as a risk factor for aggressive behavior' (*ibid*).

Finally, Jamie Ostrov has researched the link between aggression and media exposure (2005, 2006). His work and the studies he has undertaken with colleagues have brought to light some interesting issues. In one large observational study in Minnesota, USA, the watching habits of pre-schoolers were monitored and then considered in relation to their behaviour. While a possibly predictable finding was that children who watched more violent media were more prone to physical aggression, another finding was that 'the more educational media the children watched, the more relationally aggressive they were' (Bronson & Merryman 2010, p.180). Surprising? This was certainly a new idea for me to integrate into my beliefs about children and the impact of watching TV. Children who watched shows where conflict was resolved in a neat, relatively fast ending to a programme were 'increasingly bossy, controlling and manipulative'. The research was repeated in another US state and this study confirmed the results, but also showed that for children watching educational programmes it 'also increased the rate of physical aggression, almost as much as watching violent TV'(*ibid* p.181).

These educational stories, showing how the right way or the fair solution is imposed seems to teach the 'lesson' that the way to solve conflict is through 'relational and verbal aggression' (*ibid*). This encouragement to aggressive and controlling behaviour comes from, to me anyway, a surprising source. And I hadn't until now included worrying about how the media can influence our tendency to 'bullying' types of behaviours, as well as physical violence. I will certainly notice more now if educational content on TV seems to suggest that imposing my will is the way forward, rather than collaborative, consensual approaches.

A whole other topic - but now I am thinking about how I sometimes tend to take over. Influenced by Sesame Street? Or Play School perhaps? Maybe the very programmes that also taught me to be creative, moral and playful? But before we look at the positive outcomes of screen time and technology play in all its guises, I would like to return to 'bullying' behaviours - this time on the internet and social online spaces our children inhabit.

While this is not the place for an in-depth look at the concerning issue of bullying through the use of technology, it is worth exploring how our desire to play with potential identities may include playing online in ways that involve harassment and intimidation. Writing in *Understanding School Bullying*, Peter Smith (2012) feels that defining cyber-bullying is not straight-forward as it can involve a diversity of forms over a variety of media. Steen & Thomas' succinct definition is that: 'Cyber bullying involves the use of technology to repeatedly harass and bully others' (2016, p.124). They report that in 2010, cyber-bullying was half as common as face-to-face bullying; by 2013 it was more common (*ibid*). Peter Smith (2012) questions if this form of bullying is still growing or not, explaining that it is hard to record as the ways and means of digital communication continue to develop and diversify.

Smith, P. (pp.81-82) goes on to identify seven features of cyber-bullying that are different from other forms of bullying. These include the potential for the perpetrator to remain anonymous and the additional feature that the bully does not usually see the victim's reaction. These aspects mean that there is no relational feedback, or visual and immediate prompt for a compassionate response. This resonates with the dad who felt that online interactions are less likely to encourage understanding and empathy for the feelings of the other (p.118). Children do 'play at being', and online they may play at being cyber-bullies: but the experience can be very different for both bully and victim because of the nature of the internet environment. As we learned in Chapter 3, playing at being mean, powerful, and 'not nice' is important. Gupta (2011), among others in that chapter, advocates for our need to play with different possible ways of being - including being 'not nice'. Sometimes we need to have developed a wide range of skills in our behaviour repertoire.

However, in face-to-face hands-on play these behaviours are modified by the fact that:

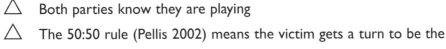

△   Both parties know they are playing

△   The 50:50 rule (Pellis 2002) means the victim gets a turn to be the
     persecutor too

△   Either participant is able to end the play by leaving the boundaries of
     the play space at any time

△   Immediate and visceral feedback leads to opportunities to 'make-up' or
     to notice our own feelings of guilt and of shame

These are four conditions that are not present online. And remember that without the first three of these conditions - the activity ceases to be play.

Shirley Turkle (2015) explains that adults also get lost in their creation of a 'version' of themselves online, and she gives the example of one of her friends who acknowledges that 'online she feels involved in her performances to the point that she has lost track of what is performance and what is not' (p.24). Worryingly, Turkle also includes an example of a schoolgirl who believed that posting cruel comments online is somehow of little relevance - it is 'just Facebook' (p.166). Turkle feels our children see 'play' online as a place where we see 'other people as objects that can't be hurt' and where we can engage in 'a kind of cruelty that doesn't count'. This space where the normal 'rules' of life do not apply again links to the 'otherness' of play; a place and time that are separate from reality. However, play has a to-and-fro rhythm, a give-and-take quality, as well as the time when 'you are not you' and 'I am not me'. Play, when it is play, is the best of times for when 'you and I become us'!

Turkle does have a remedy for online experiences that deplete us and that leave us feeling alone and without understanding from others - reclaiming face-to-face conversations. For all of our children engaging in online activity, but particularly when their experiences are toxic - and since both bully and victim are damaged by bullying, and both need restorative experiences - I prescribe regular and sustained opportunities for face-to-face play.

Already in this chapter we have heard how online social engagement and play offer positive opportunities as well as potential for harm. Let's take some time now to 'accentuate the positive'.

AND WHERE DOES IT ALL GO RIGHT?

Even the most ardent opponent of gaming would admit there are benefits - maybe limited - grudgingly - to eye-hand coordination or confident IT skills! But as well as the research supporting the benefits of video-gaming for manual dexterity and spatial awareness, other findings report the benefits for intelligence and wellbeing as well. One summary of current research suggests that 'well-designed computer games offering open-ended or problem-solving challenges to children are likely to share some of the benefits of problem-solving or constructional play with objects' (Whitebread 2012, p.24). Another of the summary findings is that children really do still have time for experiencing other problem-solving or construction play which might supply the missing play 'nutrients' not easily accessed online or on screen. 'Playing video games did not appear to take place at the expense of children's other leisure activities, social integration, and school performance' (*ibid*). The positive findings in Whitebread's summary of research keep on coming! 'A positive relationship was found between time spent on videogames and a child's intelligence' (*ibid*), while children themselves also recognise the benefits of video game playing, identifying that it is good for building self-esteem (Kane 2005, p.146).

In one survey, 19% of parents of gamers reported they believed video games have a positive influence on their child, while a further 5% noticed some negative influence and also some positive influences (Lenhart et al 2008, p.39). In the same survey on *Civic Participation in Teens*, the gamers themselves reported playing a game or games where they:

Learn about a problem in society

Explore a social issue the player cares about

Think about moral or ethical issues

Help make decisions about how a community, city or nation should be run. (p.41)

These gamers were more likely than their peers to:

    Give or raise money for charity
    Say they are committed to civic participation
    Say they are interested in politics and stay informed on current issues
    Persuade others how to vote
    Take part in a protest or demonstration   (p.45)

So pro-social gaming seems to lead to increased interest and involvement in real-life social issues and activities. Or do civically minded youngsters choose pro-social gaming more often than their less interested peers? Hard to know the answer to that one. But often it is a bit of both - I do this because that is what I am like and I am like that because of the things I have experienced. Probably true here in the gaming world too?

Another identified benefit of technological play is its egalitarian nature. Studies demonstrate that boys' and girls' time spent on media is about the same, albeit there are slightly different uses according to gender. Differences in culture, race or economic status do not separate children in their technology play experiences, and nor does being in a rural or city area. In America the access to screen machines appears to differ, according to race and economic status, but interestingly, time spent using them is roughly the same. This might seem unlikely when we see the prices of gadgets and the latest 'must-have' version that comes out every year. But if you think about it, you will probably notice that most youngsters you know talk with knowledge of the games they play and the videos they see, and across the world the push to connect children to the digital world may even mean someone has a phone or laptop but no shoes or in-house sanitation. Despite different opportunities across the economic spectrum, children seem to 'find a way' to spend as much time as each other on technology such as computers (Rideout et al 1999, p.43). Apart from anything else this shows the importance of this activity to children - 'where there's a will there's a way', and means the evident desire for connection to this world of play leads children to collaborate, persuade, cooperate and to generally 'beg, steal (temporarily) and borrow' the gadgets they need. They are employing important social skills to enter the world of social e-play.

Any good diet needs variety - play diets too!

Remembering that allowing for screen time is a great balancing act, where do we now stand in terms of the value of this sort of play?

> For most teens, gaming runs the spectrum from blow-'em-up mayhem to building communities; from cute-and-simple to complex; from brief private sessions to hours' long interactions with masses of others.
>
> *Amanda Lenhart in a press release, announcing*
> *the publication of her 2008 study* (Lenhart et al)

So within the one way of playing, the stories are varied, as are the lengths of time spent on them and the amount of potential for relating to the others involved. The type of play, where and with whom it happens, the individual vulnerability and resilience of the child and the interest and care of adults around the child are literally all 'game changers'. But most of all it is the *balance* of activities, the menu of play choices and the breadth of play experiences that inoculate against some of the minuses and ensure the pluses. It is just possible that as long as children get the same opportunities as the young son of Mike Goldsmith, (a former Editor of Playstation 2's official magazine), all may yet be well.

"I always make sure he has a mix of things to do - that he gets out there, takes the skin off his knees, comes back covered in mud".

in Kane 2005, p.146

The maxim 'everything in moderation' sums up the idea of getting a balance, of not letting anything be ruled out or for any one thing to over-rule everything else. It may be that as long as children still do all the things that children have got loads out of over years of playing, then all will be well.

So some technology play is probably good for us, some not so good, and for some of us probably bad. But another potential problem with play in cyber space is time lost to play in the concrete world. Concrete play alongside virtual play is one of the balances we must sustain. Stuart Brown (2009) tells us why. In his view, time spent on video games means we may lack some other elements of the types of play that are also important for development. He finds there is no substitute for 'hands on' play experiences. His belief is based on the experience of an American aerospace research facility, JPL (pp.9-11). The company wondered why, despite employing the best graduates from the top US universities, their younger workforce struggled with innovation and problem-solving. Looking into the backgrounds of employees, JPL found that those who tinkered, who had 'taken apart clocks to see how they worked, or made soapbox derby racers' (p.11) were able to imagine, think through, visualise the solutions to problems in a way that pure academics, and those who had not been involved with such activities as children, could not.

Other organisations have taken the findings of JPL on-board, asking job applicants about their play experiences with construction toys. And Young Engineers UK (young-engineers.co.uk) offer 'Edutainment Programs' to develop hands-on foundation skills in building, fixing and designing. How amazing is our brain? It can translate physical action into mental imagery, and apply findings from one experience (block building) to a variety of other situations (space travel, medical procedures, and so on). That really is the most powerful and advanced computer ever. It has always been mobile, you can take it everywhere, and you don't have to worry about battery life! But our brains were designed for life thousands of years ago and brain changes take time. The brilliance of our brains to convert physical experience into mental imagery took a long time to 'programme' in. Maybe it will take generations for human brains to find ways to adapt the application of online skills and learning into other real-world situations.

What we do know is that brains develop through trial and error and through making connections: in other words, through play. So as long as we are playing, our brains will (eventually) find ways to keep up.

A balanced diet is all that most people need to stay healthy (although some may need supplements, while others are intolerant of certain ingredients or food types).

Back to our question: should children be playing so much of their time online, watching screens, killing cyber monsters and meeting invisible 'friends? The research and the expert arguments are split; so maybe taken together offer balance? Gill (2011) warns us not to look through our nostalgic 'rose-tinted' glasses when considering the effects of technological advances on the experience of childhood. His argument is balanced:

> It would be wrong to say things have simply got worse for children. The truth is that children's lives have changed for the better in some ways, while becoming more challenging or difficult in others. p.5

The pluses of using computers and other screen devices need balancing against the minuses (remember our risk assessment skills in Chapter 4?). It is not helpful to have a set of tech worshipers extolling the virtues of screen time while a set of technophobes make the argument that it is the devil disguised as a household, or classroom appliance. I guess that, as with anything new and untried over time, we can proceed with caution. As playful adults we are able and willing to embrace change while retaining our cultural legacy of time-honoured play activities. We need to balance the needs of children and the applications of computers and come up with a balanced equation - maybe something like this:

$$A \times screen\ play$$
$$+$$
$$B \times social\ play$$
$$+$$
$$C \times active\ play$$
$$+$$
$$D \times rough\ and\ tumble\ play$$
$$+$$
$$E \times creative\ play$$
$$=$$
$$a\ happy,\ healthy\ child$$

Although of course this equation is by no means an exhaustive list of the play types needed to create health and happiness!.

It may be not all good, it's certainly not all bad: it's just different

> With no consoles, no laptops, no mobile phones and, in all likelihood just a single household TV with only three channels to choose from, the 1980's might initially look like a very dull place indeed for today's tech-savvy, media-aware kids.
>
> Gill 2011, p.4

Children need to know how screen machines work. Children need to be a part of their peer culture. The important thing is that cyber time is 'as well as', and not 'instead of', other play time. The good news about players is their resilience to change. The good news about play is that it will happen. The good news about screen machines is that children show them no more respect than any other of their play resources.

> Life with smart toys is much like life with dumb toys: they just generate a different kind of mischief.   Kane 2005, p.147

. . . .

and so ...

KEY POINTS

Technology both increases and decreases opportunities for play

Social face-to-face interaction cannot be replicated by cyber-space contact

Games on screens do not develop understanding of real inter-personal consequences of actions

'Playing' on devices is not always 'play,' so at those times, 'any benefits that are said to come from playing, will not apply'.   Hughes 2012, p.78

Technology play: *Where do we go from here?*

The play-full school would -

☺ Use technology in free play provision

☺ Ensure all children can play with technology and play without it

☺ Have a strong policy for encouraging and supporting families to monitor pupil's use of only age-appropriate games and films

If you want to know more, try reading

Blackboard (2008) *Teaching in the 21st Century: A Review of the Issues and Changing Models in the Teaching Profession.* Washington DC: Blackboard

Blakemore, S-J, (2010) The Developing Social Brain: Implications for Education. *Neuron.* Vol. 65:6 pp.744-747

Embrick, D., Wright, T. & Lukacs, A. Lanham (Ed) (2013) *Social Exclusion, Power, and Video Game Play: New research in digital media and technology,* MD: Lexington Books

Glenn, N., Knight, C., Holt, N. & Spence, J. (2012) Children's Views about the Meanings of Play. *Childhood* Vol. 0:0 pp.1-15 Sage

Greitemeyer, T. & Mügge, D. (2014) Video Games Do Affect Social Outcomes: A Meta-Analytic Review of the Effects of Violent and Prosocial Video Game Play. *Personality and Social Psychology Bulletin* Vol. 40:5 pp.578–589

Lenhart, A., Kahne, J., Middaugh, E., Rankin Macgil, A., Evans, C. & Vitak, J. (2008) *Teens, Video Games, and Civics.* Washington, D.C.: Pew Internet & American Life Project. Available at: pewinternet.org/files/oldmedia//Files/Reports/2008/PIP_Teens_Games_and_Civics_Report_FINAL.pdf.pdf

Ostrov, J. & Crick, N. (2005). Current directions in the study of relational aggression during early childhood. *Early Education and Development* Vol. 16 pp.109-114.

Ostrov, J., Gentile, D. & Crick, N. (2006) Media Exposure, Aggression and Prosocial Behavior During Early Childhood: A Longitudinal Study. *Social Development.* Vol. 15:4 pp.612-627

Playday (2006) playday.org.uk/playday-campaigns/previous-campaigns/2006-play-naturally.aspx

Rideout, V., Foher, U., Roberts, D. & Brodie, M., (1999) *Kids & Media @ The New Millennium.* A Kaiser Family Foundation Report. Menlo Park CA: The Henry J. Kaiser Family Foundation

If you want to understand more, try reading

Berenstain, J. & Berenstain, M. (2010) *The Berenstain Bears' Computer Trouble* NY: Harper Festival

If you want a 15 minute group or individual training, try watching

Shilo Shiv Suleman's 2011 TED talk 'Using tech to enable dreaming' on ted.com/talks or youtube.com

Chapter 6

Growing old playfully

When I was ten, I read fairy tales in secret and would have been ashamed if
I had been found doing so. Now that I am 50 I read them openly. When I
became a man I put away childish things, including the fear of childishness
and the desire to be very grown up.   C. S. Lewis 1982

I hope that like C. S. Lewis, I am someone who embraces any possibility to be
childlike, and enjoys opportunities to not be 'very grown up'. Does the sight of
snow still bring out your 'inner child'? Do you ask your daughter to go to the latest
Disney blockbuster with you, rather than the other way around? Have you spent ages
'checking' the toy you just bought for your son before wrapping it, just to make sure
that it works? While we can continue to enjoy the same play as we did earlier in our
lives, as we grow we develop new play activities and find playful ways to engage
with adult resources and work.

Every adult was once a child; and that child remains a part of who we become.
The trick is not to stop being a child, but to add to the foundation we developed as a
child, the building blocks of our adolescence, young adulthood, middle age and old age.

A tree grows because it adds rings: a train doesn't grow by leaving one
station behind and puffing on to the next.   *ibid*

As adults we are like Russian dolls: we grow layers of experience, stages of development, the 'rings' that can be counted to find out our age. The 'person' of each of our previous stages lives, unseen like buried treasure, within the containing outer shell of the fully formed grown-up. The inner Russian dolls are there - whether we allow them out or not is another matter!

Whatever our age though, play matters. It always matters, but sometimes it matters more. The importance of play is connected to the developmental needs of the brain. Different sorts of play are important at different times in life. Different amounts of play are necessary as the brain changes at different speeds.

If play can help a child to understand their world and be a rehearsal for life, then the need for play to help us understand new events, and the usefulness of having played something through before we have to actually do it never ends. Life brings challenges and change at every age.

In this chapter we will think about the role of play throughout our lives. This will include a look at some of our ideas about ages and stages of life and how play *always* matters: but sometimes for different reasons, and in different ways.

THE QUESTIONS TO CONSIDER ARE:

THREE SCORE YEARS AND TEN? HOW WE DEFINE THE STAGES OF
LIFE?
ERIKSON'S EIGHT STAGES OF DEVELOPMENT
*Looking at a useful model created by Erik Erikson (1995), do we recognise the
different life-tasks that are our focus at different stages of our lives?*

PLAYING FOR LIFE
*Different ages may offer different opportunities for play and we may need and use
play for different purposes. But why does play continue to matter, whatever our age?*

PLAYFUL PEOPLE
*Are there certain 'play types' or particular 'kinds of play? If so - who am I when I play?
And am I playful in a particular way?*

Before considering the different play stages we go through I'd like to spend a moment considering different ways of viewing the ages or eras of our lives.

THREE SCORE YEARS AND TEN?

Life is getting longer, giving more time for play you might think. While recognition that adulthood may not start until later than we thought - with 25 being a new 'cut-off' for funding streams and neuroscientists - education and the world of work stick to 16 and 18 as key ages, keeping 'childhood' as a relatively short period of our longer lives. And pension age is rising in-line with life expectancy. So it may be the busy middle bit, the work life, that is expanding in duration, leaving the number of our childhood and retirement years much the same. Any expectation that we live to 70 or 80 years of age is changing as fast as our ways of playing. In the last 50 years we have all gained about a decade in life expectancy. In 1960 the average age we could expect to reach was a little over 70. In 2010 it was just over 80. The change in longevity is reflected in changes in pensionable age. This has already risen from 60 for females and 65 for men, to 67 years of age for everyone. It may not be that long before it reaches 75. This change means that many of our expectations about life are changing. What we consider as 'old age' changes as people become fitter for longer and remain part of the workforce well into their 60s.

It's official! A UK opinion poll for the Department of Work and Pensions (Sweiry & Willitts 2012) reported that, on average, respondents thought that 'youth' ends at 41 and that 'old age' begins at 59. This means we are mostly at work for half our youth, the whole of our middle age and soon, half of our old age! In this model the things we are doing at the different ages are not the defining criteria. We don't see youth as the years before and during schooling, or middle age as the working years and old age as retirement. In the DWP model, roughly speaking:

➥ Youth is 0-40
➥ Old age is 60-80
➥ That leaves middle age as 40-60

So in this poll, youth covers a huge span of developmental change (*and how come I didn't know I was still in my youth when I was in my late 30's?*). Childhood, whether that ends at 14, 18 or 21, is a very different time of life to late 20's and 30's. It is set apart as different in legal, social and cultural ways. So perhaps describing life's journey by dividing it into more than three categories would offer more descriptions of the changes over time, and a richer way to think about how play opportunities and expectations vary over time as well.

Shakespeare famously wrote about the Seven Ages of Man in the play '*As You Like It*'. His character Jaques describes the human condition as moving from the 'puking' infant, through the 'whining' schoolboy, 'sighing' young 'lover', to the 'jealous' 'soldier' looking to make his mark (it all sounds very 'male' and of its time, but I think we get the idea). On to the 'wise' (somewhat sanctimonious) 'justice', the sixth stage of life is the failing of health and of senses into the final 'second childishness', on the one-way road to 'oblivion'. His descriptions do not fill anyone with hope for the condition of being human. Each of the stages describes the attributes of a 'man' no-one would want to be or to know!

I know babies 'puke' but they also giggle and are full of wonder about the world they find themselves in. Maybe school children 'whine' but they also joke and sing and run and jump. Young people in love sometimes sigh and other times laugh and tease and hug and care. Ambitious workers can feel jealous of other colleagues but are proud of their own achievements and create dreams of their future. Wise, seasoned employees could be smug but are often helpful, supportive, playful and droll. The older, albeit frailer people we know or meet entertain and amuse us with their stories. Play is an expression of 'where we are at' in life, whichever 'age' we are in. And it's certainly not all doom and gloom.

Erikson's Eight Stages of Development

Erik Erikson (1995, pp.222-243) identified eight ages of man by what he thought of as the 'developmental tasks' each stage of life presents, and the healthy outcomes each task can offer. The ages are only a rough guide. Erikson gave six separate developmental stages for the 'Youth' stage of the DWP report: to me they are far more descriptive of the human journey from birth to adulthood than Shakespeare's. Erikson saw life as a series of steps that had to be negotiated. His ideas create a tower of building blocks, where successful completion of each task gives a firm foundation for subsequent blocks to rest on. Because I have permission to play in this book, I have reversed the order of the stages to mirror this building process, so please read the chart from the bottom up.

LATE ADULTHOOD	60 to death	The development of wisdom
MIDDLE ADULTHOOD	5 to 60	The development of care for the next generation
YOUNG ADULTHOOD	18 to 35	The development of fidelity
ADOLESCENCE	12 to 18 years	The development of identity
SCHOOL AGE	6 to 12 years	The development of industry
PLAY AGE	3 to 5 years	The development of initiative
EARLY CHILDHOOD	18 months to 3 years	The development of autonomy
INFANCY	Birth to 18 months	The development of trust

Because we are thinking about play at different ages and stages, we can see if there is a fit between what Erikson saw us striving to develop at each stage, and the types of play that each age engages in.

PLAYING FOR LIFE

The end of play can be read as the end of personal development.

Kane 2005, p.163

Looking at Erikson's stages through the eyes of a play observer we can see why play matters in different ways at different times (*here the stages are written as Erikson (1995) gives them*).

INFANCY	WHEN PARENTS MATTER MOST
	Play develops a map of the world that gives a sense of security
EARLY CHILDHOOD	PARENTS + SIBLINGS
	Play challenges the boundaries and asserts independence
PLAY AGE	PARENTS, SIBLINGS AND WIDER FAMILY
	Play becomes purposeful, ideas are developed, ownership of play is fought over
SCHOOL AGE	PARENTS, SIBLINGS, WIDER FAMILY AND SCHOOL
	Play challenges abilities, becomes sustained and more focussed, collaboration emerges in play
ADOLESCENCE	PEERS
	Play is about social belonging, role and status and playing with identity
YOUNG ADULTHOOD	FAMILY, COLLEAGUES AND FRIENDS
	Play develops intimacy in relationships and bonds family groups
MIDDLE ADULTHOOD	FAMILY, COLLEAGUES AND FRIENDS
	Play is about wider connections, developing social networks and supporting the play of younger generations
LATE ADULTHOOD	FAMILY AND FRIENDS
	Play helps to maintain abilities (neural connections) as well as social connections and coming to terms with the final stage of life

Like any building blocks, the first bricks being solid and stable matters most, and play in the first stages of life matters more than at any other time. Once we become language-driven beings, able to contemplate and ruminate verbally, play stops being the only way we can pass the test each life stage presents. Play remains unique in what it brings to each task, but later in life, there are compensating structures for the reduction in or absence of physical play. In the first stages of life, there just aren't.

A simple, equal, if arbitrary, division of life shows the way play matters at different times. Dividing life in this way fits with childhood and education, parenthood, midlife and retirement.

0-25	Youth	play as exploration, social bonding and identity formation
25-50	The golden years	play as competition, relaxation and challenge
50-75	Payback time	play as transition, completion and continuation
75-100	Old age	play as entertainment, maintenance and resolution

The DEMOS report *Other People's Children* (Thomas & Hocking 2003, p.53) describes the stages of childhood development in terms of the *needs* of different ages in a playful, symbolic way, for example:

climbing trees:	establishing independence
running races:	learning to perform and growing up
the dressing-up box:	social networks, imagination and play

The analogies conjure up perfectly how children develop through play. We all recognise the small child's need to 'climb trees', or push their own boundaries, while challenging our need to protect them. In the middle years of childhood the network of people involved with the child is extended; friends come and go while adults responsible for the child now include school staff and club leaders, and competition kicks in. The 'dressing up box' is a powerful metaphor for the search for identity in adolescence. They are still children 'trying things on'. The dressing-up box 'represents the communal resources, tangible and intangible, that communities provide for children' (*ibid* p.57).

PLAYFUL PEOPLE

Emerging from the experimental years of the adolescent dressing-up box, our character is beginning to stabilise. As adult 'players', we often have certain play strengths or play preferences. Stuart Brown (2009, pp.65-70) lists adult play personality types as:

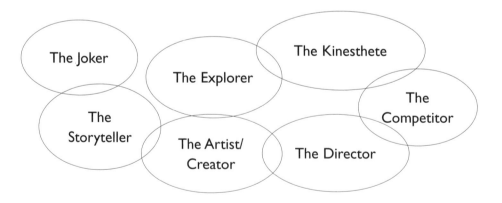

Do you trick and tease or surround yourself with sumptuous materials and sensual smells? Travel and study, or play team or individual sports? Are you a fixer and planner or a philatelist and numismatist? Are you a potter and a weaver, or a spinner of good yarns? We may be several, one or none of these players. The more flexibility our brain retains after adolescence the more types of play we may enjoy doing.

I notice that Brown's list of adult players does not include -

- perhaps an odd omission, as adolescence is the age of the risk taker and many of us struggle to leave behind that final stage of childhood, holding on to our adolescent aspirations and counter-culture membership for as long as possible. And how about other adolescent play types which remain into adulthood? Such as:

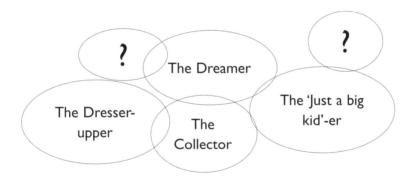

How many people do you know who buy the toys for their children that they want to play with themselves? - well before their child reaches an age where interest or ability means that they would choose that toy, or could use it even if they wanted to. Playing doesn't stop because we are no longer children. I don't believe either, as some seem to do, that later in life, it becomes only about physical exercise:

By adulthood, playing transforms itself into exercise. What up to now might have been fun, *just for the hell of it,* is no longer fun. Play is no

longer voluntrary. Now play becomes obligatory if one wants to enjoy and
survive.   L'Abate 2009, p.152

I would say play is always about survival, and that play is always essential, although
it is always also voluntary. I agree that play is not always about enjoyment and fun,
but that is no more true in middle or old age than in youth. C. S. Lewis argued that
play becomes more enjoyable as we get older - possibly because our capacity for joy
grows with our capacity for effort or for understanding:

I now enjoy the fairy tales better than I did in childhood; being now able to
put more in, of course I get more out.   Lewis, 1982

In answer to the question *"What about play in old age?"* L'Abate (2009, p.154)
answers: 'Clearly, sedentary play such as bingo won't cut it'. Bingo? Not cut it?
A game of fast reaction time, physical dexterity, competitive drive, need for
emotional self-regulation and above all highly sociable - it's got it all, never mind
'won't cut it'.

The social nature of play is again to the fore in meeting the needs of the oldest
people in society. Social networks and social contact form one of the most important
predictors of wellbeing in old age. Socialising, belonging, meeting people, having
someone to talk to, all increase the likelihood of good physical health in old age.
Even gambling has been shown to be linked with positive health outcomes in old
people because of the social aspects of playing (Desai et al, 2004). Although the
researchers warn against 'problem gambling', it appears that a few financial losses are
more than made up for by the social gains. Kestly & Badenoch (2015) advocate for
the healing power of play throughout life; and refer to research from a Harvard study
which demonstrated that 'knowing how to play' (p.534) made the most difference to

retired people's wellbeing, both their physical health and their happiness. In Chapter 15 we will think more about ways to stay playful as we grow older.

The play-full life

The most life-enhancing, health-insuring way to be, throughout life, is - playful. Being playful is an attitude or aptitude rather than an activity. It's not what you do, it's the way that you do it, as we already know from Chapter 1 and Chapter 4. Playful people are:

☺   bubbly, effervescent, sociable, intellectually curious, enthusiastic
       (Lieberman 1977)

☺   joyful, free and actively engaged with the surrounding world
       (Cornelli Sanderson 2010)

In Chapter 15 we'll come back to how important it is for us to be playful and bring that playfulness into our work and our lives. Playfulness is often equated with spontaneity; it is the ability to be flexible, not upset by surprises: open, humorous and often affectionate. It seems to have much in common with resilience - an ability to roll with the punches. Whether resilient people are playful or playful people are resilient, the two do seem to go hand in hand. Playfulness has no age or stage, but maybe we do have more time for play at the beginning and end of life. Do we enter a second childhood in old age because we are diminishing? Or because we finally have the time to play again; and have passed on to others the responsibility of looking after the younger generations of players, and can once again indulge in our own innate drive to play?

Practise what we preach

Whatever your age or stage, how much do you play? Do you need permission to play? When I ask groups of school staff the question about their own play, more often than not they talk about the play they enjoy with their child or their pet. Great opportunities for play - but sometimes they are our 'excuses' for play. Keep on playing with your children and animals and also keep playing just for you. Maybe noticing how play at different stages of Erikson's (1995) model might be important to you, or remembering how one of Brown's (2009) play types used to *be* you, will help you discover, uncover or recover powerful play in your life.

In this book I've often described my play in terms of the children in my life or my dog, but I do play lots when neither are around as well. I see myself in a few of Brown's (*ibid*) play characters: the Storyteller and the Explorer are just two that resonate with me, but I think mostly I'm the 'Sleuther'. I love working out things about people, sometimes true things and sometimes I make it all up. How about you? What do you do that you don't have to do (Twain 1992)? If the answer is 'not a lot,' then maybe you might try exercising your play 'muscle' a bit more.

Life offers endless opportunities to do things playfully - let's give it a go - let's not just run up the flight of steps, let's run up them 'as if' we were Rocky Bilbao (United Artists 1976); let's do all sorts of things 'as if' and seize the moment and go with it whenever (alright - not whenever, but whenever safe and appropriate) '*something ... tells me*' (Chapter 1 p.22) to be random, spontaneous or childlike. Let's heed the 'warning' from Jenny Joseph (1996, p.45) and not wait until we are old to be more playful in order to 'make up for the sobriety of (our) youth' and take her advice to 'practise a little now' -

... so people who know me are not too shocked and surprised.
When suddenly I am old, and start to wear purple.   (*ibid*)

and so ...

KEY POINTS

Play is important across the whole lifespan

Play changes as we grow and sometimes we grow into play and become a 'type' of player

If we are living longer we get to play more! It has never been more important to keep playing

Play across life enhances emotional wellbeing and social inclusion

Growing old playfully: *Where do we go from here?*

There are more and more play facilities for grown-up children. From ball ponds in the UK to giant sand pits with life-size diggers in the US resort of Las Vegas. If you want company, or if you like structure; if you are a 'joiner' or are not sure where or how to get started, try finding out about play opportunities in your area. For example maybe try one of these:

△   Laughter clubs
△   The Shaw Park Eco Wellness Project in Hull (and even
        create electricity as you pedal)
△   Dog yoga
△   *Jump in!* Ball pond at Pearlfisher Gallery, London

△   Playzone in Portsmouth and Swansea

△   'Grown-up' nights at Thornaby Play Factory

△   And a host of similar opportunities near you

The play-full school would -

☺   Prepare pupils for a life of play

☺   Invite families and communities in to play!

☺   Offer opportunities for play that can lead to life-long play habits

☺   Be full of playful staff

If you want to know more, try reading:

Erikson, E. (1995) *Play and Society*. London: Vintage

L'Abate, L. (2009) *The Praeger Handbook of Play Across The Life Cycle. Fun from Infancy to Old Age*. Santa Barbara Ca: ABC-CLIO, LLC

Lewis, C.S. in Hooper, W. (Ed.) (1982) *On three ways of writing for children, On Stories and Other Essays on Literature* pp.3-7 New York: Harcourt Brace Jovanovich Available at: mail. scu.edu.tw/~jmklassen/scu99b/chlitgrad/3ways.pdf

Thomas, G. & Hocking, G. (2003) *Other People's Children*. London: Demos. Available at: demos.co.uk

If you want to understand more, try reading:

Kalch, F. (2011) *Little Old Ladies* NY: Minedition (Penguin Young Readers)

If you want a 15 minute group or individual training, try playing

There is no training for play like playing itself!

Chapter 7

Adolescence: swings, round-abouts and rollercoaster rides

"I don't really play anymore just go about on my rollerblades or hang around with my friends having a laugh, telling each other jokes."

12-year-old boy in IPA Scotland 2011, p.9

In other words - playing! Play in the teenage years may look different. It may feel different. It is helping the brain develop different capacities. But while teenagers are doing things that don't need doing, it is still play. Search results for Teenage Play are almost exclusively centred on literature about either video/gaming/social media and TV, or about formalised physical activities and sport. It seems that teenagers, like the twelve year old at the start of this chapter, struggle with the word 'play' in relation to adolescent activity, as do academics, researchers and writers alike. In the *Praeger Handbook of Play Across the Life Cycle* (L'Abate 2009), just two pages are dedicated to high school and adolescence and a further two to college and early adulthood. L'Abate believes that this is an area that needs much more attention and research.

I agree, and I want to dedicate more space to adolescent and to teenagers' play. Remember in the last chapter, we looked at play for different life-stages and the needs of the brain, body and spirit at different times in our development. Well, the teenage brain is a particular phenomenon. If you have a teenager at home (or remember your teenage self), no doubt you will know what I mean! But the teenage years are a time of much change: the outwards changes we see and the brain changes we don't see, but are acutely aware of. The brain develops new pathways, new knowledge and understanding. The brain grows more connections, richer templates and maturing skills. At this crucial time in our brain's growth, it also prunes connections that are not useful or not being used.

Use it or lose it

Physical play keeps our bodies flexible and increases the range of our movements. Mental play keeps our minds agile and increases our openness to change. Social play keeps our relationships adaptable and increases the range of our friendships (remember Antonacci et al's 2010 research about how play turns a stranger into a member of the group, in Chapter 3?) C.S.Lewis (1982) felt more comfortable admitting to playing and being seen to play, but he was in his fifties. Adolescence is more tricky. Not young enough to play without giving it a second thought, and not old enough to be sure that friends and family won't think they are childish or immature. But at this confusing time, play is essential for healthy bodies, minds and relationships.

In this chapter we will think about play in the years of adolescence and why it matters that adolescents play.

THE QUESTIONS TO CONSIDER ARE:

WHAT IS ADOLESCENCE?

The last chapter highlighted the different beliefs that governments and the public have about when life stages begin and end; but whatever the age-limits at either end, what are the developmental 'tasks' of adolescence? And how might play during teenage years help children to move successfully into adulthood?

KNOWING ME, KNOWING YOU - SOCIAL SKILLS AND PEER RELATIONSHIPS IN ADOLESCENCE

What does the research tell us about the changes in the adolescent brain? And what might that mean for our expectations of teenagers, particularly in the area of their social skills?

'REBEL SEEKING A CAUSE' - IDENTITY FORMATION

Sometimes it is clear that an adolescent wants to identify with someone or something, but changes in direction are often a part of their exploration of who to be. Why is playing with ideas about who I am and who I may become so important in adolescence?

'I AIN'T BOVVERED' - RISK TAKING IN ADOLESCENCE

Risk-taking, the inaccurate perceptions of risk, the addictive thrill of the brain's chemical response to risk and the need to not (appear to) care about the dangers of risk are all more apparent during teenage and young adult years. So can play provide a 'safe' space for these important experiences?

BEING A BRAIN-WISE EDUCATOR - USING RESEARCH TO INFORM PROVISION FOR THE ADOLESCENT BRAIN

In light of what we understand about adolescents, how can neuroscience inform how we might respond to their particular needs for play in our learning spaces?

WHAT IS AN ADOLESCENT?

Adolescence encompasses the transition from childhood into adulthood. A tricky time, where often our expectations are both that the child *"Grow up"* and that the young person remember *"You're still (only) a child"*. Stuart Brown (2009, p.108) reflects on this pulling in 'opposite, incompatible directions', both in terms of the teenager's own uncertainty and of the adult's conflicting messages. He feels the American term for this age group - sophomore - describes this 'paradox' perfectly; it means 'wise foolish'. Are adolescents both wise and foolish? Or are they not yet wise but no longer foolish? Hopefully they are becoming wise but remaining foolish in a playful sense of the word 'fool'.

Erikson (1995, the creator of our Stages of Development model in Chapter 6) describes adolescence as the years between twelve and eighteen. But you may know of a ten year or twenty year old you consider to be well and truly behaving like an adolescent. The boundaries of adolescence are fluid, and differ across time and culture. Gender also plays a role in when adolescence seems to start and end. Currently there is evidence that 'the age of onset of puberty is decreasing and the age at which mature social roles are achieved is rising' (Sawyer et al 2012, p.1630). Society now allows for an extended period of 'no longer child but not yet adult' hood. If we follow the logic of the argument in the Introduction to this book, that we don't play because we are young but are younger longer so we can play more - then this extended time must be for more opportunity to play!

The ages Erikson chooses for the adolescent years fit with the current UK schooling provision of Secondary Education. Neuroscience also identifies these ages as a vital stage for brain development. At about 11 years of age there is 'a major increase of neurons in the frontal cortex' (Morgan 2005, p.27), where thinking, reasoning, and logic are seated. During adolescence increased brain potentials are explored and then pruned, until at about 17 years of age the ability for 'rational thought and sensible decision making' are achieved (*ibid* p.96). So Morgan's understanding of the brain sets adolescence firmly within the secondary school stage of education: a spurt of brain growth at 11, followed by growth and cuts which shape the brain until about age 17.

The developmental 'tasks' of adolescence

Adolescents may seem like a strange group to be called a 'special population,' as adolescence is as intrinsic to growing up as being nine or being two. However in terms of play, adolescence is special in schools, since play is not currently widely considered as relevant in secondary education settings.

> Perhaps the aims of education for adolescents might change to include abilities that are controlled by the parts of the brain that undergo most change during adolescence.   Blakemore 2010, p.747

Sarah-Jayne Blakemore (2010, 2012), a cognitive neuroscientist with a particular interest in the teenage brain, identifies several developmental areas for which teenage years are a sensitive, formative time. These include:

- *the development of social skills*
- *the development of self-awareness*

She also identifies particular drives or needs that shape behaviours during teenage years:

- *the need to belong to a peer group*
- *the biological desire to get a kick out of risk-taking*

'KNOWING ME, KNOWING YOU':
Social skills and peer relationships in adolescence

Rough-and-tumble play provides opportunity for the declaration of friendship and caring relations.   Debenedet & Cohen 2010, p.18

Play (*see* Chapters 1 & 2) is the principle medium for social bonding. Recent research, confirming Erikson's beliefs, shows that adolescence is 'a key time for the development of regions of the brain involved in social cognition' (Blakemore 2010, p.747). Social play opportunities for adolescents are important in developing areas of the brain that are working on understanding others. Here we are, back with our old friend from earlier Chapters (particularly 3 and 4) - rough-and-tumble play. Do you get the feeling R&T play *really* matters? I hope that you do. Of course social play in adolescence can carry danger for teenagers, in terms of emotional and physical injury. It can look incomprehensible, uncomfortable and disconcerting to adults. Teenage girls are still able to satisfy their need for physical touch, and while they do fight, they also hold hands, groom each other (hair, nails, make-up), drape all over each other in pairs and in groups and greet each other with kisses and hugs. Many boys find it more difficult to have close physical contact with each other outside of sports and play-fighting. For some children, school may be the only place they get to mix with peers: but opportunities for social play in schools may be scarce and are often highly regulated.

Secondary schools are not the place for children to first play rough-and-tumble. Big bodies, teenage hormones and the heightened adolescent response to the fear of shame and embarrassment make for a potent mix. However secondary school is the place for consummate rough-and-tumblers to continue to use physical play to find out who they are, what they can do, and to bond with their peers. Practised players know the 'rules'. They know that -

... a basic rule of rough-and-tumble play prohibits you from hurting other players; in a play fight, you go through some of the motions of real fighting, but you do not kick, bite, punch, or scratch.   Gray 2011, p.455

Keeping play going, feeling your own ability to control your body and your feelings, are rewards in themselves.

Studies of young animals shed light on what we are currently experiencing in classrooms and playgrounds; young animals who do not have time for physical play when they are little show 'both excessive fear and inappropriate aggression' (Gray 2011, p.456) to later situations that are stressful, threatening or uncertain. Delaney (2009, pp.132-133) describes older children who have not reached an age-appropriate level of 'play expertise' as feeling 'shame and humiliation' if they don't know how to play or if they lose in play. These pupils:

△   Spoil things for others
△   Cheat
△   Sulk
△   Take over
△   Refuse to join in
△   Argue

This makes it harder for adults to include play in secondary provision and makes it impossible for adults to give teenagers only minimal supervision when play happens.

The paradox of play here is that while it is through play that we all develop restraint, self-control and emotional regulation, we do not currently provide teenagers with enough opportunities for long periods of play that are minimally supervised. 'Extended play develops children's self-control' (Edmiston 2011, p.54), and longer periods allowing for collaborative play has been shown to 'promote(d) more kindness in daily collaborative relationships among children' (*ibid* p.58). Children who did not have a fair chance at the first bite of the play cherry in the Early Years now miss out on their second chance of success, because their very lack of skill and play-ability stops them being included in the activities that alone could fill this gap.

Research suggests that during adolescence children use the part of the brain that relies on 'gut reaction' and 'raw emotion' to recognise emotions in others (Morgan 2005, p.30). Adults can mediate the emotional reaction to others by the use of logic, by consideration of context and probability. Tests on adolescents, using photographs of facial expressions to identify emotions, suggest that they 'jump to conclusions' and often get it wrong. Their interpretation or perception of others' feelings is highly influenced by their own feelings - *and they can't help that*. It's just how their brain is working. This is not connected with cognitive ability. It is connected to being an adolescent.

So play can be a way for teenagers to test out hypotheses, as it is for all of us. Play is 'evolution's answer to the problem of uncertainty' (Lotto & O'Toole 2012). But we already knew from both Chapter 1 and Chapter 3 that play is the way to find answer to questions and quandaries. We humans don't like uncertainty. Teenagers in particular feel it is their job to know the answer, to be sure of themselves, to be permanently 'right'. So we all, and teenagers in particular, plump for our best-guess answer, rather than live with not knowing, or being seen to not have any answer. In play it feels safer to take a bit longer to work it out, to test out a few possibilities, rather than limit ourselves to the most likely, or least shame-inducing option. Play, as we already established, is a safe place to make mistakes. In play a 'mistake' becomes *'I was only joking'*, or an elbow in the ribs and a quick change of tack. In real life a mistaken guess at someone else's feelings or meanings can make the adolescent feel embarrassed, rejected, 'stupid,' or fearful of the other person's reaction to their misunderstanding.

'REBEL SEEKING A CAUSE':
Identity formation

Erikson (1995) recognised the challenge of the adolescence years was to resolve the questions *"Who am I?"* and *"What am I?"* In fact he is credited with coining the phrase 'identity crisis'. Adolescence is about the development of an identity that 'fits'. It is also about developing a sense of *'Where I fit in'*. Often this can be more about rebellion than conformity; or at least that's how it feels to us parents who watch our child 'morph' into a stranger, seemingly for the sole purpose of being different. Different to family, but alarmingly conforming to a group of their peers! Finding out where they 'fit'- or don't - into family, 'relate'- or choose not to - with their community and the wider world, preoccupies the adolescent mind. As adolescence is a time when structural and functional brain changes increase the ability to become self-aware (Blakemore 2010, p.747), it is the physiologically right time to be working at creating, or playing with possibilities of identity.

Blakemore (2012) also identifies increased self-consciousness at this stage of development. Self-awareness and self-consciousness can be confused. What adolescents need is time to explore who they are: to be, or to become, aware of their 'Self'. Self-awareness can be defined as having the ability to access a conscious knowledge of one's own personality; being able to identify your feelings, motives, and desires. Or, more usefully, awareness of 'self' is about knowing our 'story' (Badenoch 2008), being able to see a strand of 'me' threaded through our life. We will think about the development of self-awareness and the importance role-play can have in that development when we think about our PSHE curriculum in Chapter 12.

Self-awareness is developing during teenage years, but teenagers are also developing a 'Self' that defines them. This Self is open to change. The best way to try things on for size is through play. Edmiston (2011) notes how dramatic play allows for 'shifts' between characters and roles. Being in the role of various characters looking at the same scenario from differing perspectives, such as 'perpetrators, victims, and bystanders' not only allows players to think *"What sort of person am I?"*, it also affords chances to develop morality and restraint (p.54).

Adolescence is a great opportunity for choosing who and how to be. Extremes at the stage are common. If you think 'Nerd', 'Goth', 'Emo' or, in my day, 'Mod' or 'Rocker', you will no doubt picture an adolescent. Most 30-year-olds have left the more extreme external signs of 'belonging' behind. Who we are or who we want others to see us as is really important during adolescence. Play offers opportunities for both demonstrating and expressing who we are; and for trying on who we could be.

'I AIN'T BOVVERED':
Risk taking in adolescence

'Am I bovvered?', Catherine Tate's teenage character Lauren's catch phrase, gave us the 2006 word of the year (OED UK Word of the Year). I love Lauren. Would I want Lauren in my home or in my class? Briefly - maybe; long term - probably not. But the way Tate captured the insolent, bolshie, argumentative 15-year-old with 'attitude' struck a chord with teenagers and their parents and teachers. Actually though, we probably recognise that kids at this age are more bothered about lots of things than children at any other age. Bothered about friendships, bothered about appearances, bothered about the planet, and above all bothered about what others think about them. As adolescents we feel things hugely but spend inordinate amounts of energy sending out signals that say *'I ain't bovvered'*. This need to appear careless, reckless, brave and 'up for anything' plays into the particular way adolescents relate to risk.

We know that adolescents have a tendency to take risks. They do. They take more risks than children or adults, and they are particularly prone to taking risks when they're with their friends.   Blakemore, TED talk 2012

In Chapter 4 we looked at the role of play in developing our ability to *manage risk* and also at how play might be the safest place to experience perils and to gamble with outcomes because of the possibly less serious consequences of play. A sound grounding in risky play early in life pays dividends now, since there is an increased incidence of risk-taking in adolescence; and bigger kids means bigger risks, so not a time to be just starting out on judging situations and people. Such pushing of the limits (their own and ours!) also plays a part in the teenagers desire to 'be someone', and to be independent and autonomous.

No escape for the teenage brain here then. They are chemically driven to be 'particularly responsive to novel and rewarding situations that normally induce dopamine release' (Zald, BBC News 2008). Adolescent 'problem' behaviours actually 'reflect(s) changes in the brain' (Blakemore TED talk 2012). They are socially driven to appear 'wild' or 'brave', 'crazy' or 'strong', in order to 'be someone' or to 'fit in' or generally to 'assert their status' (Morgan 2005, p.86). So the adolescent has a two-fold reason for their risk-taking behaviours.

One possible further reason why adolescence is so marked by risk-taking could be evolutionary. Adolescents 'could only learn to be bold and successful later by taking risks while still protected by their parents - in other words in relative safety' (Morgan 2005, p.85). The safety to make 'valuable mistakes' (*ibid*) when still a 'child', is similar to the safety to make acceptable mistakes in play situations. In most 'good enough' homes, parents and/or play offer a safety net for the risk-taker. Morgan (p.87) recognises that extreme risk-taking may occur because 'milder' forms of risk-taking are not usually available to teenagers.

There are exceptions. The National Institute of Circus Skills in Australia (nica. com.au) certainly knows how to tap into adolescent brains to encourage them to come along; they advertise their courses by offering skills that will impress your friends and thrills from performing in front of an audience. Getting a 'buzz' from play and appearing skilful to peers in a safe place might mean walking the tightrope over a safety net replaces climbing on roofs of derelict buildings; riding a unicycle replaces joyriding in cars; and slap-stick comedy and slinging of custard pies stands in for the merciless teasing and insult-throwing of bored and unhappy kids hanging about on street corners. In Chapter 12 we will hear how Brian Sutton-Smith (2002) also sees the circus as symbolic of the fun and the 'danger' in play.

BEING A BRAIN-WISE EDUCATOR: Using research to inform provision for the adolescent brain

> Given that the primary focus of education is to maximise human potential, then a new task before us is to ensure that the conditions in which learning takes place address the very biology of our learners. Carskadon 1999, p.348

One area where neuroscience is informing education at secondary school level is in the organisation of the school day. In both America and the UK, some schools have taken up the challenge of adapting education in light of knowledge about the adolescent teenage brain. Studies by Wolfson & Carskadon (1998) show that teenagers 'internal clock' shifts to sleeping later and waking later - a 'sleep phase delay'. Schools that have trialled later start times for pupils have found that there was less absenteeism and fewer students arriving late for school. In the US, other advantages reported for students in schools taking part in the initiative include:

➡   pupils seeming more alert

➡   improvements in behaviour

➡   a decrease in reports of stress due to schoolwork

➡   a decrease in reports of stress due to difficulties in relationships at
       home and at school (*ibid*)

In my view, other areas of education would also benefit by paying heed to the latest understanding of the teenage brain. 'Learning how to stay playful, in age appropriate ways' (Brown 2009, p.110) is an important task for adolescents if they are to become playful adults, with all the health benefits and likelihood of social inclusion that playfulness imparts. 'This is a period of life where the brain is particularly adaptable and malleable' (Blakemore, 2012). The plasticity of the brain, the growing and pruning of neural pathways, the developing of brain connections and the turning on of 'a whole new set of brain genes' (Brown 2009, p.109) means that this is a time for shaping who we are to become. I believe that more time needs to be given over to the crucial tasks of becoming oneself and relating to others through play at this age stage. Schools need to find ways of including diverse, safe but challenging play opportunities for the teenagers in our care.

It takes our brains a long time to change and catch up with changes in society and technological development. Animal adolescents take risks, try out possible ways of being, and create bonds through play. This means that if they fail, they can do so in (relative) safety. We expect human adolescents to reason, think, listen and act logically. But it is not until around 17 years of age that this ability comes to the fore. Much early brain pruning happens through play - so do we provide enough play at the second big stage of brain pruning - in adolescence? Play helps us keep up with the fast changing pace of life. Playing is an experience where adolescents can both 'prune' and 'fertilise' their developing brain (*remember the brain food - BDNF, mentioned in Chapter 2 which is released through play experiences?*). It is 'feed and weed' time. *"I'll nurture my caring nature but cut out my over-dependence on others".* It is 'Miracle Grow' for human potential. It is topiary of the brain. But over-pruning at this age reduces options in later life. 'If you don't use it, you lose it' is literally true. Alongside the pruning and the shaping, the adolescent brain needs the fertilising opportunities that only play affords.

The pay-off at the end of adolescence is that 'you get better at the things you are good at' (Morgan 2005, p.27). The drawback is that after adolescence, we have fewer options and find new things much harder to do. The things that we do, the neural pathways we use, get stronger, but the things that we don't use, the neurons and synapses that appear to be redundant, get pruned (*ibid*). Play experiences, and plenty of them, leave more of the brain potential exercised and available for use. Play allows the brain to use the parts other forms of behaviour cannot reach!

Back to Lauren. Tate 'retired' her in the 2007 Christmas Special (BBC 25th December, 2007 - I think 'killed off' is the TV serial term!). Now Lauren remains an eternal teenager, and her epitaph stays true to her adolescent bravado: *"I still ain't bovvered."*

and so ...

KEY POINTS

The teenage brain is different; it is not able to process the world in the same way as that of an adult

The teenage years are a vital time for shaping the brain and the person we will become

Adolescents need lots of opportunities for exploring potential identities

There is a real correlation between adolescence and risk-taking. Risk-taking in play is a safer option for teenagers

Peer relations are of overriding importance in adolescence - schools are the ideal venue for peers to congregate and develop their networks

Adolescence - Where do we go from here?

Like any area of school provision, we look to evidence-based best practice in ways of supporting our children. And the Young Minds website, youngminds.org.uk, is a great place to start. They offer a range of resources, including:

△ Reports that give adolescents a voice to tell us how they feel

△ And a chance to tell us how they feel we could do better in
    meeting their needs!

△   Resiliency programmes

△   Information on a range of issues relevant to adolescents

The play-full secondary school would -

☺   Have annual whole school training in the evolving understanding of the adolescent brain

☺   Structure the school day in light of the knowledge of the teenage brain and include play opportunities

If you want to know more, try reading

Blakemore, S-J. (2012) *The mysterious workings of the adolescent brain*, a TED talk. Available at: ted.com/talks/sarah_jayne_blakemore_the_mysterious_workings_of_the_adolescent_brain.html

Carskadon, M. (1999) When Worlds Collide: Adolescent need for sleep versus societal Demands, *In Phi Delta Kappan Magazine*, Vol. 80:5 pp.348-353

Morgan, N. (2005) *Blame My Brain: The amazing teenage brain revealed* London: Walker Books

Wolfson, A. & Carskadon, M. (1998) Sleep Schedules and Daytime Functioning in Adolescents. *Child Development*, Vol. 69:4, pp.875-887

Zald, D. H. (2008) Evidence of 'risk-taking' brain. *BBC News* news.bbc.co.uk/1/hi/health/7802751.stm

If you want to understand more, try reading

Dr Suess (2003) *Oh, The Places You'll Go* London: Harper Collins

If you want a 15 minute group or individual training try watching

Sarah-Jayne Blakemore's 2012 TED talk 'The mysterious workings of the adolescent brain' on the TED talk website, ted.com/talks or youtube.com

Better play

SECTION 2 : PLAY IN SCHOOLS

Chapter 8

Let the children play:
play and the curriculum

Let's face it, what school usually does is continually interrupt any attempt on the part of children to recapture the highly focussed intensity of play. What we need to do is help them - and ourselves - get back on track.

Paley 1997, p.75

In many ways, the question *'How do we learn?'* reflects the debate over nature versus nurture in the broader question, *'How do we become the person we grow up to be?'* A balanced view of the nature: nurture debate - that actually we have genetic potentials (nature) that are developed or depleted by the environment (nurture) - is like a balanced view of the role of play; we have *potential* for creativity and emotional wellbeing that are *developed* through lots of varied play experiences or are *never fully expressed* because of a lack of play opportunities. We have an innate drive to explore and make sense of the world (play) which is encouraged or discouraged by educators (teaching). A description of the adult's encouragement of play as nurture fits in the Early Years, pre-school ethos. But does it sound like the mission statement for schooling for seven to 18-year-olds in your school or work setting?

Having considered what play is, we need to consider a common understanding of 'learning' and of 'education'. If we are advocating for play in schools, it is important to think about the nature of education and where play 'fits'.

In this chapter we will think about the nature and purpose of education and how that might relate to learning while at play.

THE QUESTIONS TO CONSIDER ARE:

EDUCATION, EDUCATION, EDUCATION: WHAT IS 'EDUCATION'?
What do we all hope to provide in education establishments? And can those good intentions be achieved through play?

PLAY COMES LATER
*Sometimes we seem to 'split' play and learning and offer play as a break from or reward for learning, rather than what it is: an intrinsic part of learning. Can we stop seeing **play** and **learning** as opposing activities that compete for our energy and time, and start to provide them as two closely related activities with complementary outcomes?*

DREAM A LITTLE DREAM
What role do daydreaming and play breaks have in helping us learn?

VALUING PLAY:
CHILDREN LOVE TO PLAY, AND IT IS GOOD FOR THEM!
What are our own attitudes to play? Do we value it as much as our children do? If not - should we?

This chapter ends with a few lines which look as if we might be starting to build a manifesto for play! The sections where we will draw together our learning from this chapter and previous ones are:

Let's get more precise with our use of language:

  only play is play

Let's be honest

Let's be confident

Let's be creative

Let's embrace the subversive nature of some play

Let's be 21st Century research-based practitioners

EDUCATION, EDUCATION, EDUCATION

The political war-cry suggests that education is really, really important. So what is it all about? Is education 'The transfer of knowledge and skills from teachers to pupils'? A bit maybe, but a lot more besides. Can education happen where there is no teaching? Yes, certainly: but without teaching, are there some things we could never learn? Perhaps it is the developing of cognitive abilities necessary for adult life. But would I like a world where I only learned what was 'necessary'?

UNESCO described their vision for education in the 21st Century in Delors' 1996 report, *Learning the Treasure Within*. They suggested four pillars of education that best represent what is needed to prepare children for their future.

- *Learning to live together*
- *Learning to know*
- *Learning to do*
- *Learning to be*

In other words, what I'd think of as playful learning:

➡ *Living together*, across animal species, is underpinned by playing together

➡ From birth we are programmed *to find out how to find out* - the playful exploration of the world

➡ Not only do the baby and toddler *learn what they can do* through play, through playful trial and error, they learn what they can make others do too!

➡ Play is *all about being and becoming*: it is the most expanding experience for the brain and the soul that anyone has ever discovered

Herb Kohl (2009) (who we will meet again in the next chapter since, as well as having things to say about learning, he gives us lots to think about when he talks about teachers!) believes that children must have six basic skills (pp.105-6) if they are to be 'effective and compassionate' adults:

i)   The ability to use language well and thoughtfully

ii)   The ability to think through a problem and experiment with solutions

iii) The ability to understand scientific and technological ideas, and to use tools

iv)   The ability to use imagination

v)   The ability to understand how people function in groups

vi)   The ability to know how to learn something yourself

Mmm, now - can play help here at all? Anything leaping out at you? Let's go through them one at a time.

i)   Play can help with that one   ✔

ii)   Play is probably the only way we can do that ✔

iii) Direct teaching needed here I think, with lots of practice (play)
      afterwards to consolidate ✓

iv) Absolutely, no question   ✓

v) No good talking about this one - you've got to experience it ✓

vi) A 'no-brainer'   ✓

Pramling Samuelsson & Johansson (2006, p.53) describe learning as:

> … a question of seeing, perceiving, experiencing, distinguishing or understanding something in a new and qualitatively different way, and by relating to the surrounding world in the light of this experiencing.

From birth to the first day at school, exploratory play is doing just that for the future scholar. So play = learning (Singer et al 2006), and so much more besides: play certainly 'does what it says on the learning tin'! So where do play and learning suddenly diverge in our thinking and belief about education?

PLAY COMES LATER

In schools play is sometimes used as a reward, *"Finish your work first and you can play"*; or as a break from work, *"After playtime I'll expect you to come back refreshed and ready to really work hard."* It can be seen as a means to an end or just another teaching tool:

> Classroom-based teaching should be reinforced in assemblies, homework and play periods (in class as well as in the playground).   NICE, 2008

In primary schools 'best practice' separates play from learning and may seem to imply that play is a less valued activity. NICE guidance suggests schools take over and control children's play periods. The message is: play has little value other than as a time and place to learn what society has chosen to teach.

So let's try turning that on its head - how would schools look if we believed play was more important than adult-led activity?

> The free play of children should be enriched by assemblies, homework and classroom-based teaching.

Evidence suggests that learning is more effective when it is self-chosen and relevant to the learner; in other words, teaching added on to play, rather than play directed by teachers. Brain experts understand that a child can only learn what their brain is able to take in. This learning has to be something that can connect to networks that already exist. How do we know what a child already knows? We see it in their play. How do we find out what a child is ready to learn next? We can follow their interest and notice the gaps in the things they are making sense of in their play.

> The single most important factor in learning is the existing networks of neurons in the learner's brain. Ascertain what they are and teach accordingly.
>
> Zull 2002, p.93

Nate Kornell (2012) conducted a small experiment to test the theory that only practice (work) makes perfect. He had two pairs of his students from Williams College in Massachusetts practise a new skill, and play a new game. Two students only played pool, and only practised chess, while the other two only practised pool and only played chess. In this very small experiment, the students who played games did better than those who practised skills. However Kornell notes that he believes a hybrid of play and learning are probably the best approach to getting better at things. He felt that one of the main benefits of play was that through playing you find out what you need to work at, and what you need to learn about, and that self-selected work for an identified need or reason increases motivation to learn.

> When you're new to a sport or skill, sometimes play is the best practice. Practising and playing both worked, though, and all four participants improved a great deal. But in our data, playing worked as well or better and it was more fun - and more likely to keep us motivated to continue getting better.   *ibid*

Birds of a feather, or poles apart?

Often the dynamics between school-work and play seem conflicting, opposing or irreconcilable. Kuschner (2012a, p.242) goes so far as to say that while play is natural to childhood, school is not, and that 'the tension between play and school may be a case of an irresistible force (play) meeting an immovable object (school)' (*author's italics and brackets*, p.244). But Pramling Samuelsson & Johansson believe that play and learning not only go hand in hand but are, in fact, indivisible. 'Play and learning are dimensions that stimulate each other and could be seen as an indivisible entirety, which is a part of children's experiencing, and which helps them create an understanding of their surrounding world in a life-long process' (2006, p.62). Making school playful might help the irresistible force shift the immovable object.

> If teachers approach play and learning as one (rather than two separate activities, with two separate goals), their teaching may be more effective, particularly in promoting a lifelong love of learning.   Cornelli Sanderson 2010, p.153

Happy, healthy schools acknowledge the relationship between play and work as complementary and inter-dependent. At times, work and play are threads that weave together to create a stronger whole. The two parts are often indistinguishable. Play can be the thing that makes work bearable. It can be the thing that makes a way of working unique to the worker. It may be the thing that leads the work into new, unforeseen but important areas. Imagination, creative thinking, the part that does not need doing but you just do it anyway, can change the act of work, change the outcome of the work, change your understanding or change the world! Playful work makes life fun.

> *"When I am hoovering I imagine it's my pet dog eating all the crumbs."*
>
> *in* Kapasi & Gleave 2009, p.8

Standing back and observing in any classroom, we'd all notice moments of play, and playful moments during work sessions. We're also likely to notice serious, deep thought, intense concentration, planning and absolute effort during sessions at play. 'This is how things are made, by a kind of match of playfulness and discipline' (Almond 2013). In younger age groups, we'll see jokes being exchanged, children adding complications to tasks 'just for the fun of it' or pupils staying on task but expressing unique ways of doing so. In older classrooms the play may be more subtle and less immediately obvious. The belief that daydreaming is internalised play suggests the pupil staring out of the window or poised with pen not connecting with paper may be playing, without conscious knowledge of doing so.

Play during work could be about the need for a moment of relief or release, the need to play with the matter in hand in order to inform the work task or the need to bring into consciousness something of use accessible only through the randomness of play. Psychologists believe that daydreaming is a way we review what we are already aware of, and also a way to imagine other possibilities of which we are as yet unaware (Glausiusz 2009).

However, when a child appears to be 'in a world of their own', our first thought is to bring them back to the task at hand. But reflection on the known and on the possible is how our brains work. The reverie might not be relevant, or might start off relevant but move into another area more pressing to that child's need to make sense of life, or start off as a far-fetched fantasy that amazingly gives new perspective on the given task. In life we often find that the seemingly irrelevant turns out to be helpful and the random connection solves the intractable problem.

I know it is not quite the same but I have often woken up with the answer to a crossword clear in my mind when I've fallen asleep hours after a frustrating and unsuccessful wrestle with a cryptic clue. It has happened so often I now expect my brain to come up with answers while I am doing something else, or when I think that I am thinking about nothing. These days, in a strange way, I have learned to trust my brain to play with ideas or to rough-and-tumble with a quandary, the more I give it free rein to do so. Having reached a grand old age (remember C. S. Lewis from Chapter 6 - like him I'm no longer worried about appearing childish!) I am happy in serious professional discussions to throw in a daft idea or say something that seems initially ridiculous but has just come into my head, because I believe my brain prompts these random thoughts for a reason. I also find that 'far-fetched fantasy' can be a great starting point to finding practical and realistic solutions. In Chapter 11 we'll hear about how some of the world's most creative thinkers trust their play instinct and their dreams to open up the world of possibilities.

DREAM A LITTLE DREAM

The author David Almond's call for '10% of the curriculum ... to be left a kind of space - as dream time' (2013, BBC) might in fact already be an unrecognised reality. Brain imaging of a typical 13 year old during an average school day would offer insight into the child's ability to meet his or her needs for distraction, reflection or fun. A Harvard study by Killingsworth & Gilbert in 2010 recorded that people spend 47% of their waking hours daydreaming, and other researchers agree that we spend between 15% and 50% of our time daydreaming.

Smaller children may physically play while mentally working; maybe singing aloud as they thread beads in a pattern to match their work card. The nine year old boy may nudge, tickle, gently kick and pull faces at his peers as he completes pages of multiplications. The seven year old girl twiddles hair around her finger, tries to get her tongue to touch her nose and ties and unties the bow on her dress while never taking her eyes off the page as she reads and enjoys the next chapter in her book.

Older children become more skilled at internalised play, where thinking takes the place of doing; 'imagination in adolescents and school children is play without action' (Vygotsky 1978, p.93). For some 15 year old pupils the play may be action, doodling, fiddling, or humming: in others the play may be unseen and not physically expressed in any way. Other teenage activities that King calls 'illicit play' (In Hyvonen 2011, p.66) may be called something else by school staff not versed in the vocabulary of playfulness. 'Illicit' play 'includes verbal and physical activities such as joking and fooling around'. King is aware that illicit play is not 'appreciated' by the adults in schools!

Play alongside or as a break from work may be fulfilling an important function;

"It gives you more energy."   Ten-year-old boy

"It encourages you to work hard during the week."   11-year-old boy,

"It stops you getting stressed, if you are struggling
with something in the class."   11-year-old girl
                                                      IPA Scotland, 2011, p.19

But when we regulate the time when play can happen it might not be the time when an individual needs that energising, encouragement or relaxation. Separating work from play or splitting activities into work *or* play forces us to engage in philosophical, political and cultural arguments. Acknowledging that success and progress are achieved through a match of work and play is seeing things as they really are, and changes the way we approach the provision of playful work in schools. Spontaneous and incidental learning are valuable sources of information and often more memorable. As educators we often remember the surprise findings and unanticipated results from our planned activities and lessons. And we value incidental learning enough to include it in our planning for that taught session next year!

VALUING PLAY:
children love to play, *and* it is good for them!

Attitudes to play inform the arguments around play and learning. Those of us working in schools may feel the responsibility of 'ensuring that children do actually learn through play' (Adams 2005, p.215). We are employed to work with children and young people in order that they learn. Living involves learning, so pupils will learn, whether that is because of us, with us or despite us. But we all hope to stretch that learning by what we provide each lesson, each day, each interaction.

Sometimes though we might not feel confident that we can allow for play because, if we do - is the child 'actually' learning? Moyles (2005, p.9) states that: 'play in educational settings should have *learning* consequences.' Well - here's the good news! How could play *not* have learning consequences? Play *is* the way that humans learn. Play has 'learning consequences' because:

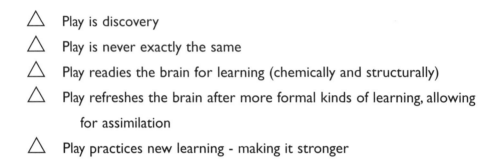

- △   Play is discovery
- △   Play is never exactly the same
- △   Play readies the brain for learning (chemically and structurally)
- △   Play refreshes the brain after more formal kinds of learning, allowing for assimilation
- △   Play practices new learning - making it stronger

Children playing *are* 'actually' learning, or just as importantly, consolidating or integrating learning. The outcome of play *is* learning.

Let's get more precise with our use of language. Only play is play

In my view, the use of the word 'play' to describe activities in the Early Years' curriculum that are planned to fit checklists and attainment targets muddies the water on the whole understanding of play provision in education. In Chapter 1 we thought a lot about what makes something play, and how sometimes we call things play that are not play and don't acknowledge things that are play as being just that. *"Let's play!"* means, *"Let's do something that we don't have to do."* How can we reconcile this with a framework which suggests a lack of understanding of what play is? The current framework guidance states:

> Each area of learning and development must be implemented through planned, purposeful play and through a mix of adult-led and child-initiated activity. Play is essential for children's development, building their

confidence as they learn to explore, to think about problems, and relate to others. Children learn by leading their own play, and by taking part in play which is guided by adults.   DfE 2014b, p.9

So the Department for Education is unequivocal in its commitment to play and fulsome in its praise of play and recognition of play's value. But it then goes on to describe play as something that can be planned. It also appears to think play can be lacking in purpose, as staff have to make the play they provide 'purposeful' (whose purpose is not clear!). The notion of adult-led, adult-guided play makes me feel that if I provide this 'play' I could be trying to sneak work in under the radar! My belief is that -

> Opportunities for each area of learning and development must be provided through a mix of planned, purposeful adult-led activity, and time for child-initiated play activity. Play is essential for children's development, building their confidence as they learn to explore, to think about problems, and relate to others. Children learn through leading their own play, joining in with play led by peers, and by adults joining in and following children's lead in their play: as well as by taking part in activities which are guided by adults.

Calling all activities 'play', whether adult planned and led or child initiated, is confusing and inaccurate. Filling a big bucket with smaller buckets to find how many small buckets equal one big bucket is play if a child decides he wants to find that out, but the same bucket and water are not playthings if I have told the child I want them to find out this answer. If 'the activities-based, adult-inspired' (Brooker 2011, p.162) work (often playfully introduced and playfully carried out) in Early Years classrooms was given the new name Brooker insists it needs, it would help us all to know when we are seeing play and when we are over-seeing this other, as yet unnamed, planned and purposeful activity.

> A discourse of 'play and learning' purports to welcome children's freedom to discover and explore through play, but such freedom is developed through objectification of the child by pedagogical gaze and scrutiny; children's freedom to discover is strictly monitored and controlled as it is essential that children are discovering the right things. Lester 2010

The girl filling the big bucket with smaller buckets may discover that as the bucket gets fuller is also gets heavier. The boy who wanted to keep playing in the home corner because he was worried about his baby brother and somehow, for some reason, putting the doll to bed and tucking it in was making him feel better, may learn that his needs are not recognised and valued by me while I am focussed on his purposeful learning.

Let's be honest

Although I would feel sneaky labelling my agenda as play, maybe children aren't fooled. Words and names don't matter to them, it is how it feels and what meaning it has that are their definition.

Mr Semple	*Today we're going to play in the construction straws.*
Ramin	*Sir, please can I finish this monster I'm building?*
Mr Semple	*You can do that later Ramin, right now I want you to come and play over here.*
Shannon	*I'm going to make a crown, I want to be a princess.*

Mr Semple	*Right. Today I'm giving each of you a pet and you are going to build it somewhere to live. Ged you've got a rabbit; Ramin yours is a budgie and Shannon you have a goldfish.*
Shannon	*I want a puppy!*
Ramin	*Ged can we swap?*
Mr Semple	*Ramin, you have to build a home for the pet I gave you. I'll be back soon to see how you're getting on.*

Ten minutes later

| Mr Semple | *How's it going? That's great Ged, I bet your rabbit will love that rabbit hutch. Shannon, where is your goldfish bowl? Haven't you started yet? That looks more like a tiara than a fish bowl. Ramin you need to think what size cage you need for that budgie.* |

Ten minutes later

| Mr Semple | *Right you three. Are we done? Great Ramin and you Ged, you can put the straws away now. Shannon you see when you put your mind to it you have lots of ideas. Well done.* |
| Ramin & Shannon | Can we ***play*** now? |

Let's be confident

In a study of Finnish teachers (Hyvonen 2011, p.71) over two-thirds of those questioned described play as a vehicle for instruction 'in which the teacher's role is to lead activities and children are to follow directions'. But even in Finland, school staff are used to calling adult-led activities 'play'. Anyone who has read much about play and learning will be used to play being described as a useful tool for learning.

Despite all the research on the value of true play, we are still anxious about allowing time for play in schools.

> *"I know that there should be playing at school, but I'm worried whether playing can meet the goals of the curriculum."*   Hyvonen 2011, p.72

This lack of confidence in play, this anxiety about the adult role - *"If the child chooses, manages and learns through their own play, then what is the point of me?"* - leads to play most often being described as 'a vehicle'. In the next chapter we will look much more at how our need to teach, or our need to feel others know we are 'doing our job', sometimes gets in the way of us doing great work. If play is a vehicle for learning, it goes without saying - the adult is in the driving seat, and our fear is that without his or her driving skill, route planning, prudence and ability to keep the rules of the road, the play vehicle could stall, career out of control, or end up at completely the wrong destination (which it might, because it does: that is the nature of play. But learning will happen. Just not the learning we planned, maybe?).

So the hijacking of play (and why wouldn't educationalists hijack such a powerful and appropriate vehicle?) has been recognised by many experts in the field (Mayall 2000; Thomas & Hocking 2003, Oksnes 2008, Lester & Russell, 2010 and Hughes 2012) as leading to play being:

> **COLONISED**
> instrumentalised
> **adulterated**
> SCHOLARISED
> sanitised
> *commercialised*

I maintain that play cannot, and should not, be harnessed, planned, directed or cut to fit. It is like fairy dust in the air that you can never collect, like a dream that lingers tantalisingly but you just can't recall, or a glimpse from the corner of your eye that disappears in the fullness of a gaze.

Let's be creative

Play is not a vehicle. It is a landscape. Learning by being driven on a planned route is important. You can later retrace your steps. I like being taken to a new place by someone who has been there before. I prefer someone else driving the first time I have to undertake a tricky, complicated, busy route. Vehicles and drivers have their place.

Learning in a landscape is different. It offers more time for reflection, allows for diversion, invites emotional engagement and lets the player choose when to leave, how far and fast to go and which parts of the landscape they are personally drawn to. James Zull (2002) seems to be talking about the landscape nature of learning as opposed to the vehicle of teaching when he advocates for more time in schools to be given over to 'random actions'.

> Maybe we should allow [students] to search around for what is out there rather than insisting that their actions be focussed on the task at hand. Maybe our job is to put things in their way and then stand back and let students discover them. After all this is the biological way. It is only through exploring, through action, that we encounter new information.
>
> Zull 2002, p.217

So perhaps our role as adults is in creating environments, landscapes, for children to be in. Then we can stand back and watch the pennies start to drop.

'There is always a conflict in education between the need for creativity and the need for mechanistic structures' (Almond 2013). The tension between outcome and process-oriented activities exists because both things are important. Both work and play have their place in education and development. Balance is the important thing. Research in Poland (Mitrega & Najgebaur 2011) confirmed that a large number of Polish pupils worked more than the 40-hour week that is legally guaranteed to adults. Not a good balance on first inspection. But no-one actually monitored the 40 hours of work the children undertook. How playful did they manage to be at any time during their week? Probably still far too many hours confined to a building, a room, a desk, but where the Polish children travelled to in their play (daydreams, jokes, resistance to the adult agenda), we do not know.

Let's embrace the subversive nature of some play

Lester (2010) refers to the different activities that are going on all around us all the time as 'dominant' and 'clandestine'. Just the word 'clandestine' makes any activity more appealing to children! Lester says that the two activities are not 'either/or' but they are intertwined behaviours that create the whole. He recognises that work informs play and play informs work. Play intrudes and interrupts work; it informs and transforms work. Play *will* happen. When children are allowed play as the 'dominant' activity, work appears in the play (funny we don't call work illicit or clandestine, when we have not asked children to do it!). In our role-play area the waiter writes out the order, checking out spellings with his friends; the astronaut calculates the distance to the next planet and how long it will take her to get there.

Let's be 21st Century research-based practitioners

Advocating for play does not mean belittling work. But the balance of provision will never be the best possible fit for children when providers know a lot more about curriculum and about how the brain learns in a taught environment, than they do about play and what children learn as they play, how the brain changes after play and why play has been important to people for much longer than education has. Balance in post-qualifying training is essential for a balanced school provision which is able to develop balanced school leavers. We are learning more and more about what play is and why playing matters, but this knowledge is not filtering into training programmes.

There are two difficulties for school staff in their understanding of and commitment to play. Training for Primary providers, and in particular Early Years, confuse the understanding of play through the interchangeable use of the term for activities that are chosen by the child and supervised solely for safety of the participants, and for activities planned, directed, overseen and assessed by the staff. Training for Secondary providers has not yet acknowledged the need for more training across the board on what it is to be human. Training about attachment and about play seem to be assigned to the world of pre-teen teaching. Teenagers' brains are at a crucial stage for retaining diversity and flexibility, yet at this very time education encourages specificity and formality. Play in teenage years keeps options open within neural networks and is of paramount importance for social bonding and the resulting emotional wellbeing.

Let's put it all together

Training for school staff has to include an emphasis on the latest understanding of how children learn. In the last chapter, we saw how listening to the research on how adolescents learn can lead to us to offer them a more conducive environment, or at least a school day that suits them much better. Decisions about *what* to teach in schools and *how* to teach should be evidence-based. Play is one of the major ways children learn. That's why we need to train and support every member of the schools staff to understand and value play. That's why we need to support play and playfulness for all ages and stages.

Research-based teacher education aims to develop teachers that are capable of using research and research-driven competencies in their ongoing teaching and decision making (Westbury et al 2005). In that aim, it should take into account research of play as well.   Hyvonen 2011, p.78

and so ...

KEY POINTS

Play is not a vehicle for learning, it is a way of being and an expression of joy

Play always results in learning, but that is not the reason for play

Play is not a tool for teaching: it is an activity where we learn what cannot be taught

*Play **is** the teacher, and adults are always learning too*

Play and learning: *Where do we go from here?*

In order for changes in practice to take place, the Play, Schools and Integrated Children's Settings Group believe that the following developments need to take place in government policy. It recommends:

> Government ensures that the value and importance of play is recognised in Ofsted inspections, and that the joint Ofsted/SkillsActive training module *Putting Play into Practice* should be reviewed, and inspectors required to attend this training.
>
> (From: Play England, 2008, *'Play in schools and integrated settings: A position statement* London: NCB

A play-full school would -

- ☺ Include opportunities for play in every area of the school curriculum
- ☺ Value incidental learning as much as learning that meets the aims and objectives of the lesson
- ☺ Support staff who are unsure and lack confidence in the use of play
- ☺ Delight in the excitement of individual discovery

If you want to know more, try reading

Glausiusz, J (2009) Devoted to Distraction. *Psychology Today*. Available at: s/200903/devoted-distraction

Killingsworth, M. & Gilbert, D. (2010) A Wandering Mind Is an Unhappy Mind. *Science Vol:* 330:6006 pp.932-932: Brevia

Kornell, N. (2012) What Does All Work and No Play Make Jack Into? *Psychology Today*. Available at: psychologytoday.com/blog/everybody-is-stupid-except-you/201209/what-does-all-work-and-no-play-make-jack

NICE (2008) *Social and emotional wellbeing in primary education*. National Institute for Care and Health Excellence.

Available at: nice.org.uk/guidance/ph12

Pramling Samuelsson, I. & Johansson, E. (2006) Play and learning - inseparable dimensions in preschool practice. *Early Child Development and Care* Vol. 176:1 pp. 47–65 Routledge

Rogers, S. (Ed.) (2011) *Rethinking Play and Pedagogy in Early Childhood Education: Concepts, contexts and cultures.* Oxford: Routledge

If you want to understand more, try reading

McCourt, L. (2000) *It's Time for School Stinky Face* NY: Scholastic Inc.

If you want a 15 minute group or individual training, try watching

Sir Ken Robinson's 2006 TED talk *Bring on the Learning Revolution!*

On the TED website ted.com/talks or on youtube.com

Chapter 9

The impact of play on the adult, and the impact of the adult on play

The play of children may strike us at times as fragile and charming, rowdy and boisterous, ingenious, just plain silly, or as disturbingly perceptive in its portrayals of adult actions and attitudes.   Garvey 1991, p.1

When we adults see children playing, we can experience a variety of feelings that can lead us to have a range of responses:

Our responses are often strong messages that encourage or inhibit the players, and not always in the way we intend! Our reactions to how and when children play may encourage resistance or defiance. Sometimes I have found that children employ subterfuge to continue their play 'behind my back'. Or maybe I just know that is what they do because it was what I did myself.

The good news about adults and play is that 79% of children interviewed for the International Play Association in Scotland (IPA 2011, p.29) thought it was good to have adults around at least sometimes when they played. The bad news is that only 45% of the children asked felt that adults thought it was important that they played!

The findings suggest that not only do children sense that adults do not value their need to play and all the things that playing does for them; but that children want us to play with them but sense that we, the adults, do not always (or maybe often?) have the time or the inclination to do so. And we all miss out: we don't get to be a child again, and children don't get to see that we remember how to play too.

In this chapter we will think about the impact of play on the adult and impact of the adult on play. While we are thinking about the most important factor for wellbeing - the relationships we build (for both children and adults) - we will look at what attachment theory has to tell us about what might be going on in relationships in school and the steps that we 'dance' when relating to others.

THE QUESTIONS TO CONSIDER ARE:

YOU MAKE ME FEEL LIKE DANCING

Attachment theory can give us some ideas about human relationships that may be helpful in understanding ourselves. How do we learn to relate in the ways we each do? Who am I in my work, and how does that influence how I act around others?

BORN TO TEACH

Why might people be 'drawn' to work with children or choose to take on a role of teacher or carer?

THE IMPACT OF PLAY ON THE ADULT

Asking ourselves questions about how play makes us feel can help us to notice that sometimes it is we who do not like what happens - the children are all having a whale of a time! How do I feel around play? Am I comfortable watching all kinds of play?

THE IMPACT OF THE ADULT ON PLAY

Are there ways we are changing children's play? Might that sometimes mean we stop the play being so deep, so rich and so beneficial?

So let's start by thinking about relationships. One model of how we relate is attachment theory; I've chosen this because I'm sure you will all be familiar with some of the ideas, and for me it often feels as if it is actually more like 'The Theory of Everything'. It really can be that informative for how we live, if we feel that it really 'speaks' to us. Taking time to consider how attachment works may give us a framework we can build on.

YOU MAKE ME FEEL LIKE DANCING

In order to for us to think about relationships in schools, it's helpful to establish a shared vocabulary. Here is a very quick glossary of terms used by people working with children and families which are about relationships, and how they can be described or sorted into 'types':

Attachment	*A pattern or style of relating to others which is usually based on our earliest experiences of relationships.*
Secure attachment	*Feeling comfortable being alone or being with people. Feeling comfortable being needed and being not needed. Feeling comfortable with asking for help and with giving help.*
Insecure attachment	*Feeling uncomfortable being alone, or being with others. Feeling uncomfortable when needed by others or when not needed by others. Having a sense of real discomfort when in need of, or being offered help, and/or not comfortable to help others or helping others in most un-helpful ways. The different patterns of insecure attachment responses have been sub-categorised (avoidant, ambivalent and disorganised, categories which change as our understanding of attachment develops) to describe the varying relational needs and discomforts different insecurely attached individuals experience.*
Attachment needs	*The relationships, experiences and environments we need in order to feel comfortable.*
Attachment behaviours	*The ways we act to get our needs met within relationships. In particular, how we ensure we are close to, or distant from, others.*

Attachment in the Classroom (Geddes 2006) is an essential guide for school staff who want to understand the way attachment influences the behaviours and learning of the child. Building on this, *Attachment Theory and the Teacher-Student Relationship* (Riley 2010) is a challenging text for school staff as it addresses the impact of the adult's attachment patterns on the children in their care. Riley considers:

➡ How adult attachment styles influence classroom and staffroom
   relationships
➡ How the attachment relationships in school between adults and
   children influence emotional responses to teaching and learning

How adult attachment needs and behaviours shape the way we manage student behaviour

In my view Riley makes a fundamental statement about anyone taking a teaching role in schools: 'the teacher needs to form a working relationship with at least one student to maintain a professional identity of 'teacher'' (2009, p.627). Harris (2012, p.42) agrees; 'Many teachers are susceptible to a destructive disease: '*Wemustimpartforyoutolearn-itus*'. In order to be a teacher we need to have someone who is willing to be taught. Teaching someone something makes me, the teacher, feel good, or useful, and successful in 'doing my job'. Pupils learning without, or despite, being 'taught' does not fulfil our professional obligation to 'teach'.

Giving over time for children to learn through play may immediately cause us professional difficulties. If the child in my classroom chooses, directs, and sustains her own learning, then what is my role? In Early Years Education this concern has been overcome by staff being trained extensively to 'teach' through play: it has been integrated into the EYs professional's role. In provision for older children, however, time for play is often organised in times when teaching staff get a break, splitting play away from the curriculum. As I mentioned previously, play is often described as a 'vehicle or a tool for learning' in literature for school staff on this subject. This clearly indicates that our current political, philosophical, cultural and professional beliefs need adults in school to be in the driving seat for play experiences, and to be 'manipulating' the play behaviours of pupils to fit with a plan or to meet an assessment target or to include a class topic or subject theme. So what has been instilled in our teachers over the years is the belief that "*If I am a teacher, I need to be teaching you!*"

Relationships are just like a waltz or a tango - we tend to follow set steps and set rhythms that we have learned. Falling in with the steps of the other person makes the dance work. When one of us quick-steps while the other one jives it sometimes feels like we can't relate to each other. Or if I'm the 'lead', I may feel that I have to force my steps on my dance partner. After all I am paid to 'lead' in my role in school, aren't I? My teacher-itus, an entrenched condition as we already heard, is always there ready to erupt. Like many of you, not only have I been trained to teach and to 'look after' children, I feel like I am doing the job I was made for! I never questioned my vocation. I wonder if you ask yourself - "*Why did I choose this work?*" or "*How come I ended up doing this?*" And now maybe you are wondering, "*Would it be a good idea to understand better what led me to where I am now?*"

BORN TO TEACH?

As adults, we may choose to work in schools because of our own positive experiences of teachers when we were at school, or perhaps in order to try and make up for or 'negate' our own negative experiences of education (Kohl 2009, p.139). The dual desires; to continue the great tradition we see of good educators, and to break the cycle of uninspiring or unkind adults we might have come across in schools are not the only sides of a coin that Kohl has found in his work with staff:

Some people choose teaching because they enjoy being with young children and watching them grow. Others need to be around young people and let their students grow for them.   *ibid*

Kohl wants us to be more aware of our motivation, because once you know why you do something, the doing of it will start to be different. Maybe 'teaching can be a way of sharing power, of convincing people to value what you value, or to explore the world with you or through you' (*ibid*). But very often, it is a way to make a better experience for the next generation. Kohl sums up the positive desires we have when we devote ourselves to teaching (pp.139-40). We hope to:

➡ Protect
➡ Nurture
➡ Serve

We also want to share our passion for learning or for Chemistry or Art so that children can also experience the wonder of our world and the amazing nature of our human potential. There are so many great reasons for wanting to teach and for wanting to work with young people. There are other reasons we may not be so aware of that can be less helpful.

For example, we all have attachment needs: they are really just plain human needs, needs I also see in my pets or watch being demonstrated on David Attenborough wildlife programmes. I need to love and to be loved, I need to feel needed and I also know I enjoy feeling powerful and in control (hopefully not too, too much of the time). My friends often quip when I tend to 'take over' - "*You can tell she's a teacher!*" I like 'knowing best' and 'helping' others because I can. Now I'm just imagining how some of these other reasons I or you chose to work in schools might come across in a job interview for an NQT:

Headteacher	*Why do you want to work with year six?*
NQT	*Because I am passionate about learning and I think I have good organisational skills and am a good communicator*

or

Headteacher	*Why do you want to work with year six?*
NQT	*Because I love having a group of ten-year-olds hanging off my every word and I think I can sort out their problems for them and make them all better.*

Some of our 'reasons' for working with children are not things we are often aware of! But they do influence our relationships and they will influence our attitudes to play. Some 'reasons' (the thing inside that 'makes' us do things) for choosing a career in schools can feel more acceptable than others. But does that mean that altruistic or selfless motivation makes a better teacher than the drive to fulfil my own need? I don't know the answer to that. There are many papers on what makes a good educator, but if I don't know myself why I want to be a good educator, I guess can't share those reasons with anyone.

What I have come to believe though is that once I can reflect on the ways I relate to other people, I can sometimes tweak the things I then see don't work for me or for them. When I start to notice the things I always do, the ways I feel about some people and the reactions I have to certain behaviours, and sorts of play, I can (sometimes) relax more because I know it is more about me and what's inside me, than it is about what is going on around me.

THE IMPACT OF PLAY ON THE ADULT

So similarly, our own experiences of and beliefs about play will also unconsciously inform our responses and reactions to it. If as children our own play was encouraged, we may grow up to be playful adults and may feel we can readily respond playfully to pupils. However, if as children our play was discouraged or limited (for many different reasons), our repertoire of playful responses may not be as wide or as easy to access. Remember the responses to play at the start of this chapter? They will be influenced by immediate factors; what sort of a day we are having, what time we went to bed last night, the fact our boss just told us she's put an extra meeting in after school, and so on. But at a more fundamental level our feelings, beliefs and thoughts about play are also influenced by our earlier experiences; liking play, worries about play and friendships, getting in trouble when play was boisterous, and so on.

How we see ourselves in our children and the children we work with influences not only our behaviours but also the language we use. 'Childish' and 'childlike' behaviours could be the same actions described by two different observers. 'Naughtiness' and 'mischief' could be indulgent or affectionate descriptions of actions, or they might be our frustrated explanations for unwanted behaviours. Remembering being the class clown, the 'Dolly daydreamer' or the creator of mayhem on the back row will influence each of us in terms of our behaviour management in class. In Chapter 8 we challenged ourselves to think again about some things like daydreaming and 'clandestine' behaviours, to maybe recognise them as play. Not recognising jokes, divergence from the task at hand and winks and nudges as play may mean we react according to our own perception of what was just going on. Now we have more information and we have more choices about responses we make.

"His work is generally very good, but I shall be glad when he outgrows a tendency to childish mischief." 1939, school report for a ten-year-old boy

Age and gender are other factors that influence our feelings and responses to children and to play. Can a ten-year-old boy be childish? Is it childish to be a child? Is 'mischief' a 'boy thing'? Some of us will feel comfortable having a child in class who spends lots of time staring out of the window or quietly doodling in every available space on their paper. Sometimes we may take it as a personal reflection on our ability to engage and to motivate pupils in lessons. Some of us will relish the banter of pupils who playfully engage in the lesson, while at other times we will see this behaviour as a challenge to our authority and a potential threat to the compliance of the class as a whole. What is expected by adults from children is bound to be inconsistent across the range of staff working in any given school. Children, just like the young of animals, learn how to be, or how and when to play, in the presence of the different adults involved in their day-to-day care.

If we have not directly observed it, most of us probably believe that a child's play may well change when an adult is around. Sometimes the play is censored:

> *"It's not good to have adults around when you're playing because they stop you doing secret stuff ... it spoils the game."*
>
> Five-year-old boy in IPA Scotland 2011, p.5

Are children's beliefs about adult's reactions to their play based on experience? Young animals at play are also sensitive to adult proximity, often based on which adult in the group is nearby; and also the mood in that moment of whichever adult it is. Children are probably using the same judgements.

Play will sometimes have an impact on us, and sometimes it won't. That can depend on how we feel that day but also on how we have experienced the world. Most of us have developed some of our own thoughts or feelings about age appropriate behaviour, gender biases in behaviours and the times and the places we think suit some kinds of play. Where and when play happens, and who is playing what, makes it feel acceptable or not to each of us according to our individual ideas about childhood and play. We may intervene differently with boys or with girls; or encourage or discourage some sorts of play differently if we are with eight-year-olds or with 13-year-olds. Do you admire physical play when boys take part but worry when it is girls? Or do you think it is OK for five-year-olds to 'cheat' at card or boardgames, but not when they are 15 or viceversa?

Our personal beliefs influence our tolerance towards play and the players and that is not a consistent template that fits everywhere in our lives either. Do you have different expectations and responses to your own child's play compared to the play of children in your professional charge? Are you more or less understanding of your child than of the child of someone else? How could you not be different to those very different groups? And if they impact differently on you then most likely you will impact differently on them, so let's take a look at that next.

THE IMPACT OF THE ADULT ON PLAY

"I love playing with my Granny and dressing up in all her clothes; we make the stairs our catwalk."

Nine-year-old girl in IPA Scotland, 2011, p.5

Adults make great playmates - sometimes. I bet we can all picture Granny and granddaughter in all of their finery enveloped in the magic of being someone else. When we join a child at play we can have a variety of responses or reactions to the play. One of us may struggle to enter the alternative universe and 'helpfully' offer, *"Well that wouldn't really happen, would it?"* Another may all too readily enter into the spirit of the game and wonder why after five minutes the child drifts away. When I 'take over' (*see above!*) the story so that I get to be the hero and the child is relegated to the powerless role of victim, or at best my side-kick, it can make the game no longer worth playing for the child who started it.

> *"If you do anything cool - OK sometimes stuff you shouldn't be because you MIGHT hurt yourself, but it is still cool - they shout at you."*
>
> 10-year-old boy in IPA Scotland 2011, p.5

Whether we worry a child might physically hurt himself or emotionally hurt someone else we often have our own clear agenda for the play of the child. Children's play can feel disturbing, uncomfortable, challenging and incomprehensible. Our answer to all or any of the above is often to distract, deflect or disrupt such play; if not to just outright prohibit it. Observing children grappling with big ideas, struggling with how to be part of things and fighting their metaphorical demons through play can feel challenging to the role of us adults. We grown-ups are carers, protectors, teachers and rescuers of children in 'real' life; and relinquishing these roles in their play takes considerable belief in the value of play and the resilience of children.

Maybe we can follow the theory more readily with children in class than with children at home? Or maybe you feel more able to be 'permissive' of play at home than you do in school? It would be surprising if we are the same players in both of these places - because most of us are not the same person in our family as we are in our work - just like we accept that a child behaves differently at school than at home. When I organise a party at work I might use the same games we play in parties at home. But it would be likely I won't feel the same as I play them. So I will impact differently on those two separate occasions. I know I am more likely to think "*Oh well ...*" at home, when a game 'careers out of control, or ends up at completely the wrong destination' (a situation we thought in the last chapter that, as school staff, we probably avoid). Whereas at school, I may ensure the rules are stuck to and we reach the end of the game just as I anticipated we would.

Once we start thinking about our responses to play and to maybe question some of the beliefs that inform our reactions, we can change the way that we are and how we impact on play. Knowing when to step in and when to stand back is a skill we can develop. Luckily for us the third option of 'stand by' is always available!

... when the child has not asked for a play-worker to intervene, but is clearly unhappy, distressed or isolated. An intervention here requires great sensitivity. Children, even when feeling bad, do not always want a cuddle or to be asked what is wrong with them, or *"Is there anything I can do?"* An insensitive intervention in this context is often more about what the playworker needs than it is about what the child needs. It is quite common for children to come to the play space to be miserable in peace ...

Hughes 2012, p.283

How much adults should be involved in the child's play is a question that can only be considered once the questions 'What is play?', and 'Why does play matter?' have been answered. Bob Hughes (2012, p.126) poses and answers the question:

How much can or should adults legitimately intervene in children's play? My judgement would suggest a sliding scale from 'not at all' to 'as little as necessary'.

In therapeutic play sessions, Play Therapy UK describes the adult role in setting limits around play as providing 'as few limits as possible but as many as necessary'

(PTUK 2011) (*I will return to this and look at practical ways of providing clear, consistent limits in* Chapter 17). Playlink (playlink.org/), an independent company which aims 'to address the policy and practice issues that affect the planning and delivery of best possible play opportunities for children and - of massive importance - young people' (*in* Whitebread 2012, pp.45-46) recommends adults adopt a 'low intervention, high response' approach to play. One 11-year-old girl recognises both the need adults have to take on a safeguarding role, and also the need she has for personal development through play: "*You need to be protected but not that much that you can't learn anything.*" (IPA Scotland 2011, p.5).

Playing better

Once we believe that children need to play, that children can manage their play and that they learn just as much from failure and frustration in play as they do from fun and fairness, our feelings about what we see and hear will change. When our feelings change, so do our responses and reactions. When we learn to tolerate the impact play has on us, the impact we have on play will be more tolerable for the players. Bredikyte (2012) worked with trainee school staff on a project to improve adult's play involvement and children's play experiences. Her students reported that they had to learn the 'language' of play (more on this study in Chapter 14). In joint adult-child play everyone is a learner. And for those of us who want to know more about how to play we are in the right place to find out. In playgrounds and in the classrooms, we are surrounded by play experts.

At worst, we grown-ups 'adulterate' and 'contaminate' play (Else & Sturrock 1998). At best we can facilitate a feeling of acceptance in order for children to explore their feelings and fears in safety. The quality and the purpose of our involvement as adults is key; as is our sensitivity to the child's agenda. Children have ideas about how they want adults to get involved: these may not always be the same ideas as those of the adult. The main thing children seek in an adult is that we PLAY! Not direct, scaffold, divert, instruct, or dominate, but that we catch the magic and experience the joy of the moment.

> *"Adults are boring - they don't do much. When I'm out on my bike, he just walks with me - they should come out and play - be like a little kid."*
>
> Ten-year-old boy *in* IPA Scotland, 2011, p.5

The benefits adults get out of play are many, and we know playing with our children is important in lots of ways. I imagine children sometimes wonder about us adults and what play is doing for us.

> *"Adults think it is important so they can get out of work by playing with their children!"*   Six-year-old girl *ibid* p.24

Or maybe we just enjoy playing as much as they do!

KEY POINTS

Often 'least said, soonest mended' is a good axiom for adults observing play

Adult intervention in play alters the play to varying degrees

Adult-eration of play means lost opportunities for the players

Adults can have strong emotional reactions to play that may say more about their needs than the needs of the players

Children like adults who play to 'really play', not to teach or to preach

If we've forgotten how to play, children are very patient teachers

If we're not confident players that's great - just follow the lead of an expert!

The impact of play on the adult, and the impact of the adult on play: *Where do we go from here?*

If we adopt Play Wales 2013 guidance on 'The Role of Adult's in Children's Play', downloadable from www.playwales.org.uk we will do (and not do) just the things that children need from us.

The play-full school would -

☺ Provide consultancy supervision for all staff, in line with provision in other caring professions

☺ Have whole school staff training on attachment, considering both child and adult attachment theories

☺ Understand that staff personal development is as important as their professional development

If you want to know more, try reading

Gussin Paley, V., (1997) *The Girl with the Brown Crayon* Cambridge Mass: Harvard University Press

If you want to understand more, try reading

Jonelle, L., & Mathers, P., (2000) *Mommy Go Away!* NY: The Penguin Group

Medermid, V. (2012) *My Granny is a Pirate* London: Orchard Books

If you want a 15 minute training, try watching

Play Wales' short 2015 video 'CHWAREA' on youtube.com Watch children play without having to be 'in charge' and listen to their views on why play matters so much, and why we sometimes spoil it for them!

Chapter 10

The where and when of play: a time and a place for playfulness

I hope you'll now be with me in recognising that play is not an activity that can be separated from non-play activities. Playfulness is an attitude to life that bubbles up in any place, at any time. Play is the answer to uncertainty (Lotto and O'Toole 2012) - and yes, I know I've said this before, a few times, but it is so true; play fills awkward gaps, and cements social relationships.

In this chapter we will think about *where* and *when* play happens, including looking more closely at the spaces and the times that play can improve the lives of children in schools.

THE QUESTIONS TO CONSIDER ARE:

THE PLACE: WHERE DO WE PLAY?
Are there favourite play spaces for children? But when there is no, or very little space, can play happen anyway?

SPACE FOR PLAY IN SCHOOLS
What do we know about the importance of 'playtime' in the school playground? And how do moments of play throughout the school day help children to connect to others, release their feelings and prepare for the next bit of the day?

THE TIME
Does play only happen at 'playtime'? If playtime gets curtailed within the school day, what are children missing out on? Because not all homes and families are the same, do some children need more playtime in schools than others?

THE PLACE

> *"Over time, I have come to realise that a few intimate places mean more to my children, and to others, than all the glorious panorama I could ever show them."*
>
> Nabhan & Trimble 1994, p.6

That is a sentiment that resonates with me. I remember lots of holidays and visits with my family as a child, but the places that I have the most nostalgia for are the garden of my childhood house where I furnished shoebox houses with mushroom table and chairs; my grandparents' house and the smell of their warm creosoted shed on a hot sunny day, and the derelict house and grounds on the walk to school where we played hide-and-seek.

A study by Wheway & Millward (1997) asked children which places they used for 'hanging out' and for play. The places included:

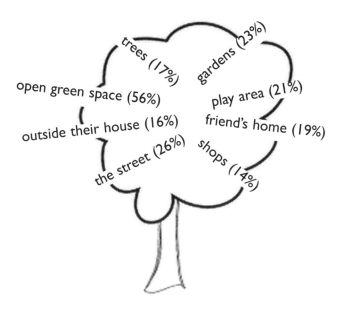

In other words, 'children play anywhere and everywhere' (Ward 1978, p.204).

For many play theorists the play space is more of a metaphorical idea than a physical place. All the places listed above could be enticing play spaces or mundane, adult-oriented practical areas. Kaplan (1995, p.173) describes going somewhere else as a 'conceptual rather than a physical transformation'. In play you may be somewhere; but you could be anywhere. As children transition between home and school on foot, we see children jumping in puddles, hiding from friends, kicking through leaves or kicking an old can along while joking with classmates. Walking to and from school you may see a pupil:

walking on walls rather than pavements not stepping on the cracks between the paving stones balancing along the kerbstones   Lester 2012, p.4

Watching pairs or groups of children on the streets before or after school you see them pushing, chasing, teasing, racing and jostling each other. 'Grab the school bag' is often a favourite game among teenagers, or 'piggy in the middle' with someone's blazer. Mini-superheroes emerge from the primary school gates, with jumper over the head, arms stretched out wide and a whoop of delight at the end of the day.

Travelling to and from school in the car or on the bus also provides opportunities for play:

> *"I play 'Wink wink murder' in the car on the way to school with my brother.*
> [But how do you play Wink wink murder with one person?]
> *If we see people walking on the way to school we wink at them and see if they fall over."*   Kapasi & Gleave 2009, p.21

Once inside, more opportunities arise for illicit play; in the school corridor children 'tag, hit, joke, make funny faces at each other' (Lester 2012, p.4) as they move around the school, shaking off the last lesson and preparing for the next. In the classroom 'clandestine' (Lester 2014) play is the age-old practice of many activities that we as school staff continue, unsuccessfully, to try and eradicate. Pupils:

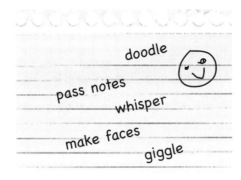

and on occasion mock and satirize adults (Sutton-Smith 1997, p.11). 'Such acts of playing are not transcendental or major events, but are marked by their very ordinariness, brief fleeting moments woven into the fabric of mundane routines' (Lester 2012, p.4).

There are moments when playing erupts simply to enliven the practicalities of everyday life and produce a different form of 'utopian hope' which says that things can be different, that life can be momentarily better and can simply go on, producing greater satisfaction in being alive and maintaining a sense of optimism about the near-future.

Sutton-Smith 2003, *in* Lester 2012, p.4

SPACES FOR PLAY IN SCHOOLS

School is a space for play. Wherever children congregate they will play, often despite our best efforts to stop them! (I think the term I often use is 'channel that energy into something more worthwhile'. The play experts like Jak Panksepp, Marc Bekoff and Isabel Behncke would certainly take issue with me, as actually there is *nothing* more worthwhile, but maybe sometimes there is a more *appropriate* activity!). The way to school and the journey home from school both provide important social 'being together' time. During the hours of the school day so too do our playgrounds, classrooms and everywhere in-between.

Children slip playing into these grey areas, the in-between spaces that are left after we have cut out the clean circles of defined time and space, the areas that are dedicated to precise purposes of the society around them.

Wilson 2012, p.32

Wilson (*ibid* p.31) feels that these 'undefined moments of activity, these unquantifiable hours', are a time that playful people unknowingly make the most of.   Children might look as if they are playing around in their moments of 'down-time' (which hopefully they are) but their brain is probably working away, reflecting, assimilating, accommodating, adjusting, rejecting, accepting and collecting new thoughts; matching them to existing knowledge and then getting to 'manipulate them into patterns that make sense' (like completing a rubic cube or jigsaw to reveal order or a clearer picture).

Remember the days of the old schoolyard?

The school playground has a different quality to the classrooms and corridors inside the building. It is a designated play space, and as such can free children to play; or take away their very reason for playing - an act of defiance to authority, "*I'm not going to play because I can choose what I do*". Some children (people) make the most of opportunities for not doing what seems expected of them! Blatchford (1998) recognises that while school playtime is one of the few occasions when children can socialise and create their own activities, without overbearing control from adults (ouch!), it is also a provision that is under threat in terms of decreasing amounts of time given over to being on the playground and in terms of increasing adult direction and prohibitions. School playtimes are important because, as we learned, or reminded ourselves in Chapter 2, it 'feeds' us, revives us and gives our brains a chance to organise and integrate learning. In other words, file the learning from before playtime, top up our self-care and prepare for learning after the break.

> Studies of more than 10,000 children found that children with recess had higher behaviour scores in classrooms than those with little or no recess.
>
> Frost 2010, p.257

Different groups have differing views about the value of school playtime (Gleave & Cole-Hamilton 2012, p.20):

> Most *children* regard playtimes positively and see them as 'freedom'. Some *adults* regard playtimes as 'a waste of time that could be spent on academic forms of learning'.   *ibid*

Research suggests that 'playful,' unstructured breaks from learning can improve cognitive performance (Pellegrini 2008). So in fact the child's 'freedom' helps their academic learning! The *Benefits of School Playtime* fact sheet provided by The Children's Play Information Service (Newstead 2010) explores the reasons why playtime is decreasing in schools, as well as explaining how this impacts detrimentally on children. The reasons playtime is under threat include;

- Increased pressure for curriculum time
- The perceived deterioration of pupil behaviour during unstructured time
- Concerns over health and safety

The lost opportunities identified when playtime is decreased include:

- Less time spent on physical exercise
- A reduction in opportunities for stress-busting activity
- Decreased opportunities for experiences of success
- Less time for developing a peer culture and peer relationships
- Missed opportunities for inclusion
- A reduction in learning opportunities
- No chance to revive the brain in readiness for concentrating in class

While playtime as part of school play provision helps:

> children's adjustment to school
> classroom behaviour
> approaches to learning
> attention to other tasks
> recovery from 'mental fatigue   Lester, Jones & Russell 2011, p.18

I think current policy makers recognise that any reduction in outdoor play in schools will impact on childhood obesity levels, but I'm not sure there is the same recognition that on a wet 'indoor play' day, the same reduction in playtime impacts on the child in other and equally significant ways. We know that true play is the way children learn to manage risk and to develop skills to keep themselves safe. It provides the space for making friendships and for re-energising brains. Playing matters, because it facilitates pro-social behaviour and creates children who know what to do when freedom presents itself. Sometimes in the UK, rather than noticing how playtimes benefit learning and behaviours we seem to notice how breaks on the playground disrupt classroom time. Our sense about the 'problems with playtimes' is that it causes:

➡ Lost time in class when pupils return slowly or bring unresolved
    issues back into class
➡ Lost concentration as children come back 'carried away' with
    the excitement of play

The 'perceived deterioration of pupil behaviour during unstructured time' (Newstead 2010), an often stated reason for *not* providing school playtimes, and the attendant results when children are deprived of the opportunities it affords, are circular arguments.

Breaktime and the free time in the lunch 'hour' are decreasing in the UK. In Finland, schools have lesson times of 45 minutes with a 15 minute break between each lesson, when children are sometimes expected, other times encouraged, to go outside and play in the playground. If the many research surveys collected by Lester et al (2011) are right, then Finnish children may be happier and more able to learn than children in UK schools. A United Nations report conducted by Pearson in 2012 (Huffington Post 2012) cited Finland as the second happiest country in the world; while the UNICEF 2013 report on child wellbeing ranked Finland fourth for overall wellbeing and for education. The 2012 Pearson report concluded Finland was at the top of the world ranking for education. I wonder how much of this can be attributed to Finland's beliefs about play.

Corridors, canteens and classrooms

While children have to 'walk and not run', and there is 'no fighting' allowed, transitions between lessons and the walk to the canteen and back are brief moments of down-time: relaxing for many but anxiety provoking for others. School corridors are teeming with children changing places. For some, transitions are inherently stressful experiences. Change brings anticipation and some measure of uncertainty.

Our brains and bodies are programmed to act in ways that increase our chances of survival and then increase our feelings of comfort. Sensory information from the environment and our interface with the world, our skin, eyes and ears, warn us of potential dangers or distress. Even our stomachs are on the 'look out' - the human gut actually has a 'brain' of its own - with neurons just like the brain that can alert us to danger. Transitions can bring release from one situation or herald entry into another. Transitions mean chemicals start circulating to help us to survive change or to adapt to change.

Sounds extreme? Well, moving from one class to another is not like changing schools. But for some pupils, some moves around school can be difficult. There are several areas of the brain involved in navigating uncertainty; and various chemicals (neurotransmitters):

Dopamine	plays a role in the reward system, how to feel pleasure and avoid pain
Acetylcholine	plays a role in attention and arousal and prepares muscles for action
Norepinephrine	increases anxiety

Our bodies and brains are telling us to act. How our actions are interpreted by others can be very different. How our chemically-induced behaviours are responded to helps us to regain equilibrium or causes our stress levels to soar. 'Banter' between pupils or remarks made to adults by children can be perceived as:

Cheeky	or	insolent
Inappropriate	or	'normal', every day interactions
Disrespectful	or	socially clumsy and inept
Funny	or	hurtful

School corridors and classrooms full of pupils at the start or finish of lessons can be 'flash points' for arguments and fights. But they are also the moments for touching base with old friends, making exploratory advances to potential new friends and brief opportunities for physical and social play. The underlying feeling could be:

Anxiety ☹ Uncertainty 😐 Fear ☹ Excitement ☺

The motivation could be (and here, let's practice our new-found skill of seeing the need behind the behaviours, shall we?):

> *I am feeling scared but I want to appear confident or like I'm not*
> *bothered* (yes, just like our lovely Lauren in Chapter 7!)

> *I want to connect to you, this is the only way I know how*
> (our need to 'belong', *see* Chapter 17 p.356, on *connect* as one of the
> 'Crucial C's', and, also discussed in Chapter 7 in terms of adolescents)

> *I feel invisible, I really want attention to confirm I am important - I'm*
> *here - notice me* (meet my need to '*count*'; another of the 'Crucial C's')

Remember the Finnish school day? 15 minutes to connect between every lesson? In our immediate change-over between lessons or teachers, the throwing of a pencil case, or the throwing of a comment may be the only way to connect with someone on the other side of the room. I believe we can connect in less time than our Finnish schools 15 minutes: usually we can shake-off one state in quite a brief space of time, and get ourselves ready for the next (however this does *not* mean I wouldn't love to have the full 15 minutes between every lesson here in the UK, just that I believe we can make the most of what we already have if we want to).

> *I recently took part in an activity on a training course and we partnered*
> *up and listened to each other with our very best listening skills for three*
> *minutes. I truly felt after just two minutes my need to have someone*
> *'just listen' had been satisfied. Any need or hunger to feel connected,*
> *valued and really heard had been met. Just two minutes changed my*

emotional state. I guess medical technology would have proved my physiological state had changed too.

It is not the length of the time we have, it is the quality of the experience. Exchanging a joke or a hug can be enough to make me feel calmer and more included.

THE TIME

Lester believes that even 'playful moments, woven into the fabric of everyday life' (2011, p.9) in brief times and small spaces are important for emotional wellbeing. Every moment spent in play is a moment well spent. Even fleeting, snatched opportunities for playfulness feed our need for expression and for 'soul food'. Research in animals has shown that early in life some species only need short bursts of social play if they are to become socially competent and integrated adults. In the case of dogs, Bekoff & Allen (2002) observed that four 20 minute play sessions a week were sufficient for puppies to gain social skills and be able to interact with other dogs later in life. Looking at adult animal play, and presumably being as true for the play of adolescents, Antonacci, Norscia & Palagi (2010, p.2) found that:

> … what is really important in adult-adult play is animals' ability to opportunistically use play in the most appropriate way. Consequently, play effectiveness does not lie on quantity (how much adults play) but on quality, that is how (social context), with whom (play-mate choice), and when (timing) adults play.

In humans, brain research demonstrates that just half an hour of play makes a significant difference (Panksepp 2007) in the 'healthy development of pro-social minds'. The activity of a large number of brain genes are 'significantly modified' by play within an hour of a thirty minute play session. These 'dynamic brain changes evoked by play facilitate brain growth and maturation' (*ibid*).

The proof is in the pudding

I feel quite ambivalent presenting 'evidence' for lots of play time: to my mind it should need no justification. But I found it helped me to feel confident and secure to advocate for play in school when I could tell anyone who was less sure of the 'worthwhileness' of time spent playing, that research had shown that play was doing amazing things and educational things for the players. However I have had times when giving time over to play and playfulness has created anxiety in colleagues who imagine (maybe rightly, but possibly not?) that they are under pressure from management, LEAs, Government, parents, all or any of the above, to concentrate on academic learning. At times I think we have good reason to feel those in authority want 'more work and less play'.

In England in 2013, Michael Gove, the then Education Secretary, put forward a plan for longer days in schools and less holiday time. The changes did not happen, but we have not yet matched other education systems. I think that it could be a great opportunity to use school buildings for offering more support for families and more fun for children if we can find ways to make children feel any additional provision is for 'time to choose' rather than time to be 'done to' (taught, organised, have horizons broadened or citizenship developed - not that those things won't happen, but only for a child if and when she chooses that).

Those of us who work in schools know that there can be a tension between school day provision, and before- and after-school provision: sharing space and resources with little time for turn-arounds is a complicated feat, and those of us who go to school might also struggle with the *now it's structure/now it's freedom* ways of being in the one space. Time away from school can be a great thing (Finland seems to illustrate that) but time away from school needs to be time well spent. Lots of that 'spending well' should be play with time also for being taken places where learning happens, because we are born to notice, reflect on and file away new experiences: and, as said above, slot them into patterns where they fit or expand what we already know, strengthening existing connections in our brains and building new ones.

For those whose environment does not support spending time well, getting to play or getting to go places, time out of the classroom, particularly over extended periods, is not so good. The book *Outliers* by Malcom Gladwell (2008) looks at why some 'succeed' in life while others don't, and one of his findings is that while American schools are serving their pupils well, the summer vacation is not. For the least wealthy and privileged in his native US, Gladwell found that:

> Virtually all of the advantage that wealthy students have over poor students
> is the result of differences in the way privileged kids learn while they are
> *not* in school.   *ibid* p.258

So while I advocate for leisure time, at best away from school, I hope for other provisions to be put in place to offer time well spent for all, not just for some, as currently appears to be the case.

Serious fun

> The entire realm of small, banal, low-key, daft, happenstance things,
> moments, events, practices, experiences, emotions, complexities, quirks,
> details and who-knows-what-else in and of everyday lives ... ought to be
> taken far more seriously.   Horton & Kraftl 2005, p.133

Play spaces and the time to enjoy them are crucial in schools. So are playful adults. How spaces and time are managed and how playful interactions are sustained without learning being diminished is down to the knowledge, understanding, training and commitment of staff. Children's 'playful disturbances' (Lester 2010) happen for a reason. The behaviour, wriggling, giggling, fiddling and quibbling, may distract others but be helpful to the child. It is this balance of needs in the classroom that is a constant challenge for school staff.

and so ...

In other words, can we integrate 'playful disturbances' into the school day without detracting from the learning of the group? Having an opportunity to think differently about what happens, why it happens and what benefits the 'disturbance' (quip, random action, 'off task' comments and so on) may have, can help our tolerance of momentary disruptions. There are also some techniques that we can include in our professional toolbox that may help. We'll come to those in the next section. There are ideas for both how to be during sustained and timetabled play experiences, and for responding to the daft, quirky and happenstance things of everyday life in Chapters 14-17.

> We need to mind the gaps, the twilight zones, and the time between dreaming and waking; ... What we need to do is to find the circumstances in which real, everyday playability thrives for children ... and then treasure and nurture them until they grow to be big, strong, and playful.   Wilson 2012, p.35

KEY POINTS

Play happens everywhere and always

Play can be momentary and fleeting

It is vital there are also opportunities for extended play

A mix of indoor and outdoor play opportunities provide for the maximum diversity in play

Time spent at play has benefits for other school activities

Where and when moments: *Where do we go from here?*

In order for changes in practice to take place, the Play, Schools and Integrated Children's Settings Group believes that the following developments need to take place in government policy. It recommends:

➡ Government issues more detailed guidance on developing outdoor, inclusive, play-friendly environments in schools and integrated children's settings. It would be beneficial for this to be a statutory requirement for all new-build and refurbishment projects, for example through *Building Schools for the Future*.

➡ Primary and secondary school grounds, Children's Centres and Early Years settings should be judged and developed against the play environment criteria set out in *Best Play: What play provision should do for children*.

➥ Government amends the Early Years Foundation Stage to require all Early Years settings to provide children with good access to high-quality outdoor play space adjoining the premises.

(*from* Play England, 2008, *Play in schools and integrated settings: A position statement* London: NCB)

· ·

The play-full school would -

☺ Ensure staff have opportunities to attend CPD on play whatever their area of responsibility

☺ Have annual whole school training in the evolving understanding of the role of play in development

· ·

If you want to know more, try reading

Blatchford, P. (1998) The State of Play in Schools. *Child Psychology and Psychiatry Review* Vol. 3:2 pp.58-67

Brown, S. (2009) *Play: how it shapes the brain, opens the imagination and invigorates the soul* New York: Avery

Horton, J. & Kraftl, P. (2005) For More than Usefulness: Six overlapping points about Children's Geographies. *Children's Geographies* Vol. 3:3 pp.131-143

Kaplan, S. (1995) 'The Restorative Benefits of Nature: Toward an integrative framework', *Journal of Environmental Psychology* Vol.15 pp.169-182.

Nabhan, G. & Trimble, S. (1994) *The Geography of Childhood*. Boston: Beacon Press

Newstead, S. (2010) *The Benefits of School Playtime*. Fact sheet 15 provided by The Children's Play Information Service. London: NCB

Pellegrini, A (2008) The Recess Debate: A disjunction between educational policy and scientific research. *American Journal of Play* Vol. 1:2 pp.181–191

Wheway, R. & Millward, A. (1997) *Facilitating Play on Housing Estates*. York: Joseph Rowntree Foundation

Wilson, P. (2012) Beyond the Gaudy Fence. *International Journal of Play*. Vol. 1:1 pp.30-36

If you want to understand more, try reading

Murphy, J. (2007) *On the Way Home* London: Macmillan Children's Books

If you want a 15 minute group or individual training, try watching

Mark Bekoff's 2011 talk on for Play Wales available from their website, playwales.org.uk/eng/ipa2011video

Chapter 11

The art and the science of play

> Artists are taught to be walking singularities, scientists are focussed on repeatability.   Andrew Zaretsky *in* Hussain 2000, pp.7-8

The individualistic nature of art and the uniform predictability of science are generalisations, but also, in the context of how play fits in both areas, they may be helpful. Play is the way we explore, learn about and come to terms with the *external* world. Play is also the way we explore, learn about and come to terms with our *internal* world. We learn about the physical world through play. Exploratory play is the way young children and babies find out where they end, where the world to be explored begins and what the physical certainties 'out there' are. From birth our brains are designed to 'work it out'. We are born scientists.

We also learn about the emotional and social world through play. Imaginative play is the way children and young people find out how they are different, and how to express that individuality. From early in life we are driven to 'tell our story'. We are born artists.

Let's take a closer look at the way we learn through play what no-one can teach us in the areas of Art & Science.

In this chapter we will think about how play develops the artist in us and how play is our scientific exploration of the world.

THE QUESTIONS TO CONSIDER ARE:

PLAY - THE SCIENCE OF FINDING OUT

How can playful science be included in the curriculum?

PLAY: THE SCIENCE OF PLATES

How do playful scientists translate 'playful disturbances' (remember in Chapter 10 those moments or happenings that seem to be not 'on task'?) or 'idle' daydreams (we reflected how important they can actually be for discovery and for problem-solving in Chapter 8) into new understandings of the physical world?

PLAY - THE ART OF EXPRESSING YOURSELF

How are Arts taught in our schools? Could we give more 'wiggle room' for self-determined creativity in the school curriculum?

READING AND WRITING

In this section we will think about literacy in particular and the link with play. And I will introduce you to one of my very favourite teachers who listens and learns from her pupils, who explains that writing and drawing mean so much more when they are chosen by the children. Hopefully this will help us to find new answers to the question - 'How can literacy be developed through play?'

PLAY - THE SCIENCE OF FINDING OUT

What if …? is *the* question of science and of play.   Lotto & O'Toole 2012

From our most iconic historical figures in the world of science, to the most current and innovative scientists of today, play is often part of the vocabulary of their scientific work. Einstein believed that 'play is the highest form of research' and Newton believed that 'to myself I am only a child playing on the beach, while vast oceans of truth lie undiscovered before me'. Our folklore on the breakthroughs of our great scientists illustrate Hughes' (2012, p.112) description of the *'Aha!'* reaction of play discoveries. The 'Eureka' moments of finding out 'by accident' about the displacement of water in a bath (Archimedes), the pull of gravity on a falling apple (Newton) or the theory of relativity born of the 'playful musing of a sixteen year old' (Norton 2012, p.123) who imagined himself chasing a beam of light (Einstein), all of these are examples of 'giant leaps for mankind' developed from the 'happenstance' of play.

Coming seventh out of 30 in a class of Grammar School pupils in 1939, a twelve year old pupil's school report stated:

> Physics: *Not good enough - he is somewhat inattentive and playful during laboratory periods.*

Another teacher, this time a teacher of chemistry in the 1960s, felt differently about the link between play and science learning in the lab. Kary Mullis (1998, p.27), a Nobel Prize winning chemist, describes how in his senior school, 'our teacher would leave the lab open so [my friend] and I could play in there'. By play, Mullis presumably meant that he and his friend experimented with ideas and tried out their ideas on resources through trial and error. For Mullis, science equals play, and for him 'a lab is just another place to play' (p.26).

To boldly go where no man has gone before!

Play is innovative, original and new, just like science. 'Science is cool and fun because you get to do stuff that no-one has ever done before' (Blackawton & Lotto 2011, p.172). Science is cool when you 'get to do', not 'have to do'. Making science playful makes it exciting and enjoyable. We have seen that one of the important elements of play is that it is owned by the player. Unless the child has ownership of an activity it cannot be play. Feeling that a problem is yours to solve as you will certainly encourages divergent thinking and creativity; and it will often increase motivation. Maths can appear to be a subject that needs strict adherence to someone else's rules and directions. But children don't see it that way:

> *"You need to look for different ways to do it. There is more than one way*
> *to do maths. You get to experiment and do it your own way."*
>   Middle Years (9-12) maths student *in* Caswell 2005, p.222

In fact maths can be child's play, when 'you muck around with things and discover something about maths (*ibid*). Kamii (2000) believes that children use materials as they explore and 'reinvent arithmetic'. They find out something for the very first time. To the playing child the discovery of number, shape, size and fit is brand new knowledge.

Much of Caswell's (2005) work for her research into 'the value of play to enhance mathematical learning in the middle years of schooling' used game playing. Lotto (Blackawton & Lotto 2011, p.168) reflects on the nature of play and games:

> The process of science is little different from the deeply resonant, natural
> processes of play ... When one adds rules to play, a game is created. This
> is science: the process of playing with rules that enables one to reveal
> previously unseen patterns of relationships.

Hughes (2012) recognises that an individual's life journey is a scientific experiment, with each unique person starting at the beginning of an investigation:

It is as if they are embarking on a research programme, where they are collecting and analysing data, and constructing and testing their own theories of what life is all about.   p.79

PLAY: THE SCIENCE OF PLATES
(not tectonic, just dinner!)

Like Sir Issac Newton, we are all 'on the seashore' exploring with wonder the world around and within us. Richard Feynman writes compellingly of the link between science and play:

> Physics disgusts me a little bit now, but I used to *enjoy* doing physics. Why did I enjoy it? I used to *play* with it. I used to do whatever I felt like doing - it didn't have to do with whether it was important for the development of nuclear physics, but whether it was interesting and amusing for me to play with.   1985, p.157

Feynman no longer felt like pursuing his illustrious career when it was no longer fun and no longer play. The creator of the theory of quantum electrodynamics attributed his Nobel prize to rediscovering his joy and his drive through 'piddling around with [a] wobbling plate' (p.158). Having lost his electrodynamics mojo, Feynman became fascinated by how and why a plate was rotating when a student in the college refectory threw it up in the air. His desire to make sense of something that interested him led onto his discovery of a new physical law. That, in turn, led to Feynman's international recognition; and to our increased knowledge and understanding of the laws which govern the natural world.

> I'm going to *play* with physics, whenever I want to, without worrying about
> any importance whatsoever.   *ibid* p.157

Less than a week after renewing his commitment to *play*, Feynman was *working* on the greatest discovery of his career.

The science paper '*Blackawton Bees*' (Blackawton & Lotto, 2011) demonstrates the relationship between art and science and how they depend on each other if each is to make any kind of sense in our lives. Discoveries need to be shared. The young eight to ten year olds involved in the Blackawton research needed to engage with both the science of finding out and the art of expressing their discovery.

> *They* asked the questions, hypothesised the answers, designed the games
> (in other words, the experiments) to test these hypotheses and analysed the
> data. They also drew the figures (in coloured pencil) and wrote the paper.
>   *ibid p.168*

PLAY - the art of expressing yourself

The Arts include literature, fine art and music amongst other subject areas. Sometimes we call these subjects the 'expressive' arts. In schools, play and the Arts seem to be two different entities. Art is for the classroom in lesson time, and play is for the playground and free time. The 'irresistible force' (Kuschner 2012, p.242) of play, the need to express through art, and create new, individual artistic responses to the world, meets the *immovable object* (*ibid*) of the curriculum, the aims, objectives, and plan for the lesson. The link between play and Arts is different to that of play's relationship to Science.

Important affective processes that occur in both pretend play and creativity include producing affect themes in fantasy and memory, experiencing emotion (especially positive emotion), cognitive integration of affect, and experiencing joy in creative expression.

Russ & Wallace 2013, p.137

Affect, or emotion, is the inspiration of many artistic endeavours and also the result. An artist expresses an emotion in their music, sculpture or painting, while the audience feels an emotion in response to the sights and sounds of the piece. We all know that the artist's inspiration can be despair and our response can be sadness, but it is also true that creating things can be a joyful experience.

We instinctively provide arts materials for young children. Paints, modelling clay, musical instruments, collage materials, our nurseries, play schools and Early Years classrooms are stocked with them all. And if you are a visitor to one of these spaces you will have seen artists immersed in the creative experience. As time goes by the freedom of creativity may be replaced by a more 'painting by numbers' approach. Now I loved my painting by numbers packs, but I chose to do them when I wanted that particular structure and challenge.

Even at a very young age, children's experience of the Arts in school is often constrained by our need to be seen to be outcome-focussed. The area of Art we have most prescribed, assessed, designed, standardised and picked over is Literacy. For very good reasons, being literate underpins much of the other aspects of schooling, and is the most helpful skill we take away from our school days to serve us through life. So, is there room for a more playful approach to literacy in schools? Let's see what playful educators have to say on the matter:

READING

How are readers also players, or how are readers playing?

Morgenstern 2010, p.392

As an adult I think of reading as one of the ways that I play. Morgenstern (2010, p.394) agrees that an adult reading a novel is an adult at play who, through reading, is 'vicariously participating in a form of play' and indeed agrees with Mark Twain's (1992) definition (*remember* Chapter 1?) saying that 'in the most general sense, reading a novel is play in that it is not work' (*ibid*). Morgenstern argues that for children the children's novel 'replaces' their nonsense play. He sees that children's imagination can both reside in the novel and be opened up by the novel. Adult Fantasy novels, with created alternative worlds, altered realities and impossible possibilities, are hugely popular with people of many ages. Escapism? Maybe, or perhaps a return to the childhood pleasures of play.

So reading can be play. Do we think of reading as play in our schools? And do we allow for lots of play to develop reading skills in our younger classrooms and time for reading for pleasure in our older age groups? 'A good approach to teaching reading is through play' (Ali et al 2011, p.17). Much of our teaching of teachers still includes the idea that we should be 'teaching *through* play'. I love that we want play as part of our education, but maybe we should teach *alongside* it? Our current use of the word 'play' reminds me of having medicine in a spoonful of jam as a child, sneaking the thing I had to have for my own good, into something I thought was a treat!

Ali et al designed a research project to trial some reading games with pre-readers to see if children can 'learn reading through play'. They found that just over half the teachers involved strongly agreed that teaching reading through play improved the skills of their pupils (p.18). The results also demonstrated that the children 'thoroughly' enjoyed the activities. So nothing like medicine, just an enjoyable activity, doing a job that needs doing, but given a name that confuses children and educators alike. We already heard in Chapter 1 how Liz Brooker (2011) thought our confused language does no-one any favours. She clearly recognises the effort, passion and dedication school staff put into planning activities and ensuring learning is fun, but really wishes we could simply find a new way to describe them so 'play' could just mean play.

… AND WRITING

> Good practice ensures that a child's early writing is promoted through planned purposeful play.
>
> Rose 2009, p.66

A child can plan and be purposeful in play, but educators cannot plan for purposeful play that will develop early writing. In Chapter 1 we considered the nature of play. I hope that you agree with those who advocate that play is a freely chosen activity and belongs to the player; lesson plans belong to the adult and, when they are implemented, involve shaping or instructions from 'above'. Like Brooker (*see above*) I wish we had not started to use the word play for any activity that involves beads, buckets or bricks! This is one of the big themes of this book. Play deserves a name all to itself. So too do the effective, fun, practical activities that school staff provide.

Our most respected education experts and our most highly regarded consultancy documents talk about play in a way that suggests they are non-believers in the truths of play. The outcome of 'planned purposeful play' has actually not been enthusiastic, able learners, but rather bored, frustrated avoiders of writing. My own experience of school was that I struggled with English language studies, and scraped through with a bare pass at English A level: this despite being an avid reader and a hobby writer of humorous accounts. My teachers did not see any potential in me in the area of literacy. The set tasks were either of very little interest to me, or my 'bending' of the rules and the 'illicit' inclusion of personally relevant material were not well received (in Chapter 8 we wondered if there were alternative ways to respond to children like me! Possibly a more playful response could have recognised the glimmer of a talent and encouraged a return to the task at hand. News ways of responding to pupils and ways to be a more playful adult coming soon! The third section of this book, Chapters 14-17 in particular, will be all about skills and practice issues). Luckily my need to write for the fun of it, and my enjoyment (the joy of creating as described by Russ & Wallace 2013) of writing survived. The summer I left school I had a long, irreverent article accepted for a sports magazine; and I got paid for it!

Jarvis & George (2009, p.265) found that pupils' views of writing were that:

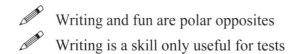 Writing and fun are polar opposites

Writing is a skill only useful for tests

On the positive side, Jones & Reynolds (2011, p.14) believe that, when conditions support playful expression, children 'invent writing' in much the same way as they learn to talk. And much the same way as Kamii (2000) sees them 'reinventing' maths! Writing starts off as fun. It begins with scribbles that say *"I want to see how this writing thing feels,"* and *"I am making my mark for all the world to see."* 'Future writers' (Jones & Reynolds 2011, p.70) are eager, choose to write, and are excited by writing (*ibid*). So although we sometimes get it wrong and leave children thinking writing is a purely practical necessity and boring to boot; other times we don't. Teaching *alongside* play, working *with* play, educating playfully can maintain the excitement.

When writing has a meaning for the child, there is an incentive to join in. When 'literacy gives power' *(ibid)* to the writer, it is its own reward. Writing for a purpose, *"I want to tell the world"* (or my best friend or my Nan), suggests the element of choice. Writing for a test, or practicing writing because it matters for tests, does not. Not everyone is as wise as Vivian Gussin Paley. One of her Kindergarten pupils wants her to understand how the imposition of writing detracts from his creative experience:

> *"Like when I don't want to do that picture-writing and you tell me 'Try it, maybe it'll be fun' but it never is. And it always spoils my picture and I can't keep thinking about my picture!"*   *in* Paley 1997, p.45

Paley responds by telling him she now understands his needs and that she will trust in the process and wait until he is ready: *"You know, until you are curious about doing it. You might even figure out a different way."* (*ibid* p.46)

In Chapter 16 there are more examples of how to respond to pupils who are trying to help us to understand their experience and how it feels to be them right at that moment. A little 'heads-up'- it won't be all about letting the child off or agreeing with everything that they say, but it will include conveying our understanding of the child, as well as what is expected of him or her.

· ·

and so ...

Alongside skills training such as handwriting, following a musical score, following a recipe and colouring inside the lines, the Arts in Education need to follow the individual. Reading and writing seem further and further from the everyday lives of our TV watching, texting, FaceTiming, SMS-ing, snap-chatting children. But the art of communicating is still going strong. In a time when anyone can self-publish, camera-taken images can be photo-shopped and music can be digitally enhanced, the worlds of art and science are merging in an Information Technology soup. But the art of individualistic, creative expression has never been more accessible and diverse. In a world, where more than ever, anything is possible, play is the way those possibilities come into being.

KEY POINTS

We are born scientists

We are born artists

Insensitive schooling can frighten the emergent scientist or artist into long-term hiding!

The Art and the Science of Play: *Where do we go from here?*
When researchers look at what goes on in our brains when we communicate with others, look at great art or make emotive music, they find out the science of our artistic endeavours and experiences. When researchers write with wit, poetry and beauty about their scientific discoveries and explorations, there is an art to the presentation of ideas.

➡   Let's all notice more when we use arts and sciences together in our everyday lives

➡   Let's notice too when children try activities they are not so often engaged with

➡   Let's try not to classify children's activities into narrow bands or subject types (I notice often how the scientist in me (and surely in all of us) cannot help sorting things into 'boxes' or 'types') but instead, let's support discovery and self expression in all areas of the curriculum.

· ·

The play-full school would -

☺   Play with Science

☺   Play with Art

☺   Allow the scientist in each of us to develop

☺   Allow the artist in each of us to develop

· ·

If you want to know more, try reading

Ali, A., Zahara Aziz, Z & Majzub, R (2011) Teaching and Learning Reading Through Play. *World Applied Sciences Journal* Vol.14 (Learning Innovation and Intervention for Diverse Learners): pp.15-20

Caswell, R. (2005) *The Value of Play to Enhance Mathematical Learning in the Middle Years of Schooling.* Conference paper presented at: Building connections: theory, research and practice: proceedings of the 28th annual conference of the Mathematics Education Research Group of Australasia. Available at: merga.net.au/documents/RP202005.pdf

Feynman, R., (1992) *Surely You're Joking Mr Feynman (Adventures of a curious character)* NY: WW Norton

Hussain, Z. (2000) Science as Art Unites Disciplines: Artists use microbiology as a medium for art *The Tech* Vol. 120: 26 pp.7-8 MIT

Kamii, C. (2000) *Young Children Reinvent Arithmetic: Implications of Piaget's theory (2nd edition)* NY: Teachers College Press

Morgenstern, J. (2010) The Children's Novel as a Gateway to Play: An Interview with John Morgenstern. *American Journal of Play.* Vol. 2:4 pp.391-400

Rose, J. (2009) *Independent Review of the Primary Curriculum: Final Report.* Nottingham: DCSF Publications

Russ, S. & Wallace, C. (2013) Pretend Play and Creative Processes *American Journal of Play*. 6:1 pp.136-48. Available at: journalofplay.org/sites/journalofplay.org/files/pdf-articles/6-1-article-pretend-play.pdf

If you want to understand more, try reading

Blackawton Primary School & Lotto, R. B., (2011) Colour and Spatial Relationships in Bees, *in Biology Letters* Vol. 7 pp.168-172

For a 15 minute training, try watching

Beau Lotto & Amy O'Toole's 2012 Ted Talk on *Science is for everyone, kids included* on the TED website, ted.com/talks, or on youtube.com

Chapter 12

Play and Personal, Social and Health Education

PSHE is an important and necessary part of all pupils' education. All
schools should teach PSHE, drawing on good practice.   DfE 2013b

The elements that schools should cover include:

drug education

financial education

sex and relationship education (SRE)

the importance of physical activity and diet for a healthy lifestyle   *ibid*

These elements sound very concrete and 'teachable'. They are content driven and
have measurable outcomes; whether through testing - how many multiple choice
questions a child gets right after following a set syllabus; or through longer term
outcomes - monitoring the numbers of unwanted pregnancies, families in debt or
adult obesity.

Without practice, through experiencing, pretending, imagining, and until we use our invitation to play (with ideas) question *'What if ...?'*, then learning remains theoretical and may not feel that it means anything, or matters or applies to us. I hope that by now it is clear that all work and no play is not an 'access all areas' way to nurture growth and development. Not only would 'Jack' be dull, (remember Kapasi & Gleave (2009, p.18) in Chapter 1: *'If children don't play it makes them yuk and boring'?*) but Jack, and Jill, will not have the flexible, unteachable, ability to respond to the novel, unexpected, unrehearsed and unforeseen threats to personal, social, physical and financial wellbeing that our PSHE curriculum is designed to support. Without the information part of the learning equation, knowledge (the facts) + play (the possibilities, the confident application of theory into practice) the player cannot manage risk or make wise decisions.

In this chapter we will think how play might be our own in-built personal development curriculum.

THE QUESTIONS TO CONSIDER ARE:

PLAY VERSUS INFORMATION
When we plan for our personal and social curriculum, do we choose to deliver through play or through work?

HEARTS AND MINDS: USE YOUR HEAD AND FOLLOW YOUR HEART
Or, can we choose to plan and deliver the powerful combination of play and work? Is it having the facts at our fingertips and the wisdom to apply them - use your head and follow your heart - that works best?

THE SOCIAL AND EMOTIONAL ASPECTS OF LEARNING (SEAL)
Can play fill in the gaps that teaching PSHE through SEAL and other such programmes can't quite reach?

SEAL has been around for a while and includes curriculum material for secondary as well as primary schools. I have chosen to look at SEAL in some depth and how it can relate to play, but the strands of SEAL, explored later in this chapter, are important areas of personal development, whether within a SEAL programme or other similar interventions like PATHS® (more on this later too), or as skills and qualities I think we may all agree are important for wellbeing and achievement.

HOW DOES PLAY SUPPORT THE DEVELOPMENT OF EACH OF THE INDIVIDUAL AREAS OF SEAL?

Self-awareness

Self-regulation (managing feelings)

Motivation

Empathy

Social skills

SO HOW ARE WE DOING WITH PSHE PROVISION IN SCHOOLS?

Looking at some results of current PSHE delivery in schools, can we improve the provision of the social-emotional curriculum in schools by giving children more time to play?

PLAY VERSUS INFORMATION?

Could play have a role in supporting formal knowledge-based PSHE? Lilith, a fifteen year-old girl may 'know' that drugs are dangerous, but may 'feel' that they are worth the risk, and 'believe' that to fit in she has to take part. She may have the knowledge but not have the skills - how to say no, for example, or the personal qualities, such as confidence and self-esteem, to back up that knowledge.

How are schools addressing the 'personal' and the 'social' aspects in PSHE as described in the Government's four targeted areas of drugs, finance, intimate relationships and physical fitness? Are there other areas of social and emotional development that schools are expected to include in their curriculum provision? How does Lilith get support, information and experiences at school that mean she develops the social skills and emotional strengths to meet the challenges life brings?

Alongside PSHE, the UK government advocates a teaching curriculum for pupils' spiritual and moral development:

> All National Curriculum subjects provide opportunities to promote pupils' spiritual, moral, social and cultural development. Explicit opportunities to promote pupils' development in these areas are provided in religious education and the non-statutory framework for personal, social and health education (PSHE) and citizenship. A significant contribution is also made by school ethos, [and] effective relationships throughout the school.
>
> DfE 2013c, *my parentheses*

The spiritual and moral development of pupils is also broken down into four areas:

- **Spiritual:** *sense of self, their unique potential, their understanding of their strengths and weaknesses, and their will to achieve.   It is about their inner lives and non-material wellbeing.*

- **Moral:** *an understanding of the difference between right and wrong, a concern for others and an ability to reflect on the consequences of their actions.*

- **Social:** *sense of belonging, active participation, an understanding of the responsibilities and rights of being members of families and communities, and an ability to relate to others and to work with others for the common good.*

●   ***Cultural:*** *an understanding of cultural traditions and an ability to appreciate and respond to a variety of aesthetic experiences, a respect for their own culture and that of others, a curiosity about differences. It is about appreciation and contribution.*   *ibid*

These elements sound far more abstract and 'unteachable' than the four targeted areas of the PSHE curriculum set out by the DfE in 2013. They are about 'how to be' rather than 'knowing what to do'. They are about feeling and believing. Measuring is qualitative rather than quantitative; not how many but how well. Dealing with life's challenges is about being resilient, the ability to adapt and adjust. It is about not just coping but doing better than coping. These life skills are hard to 'teach' and hard to measure, but very hard to live without.

I wonder if you can remember a time when you 'did the right thing'? Or an incident when you 'just knew' what had to happen? I imagine, like me, you accepted that you had an innate knowledge, or a 'hard-wired' sense of fairness, or maybe now you are thinking you must have a 'good person' gene? But if I reflect more on how I got to have the 'sense' that I have, I can remember the 'schooling' I had from my family, in giving up my seat for older people on the bus when I was a child, and the feeling I felt when I was kind to my friends when we were playing out and no adults were looking. Choices which I believe are right, that I was taught and still make: choices I make because other times I made the same choice it felt good to be me doing those things. Play has a vital role in spiritual and moral development; it is both spiritual self-discovery and expression and the time and the space where our personal moral compass is set.

HEARTS AND MINDS - use your head and follow your heart

The dual approach to PSHE, teaching knowledge and developing qualities, is an ideal that is highlighted by respondents to a DfE consultation on PSHE (2013d, pp.5-7). The responses suggest that school staff believe children need the facts and the knowledge for 'making healthy lifestyle choices'. The areas in which respondents wanted knowledge to be imparted and facts to be taught were:

- Physical fitness
- Maintaining healthy weight
- Sexual safety
- Managing money effectively
- Drug and alcohol abuse
- Career and employment education

As a young person, through years of play experiences, Tyler might have become someone who enjoys being with other people, who can make pretty canny assessments about others who are likely to be kind and reliable, or controlling and disloyal. He may be ready to develop intimate emotional relationships. But he needs the information about intimate physical relationships to inform his choices, so that he can add the 'facts' bit (on the risks of unplanned pregnancies and sexually transmitted diseases) into his decision-making process.

Looking at higher education options, Sureya might have discovered through play that she likes finding things out, creating things, experimenting, managing risk and exploring the environment. She may have thought that a straight Engineering degree was her obvious choice. Without careers advice on a wider choice of courses like Chemical Engineering, Civil Engineering or Applied Environmental Geoscience, Sureya could not consider the options available in light of the likelihood of employment or opportunities for study in the workplace.

Do the Math!

> taught knowledge (the facts)
>
> +
>
> play discovery (the aptitude)
>
> =
>
> informed decision making that is right for you

The attitudes and values the school staff (DfE 2013d, pp.5-7) wanted children to develop were acknowledged as different to, and often more important than, the facts and knowledge. The respondents felt that through PSHE opportunities children needed to develop:

Awareness ☆ Integrity ☆ Responsibility ☆ Values ☆ Relationship skills

Resilience ☆ Self-esteem ☆ Self-confidence

Independence ☆ Self-worth ☆ Personal identity ☆ Understanding of difference

Not imparted, passed down, 'teaching' of knowledge; but rather the blossoming of attitudes, aptitudes and personal qualities that are nurtured rather than taught. From birth we learn through mostly observing, playing, testing and through trial and error. We all recognise that children watch adults and cannot be fobbed off with *"Do as I say; not as I do"*. Modelling how to be; creating the space that supports exploration and enhancing play (more of that in the skills section) are the roles of the adult in the experiential learning half of the PSHE equation. 33% of respondents to the consultation said that:

> … although the knowledge of facts was important, the skills needed for emotional health and wellbeing such as mediation, listening, assertiveness, resilience and negotiation were core to PSHE education. p.5

Looking at this set of aptitudes and skills I see certain words leaping out describing how that outcome can be achieved. None of those words though, are 'teach'. The roles for the adult in providing an environment that supports the learning of these skills and aptitudes are to (maybe, not exclusively and not perfectly, but a 'good enough' fit):

Develop	awareness
Cultivate	integrity
Foster	responsibility
Embody	values
Support	relationship skills
Encourage	resilience
Nurture	self-esteem
Develop	self-confidence
Promote	independence
Enhance	self-worth
Appreciate	personal identity
Cherish	understanding of difference

I think *foster* or *nurture* would be the most appropriate words for describing the adult role in advancing all these hoped-for outcomes. I notice that the role of the adult in school in supporting the maturing child in these areas is like a 'parenting' role of nurture, and that we also have the key role of modelling, living, embodying the things we hope our pupils will become. Adults have always educated children by example: it is indeed a powerful medium for teaching and learning.

TALES FROM OZ 🐾

I notice when I watch my dogs that the mother allows her pups space and time to play, only intervening when the play stops being play and one pup starts to not take turns, or abide by the 'this is only play' rule. Her message is that she trusts her pups to manage mostly and to follow their instincts, and have good enough self-control and a strong enough desire to relate to their siblings to play without adult supervision. She also knows that she modelled playful rough-and-tumble to them herself so they had a template for 'no real biting', and for '... but if you do bite by mistake I'll still love you!'

In Chapter 16 we will take time to think about how we communicate and the messages we can give by the things that we say and the way that we say them. Then, in Chapter 17 we will learn more about how and when to step in when children play, as well as think a lot more about when and why not to. Putting these two ways of interacting together, we can create new opportunities for children to grow and to develop maturity and confidence.

Appleton (1910, p.11) sums up the intangible benefits of play in the development of personal, spiritual, moral and social qualities, when he suggests that play develops 'the growth necessary for the function of adult instincts'. Healthy, confident people operate by including 'gut instinct' into their assessments of people and situations. *"Something just tells me"; "I've just got a feeling about this"; "I'm going on a hunch"*; important, unteachable information when making choices. I guess education is all about increasing our choices in life and at the same time increasing our skills for managing the choices life presents. Believing in myself, and trusting my inner voice are important personal attributes to model in the classroom.

In a DfE consultation, 52% of respondents saw PSHE as preparation for negotiating 'the challenges that life presents':

> the most important core outcome was that pupils were able to make informed choices, recognise and manage risk, and have the knowledge and awareness to make safe decisions.   DfE 2013d

Part of the ability to manage life's challenges is to rely on your own judgement, trust your instincts. Without self-awareness and self-belief we do not notice or act on our instincts. If we cannot attune to our own thoughts and feelings we will never attune to the thoughts and feelings of others. That is unless we have become so exquisitely attuned to the feelings and needs of others it drowns out our ability to hear or to act on our own inner voice. All the way back in 1910, Appleton recognised that when we play we allow ourselves to follow our own thoughts and to not censor ourselves.

When a child plays, he or she acts on impulse. Impulsive behaviour is built into our repertoire of actions, and in the past it will have been useful to us. Yet 'impulsive' is a damning word on the end of term report, and impulsive behaviour does not fit well with structured activities and fixed outcomes. Physical impulsiveness can be seriously bad for our health, and children need to develop strategies for thinking through and weighing up. But not being attuned to our instincts can also have serious implications for our wellbeing. *"Listen to your gut instincts"* is good advice, but may fall on deaf ears when lack of play means that we miss out on opportunities to develop a mature ability to listen to our 'gut'.

There is a paradox in my appreciation of Appleton's ideas and my own belief that we adults 'school' ourselves out of our ability to listen to the inner voice that is more apparent in our childhoods. Samples (1976, p.26) tells us that Einstein saw intuition as 'a sacred gift' and that rationality should be 'a faithful servant' to our instincts. Whether we believe intuition or rationality to be our master, the need for our inner beliefs and gut feelings to work together with our knowledge and cool calculations mean we need play and formal teaching to be combined in developing our PSHE programmes.

Time now to consider the content of our PSHE curriculum through a look at the SEAL programme and other programmes that are clearly closely related.

THE SOCIAL AND EMOTIONAL ASPECTS OF LEARNING (SEAL)

The five strands of The Social and Emotional Aspects of Learning (SEAL) (DfE 2011) reflect much more roundly the potential of a PSHE curriculum than the latest Government direction on the four factual areas to be covered. It focuses on who we want our children *to become* - rather than what we need our children *to know* (*see* p.245 *the five strands*).

Other models of personal development now also being used in some schools, include:

Promoting Alternative Thinking Strategies   (PATHS®) (Channing Bete)

Five Ways to Wellbeing   (new economics foundation 2008)

The Welsh Government is committed to 'fund training in well evaluated behaviour management programmes' (Welsh Government 2011). They recommended the use of SEAL and/or PATHS® as part of their 2011-13 initiative to improve attendance and behaviour in schools. The PATHS® programme covers five 'conceptual domains':

➡ Interpersonal problem-solving skills
➡ Self-control
➡ Positive self-esteem
➡ Emotional understanding
➡ Relationships

I think that PATHS®' *emotional understanding* relates to *self-awareness* and *empathy* in SEAL, and *relationships and interpersonal problem-solving skills* may relate to SEAL's *social skills*: while SEAL's *self-regulation* may fit within PATHS®' *interpersonal problem-solving skills* and/or within *emotional understanding*. It looks as though both interventions agree on the importance of the same skills and attributes, although *motivation* is highlighted in SEAL but not directly referred to in the PATHS® strands.

The Good Childhood Report (The Children's Society 2013) looked at the new economics foundation's *Five Ways to Wellbeing* for children and young people:

➡ Connect
➡ Be active
➡ Take notice
➡ Keep learning
➡ Give

The 'five ways' do correlate in some ways to the 'five strands' of SEAL.

➡   Take notice   - *self-awareness* and *empathy*
                   (awareness of internal self and external others)
➡   Keep learning - *motivation* (possibly also *be active*)
➡   Connect   - *social skills*

The *Good Childhood Report* found that the NEF 'fifth way' - *'Give'* was not so readily applicable for children, particularly younger ones. They argue instead for 'another activity which represents a clearer fifth way to wellbeing for children'. They suggest that this missing way could be play!

> Our focus group discussions pointed towards a set of activities around
> creativity, imagination and perhaps simply play.   2013, p.43

Although there is actually nothing more motivating than play, play *is* the way we connect and relate, discover things about ourselves and develop empathy. So play is already represented in the four strands remaining if you take away *'give'*. The report suggests that in considering children and their wellbeing we *cannot* omit the value of play.

> It is in playing, and only in playing, that the individual child or adult is
> able to be creative and to use the whole personality, and it is only in being
> creative that the individual discovers the self.
>   Theodore Roosevelt, *in* Ulanov 2001, p.164

So it seems to me that there is some consensus about the elements we should be including in school PSHE content, although the *Five Ways to Wellbeing* does not include self-regulation, and PATHS® does not include *motivation*. The inclusion of *give* was questioned by the *Good Childhood* Report, and not explicitly mentioned in SEAL or PATHS®, but perhaps if you have *empathy* for others and you have good *social skills* then giving will be a natural response to the needs of others.

I hope I have convinced you that the SEAL strands seem to represent a set of attributes and skills which, as they are reflected in other programmes too, lots of us feel are important for our PSHE curriculum. I am using them as a way of looking at personal and social development through individual elements or strengths that are good for us and good for others. I will also demonstrate that each of the five strands of SEAL is a perfect fit with play.

PLAY AND THE FIVE STRANDS OF SEAL
Self-awareness

Play helps us notice things about ourselves. During play we allow ourselves to wallow in feelings, because we feel safe. We scare ourselves playfully, and see how it feels to be the sort of person who scares others (playfully!). We notice who we feel we are and tolerate others telling us playfully who they feel we are. Self-awareness includes being willing to allow thoughts and feelings to surface. To be self-aware is to notice how we feel, and to recognise thoughts as they cross our minds.

Once we have a collection of thoughts and feelings we need to create a pattern or picture that makes sense of who we are, or how we feel. Badenoch (2008) describes a self-aware person as someone who is able to:

... have a developing sense of meaning about (their) pathway through life.

(p.31)

Self-awareness is developed firstly through a sensory experience of being. *"I am hot"*, *"I feel hungry"*, *"I am tired"* are early physical pre-cursors to a sense of emotional experiencing of self within the world. Initially, of course when we are young and the story of our life is still short, the self we are aware of is a self 'in the moment'. Self-awareness in this case is about sensory experience. Without this basic understanding of *"I am me"; "I feel"; "I tune into my body to find out about me in the world"*, more mature self awareness is hard to develop later. Infant awareness relies on us as adults (accurately) tuning in *to the child* and sharing our knowledge and language to process the experience *for the child.*

How we are so good at this is one of the miracles of parenting. I don't think anyone tells us to notice the way our babies look or act and then offer them feedback loops of commentary: *"You're so tired"; "Brrr, feeling cold"; "Mmm, rusks, yummy - feeling better now"*. An adult's awareness of a child's feelings and experiences is packaged into language, verbal and body language, then offered to the baby or toddler without parents being trained to do so. But this is the finest of teaching, and is PSHE curriculum in action for pre-schoolers. This giving of words and mirroring of actions is a skill we will return to in Chapter 16 in the skills section of the book.

"I feel sad" is a much more nuanced awareness. Basic needs and their relief: hunger, and food; hot, and being cooled; tired, and sleep, are physical sensations with an antidote that once experienced is recognised as the solution that changes an uncomfortable feeling to a feeling of satisfaction or comfort. Sadness is more complex and more difficult to pin down in the body or through language: and if we had an answer to it we might all be a lot happier (sorry Brian Sutton-Smith, I know your answer would be - play!).

Self-awareness is about awareness of *how I am* but also awareness of *who I am*. The 'momentary experience', the *'I'* of physical feeling, passing emotions; and the 'enduring traits', the *'I'* that is me. The 'me' of *"Take me as I am"*, of *"That's me"* -

the self across time, and the *'I'* of *"I feel bored now"* - are located in different areas of the brain (Farb et al 2007). Both are important for wellbeing. Choices about taking off a jumper in order not to overheat matter; so do choices about avoiding people who make us feel useless, and seeking out opportunities for activities that make us feel good.

In order to be aware of our feelings, our abilities, our hopes and our fears, we need time and space to just be. Self-awareness can be about 'soul-searching' and trying to find out about our identity. But it is often about noticing when suddenly something emerges from deep inside, bubbles up, or blurts out. In play we don't decide to learn, we find out, try out, and sometimes speak out. Or sometimes a child picks up something during play and it symbolically speaks to them.

> *This (spider) is me, I have to clean up all the house, get rid of all the flies, and make it nice for everyone.*
>
> Eight-year-old boy *in* Woolf 2010, p.425

Self-knowledge can hit us like a bolt from the blue or it can seep into consciousness, creeping up on us and becoming evident without any need for effort on the part of our intellect.

> *It's like we have been looking for treasure our whole lives and what is buried in our mind has come through*
>
> 11-year-old boy *in* Smith, D. 2012, p.12

Next time a child a child says, *"When I'm playing in the dressing-up area, it's the only time I get to just be me,"* notice the paradox of play: sometimes getting to be me is about being someone else for a while. Sometimes the 'me' we are or want to be is not the 'me' others confine us into. When we think we know who 'me' is, it is only by playful pretence to be someone else that we find that actually the cap fits, and given half a chance, *"Yes, I do want to wear it!"*

Self-regulation (managing feelings)

Sutton-Smith (2002) believes that play helps children explore, come to terms with and 'mediate feelings'. In play he sees children be:

> 'angry' but not violent
> 'fearful' but not terrified
> 'sad' but not overwhelmed

Play seems to be a 'toned-down' reality. It is a safe place because the child has control; it is a contained space because the child can leave or stop and make feelings bigger or smaller until they feel manageable. Play is 'another place'; it is a fantasy world where a child can import doses of reality to unpack and unpick. Playing at being angry, scared or sad is practice for the real thing, or re-creation of past experience, and is still 'just play'. Sutton Smith *(ibid.)* believes that children at play find answers to difficult feelings:

> For anger, they find 'strategy and control'
> For fear, they find 'courage and resilience'
> For sadness, they find 'bonding' and belonging

In Chapter 7 I asked if you had noticed how rough-and-tumble play seems to keep appearing as one of the answers to everything (almost). Here we are again, looking at how important physical play is for brains, bodies, hearts and souls. Young mammals who enjoy R&T play 'are creating important neural connections' (Jarvis et al 2014, p.61) that are associated with emotion and social skills. Brain science confirms what theorists and practitioners have long since believed to be true:

> Interactive play can enhance the emotion-regulating functions in the frontal
> lobes, helping children to manage their feelings better.
>
> Sunderland 2006, p.104

We often hear complaints by older people about the way younger people behave; about how childhood has changed, how children don't 'play' anymore. If this were true, what might it mean for our younger generation's development of social and emotional maturity? Some research confirms these observations. 'The seven-year-olds of today have self-regulation levels more like those of the pre-school children of the 1940's' (Smirnova & Gudareva 2004, *in* Bodrava & Leong 2010, p.66). Researchers believe that changes in children's behaviours and in their ability to manage feelings are due to 'the changes in the way children play both at home and in the classroom' (*ibid*).

Most writers and social commentators agree that there are fewer opportunities for play now than there were. We have considered some of the causes; risk-aversion, reduced school playtimes, more social isolation due to reasons such as distance from friends, technology devices in bedrooms, pace of modern-day life and so on. As someone who has been in school most of her life - on one side of the desk or the other - I have an impression of less play now than then.

> *While schooling might have been more formal in say the '60s when I*
> *was in primary school, there were some things about education that were*
> *freer. What was taught, how it was taught, the time taken by subject*
> *areas - these were individual choices for schools or for staff members.*

English and Maths seemed highly valued and each morning was given over to them no matter whose class I was in. But afternoons seemed more random, with one teacher giving us sewing activities again and again, while another read us magical and fantastical stories from Greek mythology. And Friday afternoons were 'bring a toy' time! The one I remember most clearly was taking my bedroom rug in to school, a brown rectangle picture from Lady and the Tramp.

In terms of my memories of freedom and of play, I remember the huge size of our school playing field and walking the boundary with a few friends, far away from adult eyes and voices. My own experiences suggest that play opportunities associated with school have changed, but the time I remember most when I was free to play, talk, run, explore and have fun was on the walk to and from school. The day I took my rug in I can still clearly remember spreading it out on the pavement on the way home and a group of us sitting on it for a magic carpet ride: what a picture we must have made. What a strong memory that moment created. It makes me think of the 'quirkiness, flexibility, unpredictability and sloppiness' that Lester & Russell (2010, p.16) see as the 'essence' of play. The rug was certainly flexible, it could be a venue for a tea party; a cover to curl up into like a sausage roll; the roof of a den; a contained space to be 'out' or 'in' in a game of tag.

Apart from games of pretence, the way home included chances to hunt for wild animals in the grounds of a large ruined house, race down different routes to see which was quickest, hide from my brother who was supposed to keep an eye on me and time to chat with friends about football and fashion or pop stars and pets. Four miles every day with no adults, very little traffic and pupils from all ages of the school to mix with, avoid, annoy and emulate. A good hour and more a day of freedom, social opportunities, time to be alone, and space to be me.

Time to play, according to Lester & Russell (2010), really is one of the important factors for us in being able to develop ability to manage and cope with our feelings.

> Play may lead to the enhancement of emotion and stress response systems that avoid overreaction to novelty, and produce a more subtle and graded response rather than impulse-driven over- and under-reactions.   p.22

One way children learn self-regulation through play is the way that they 'talk themselves through' a choice or a strategy. Most of us grown-ups rehearse or walk through how to manage a situation silently in our heads. We have internal, abstract processing abilities. Observing a child at play we often hear them 'think out loud' (Howard & McInnes 2013, p.135). They talk through the things they are doing, feeling, planning and seeing. This helps them to anticipate, control, choose and change what happens; making sure that they can 'cope' with their play, stretch their coping abilities and feel rising and falling levels of anxiety, fear, excitement, courage, sadness or joy, and experience a sense that they managed.

> The experience of stress under playful conditions, with associated temporary elevations of cortisol (an important neurochemical involved in responding to stress), leads to neural re-organisation. This enables new connections that will be able to cope with the demands of an unpredictable environment (Flinn 2006) and energise activity (Greenberg 2004).
>
> Lester & Russell 2010, p.21

Children's self-regulation during this live self-commentary happens externally (Howard & McInnes 2013, p.135). Like most things we learn as we mature, the first step is necessary before the next step follows on. Parents support and manage their children's emotional responses, and then 'through identification, the child eventually responds to its own rages in the same firm, but loving, manner as its parents' (Siegel 1996, p.41). Without lots of external regulation from us adults for our youngest charges, they won't develop their own capacity for 'external' self-regulation, which over time becomes an internal, silent, unobserved but effective support to them. And research suggests that play is where lots of this good stuff happens. 'Children use more self-regulatory language in activities they see as play rather than not play' (Whitebread 2010, *in* Howard & McInnes 2013, p.136). Providing the right play experiences can improve levels of children's ability to manage their emotions.

> Children in a non-directed play condition over a period of weeks showed a significant increase in self-regulation.
>
> Ogan & Berg 2009, *in* Russ & Niec 2011, p.329

It seems that self regulation - managing emotions - is more readily researched than motivation and self-awareness. The brain science and the quantitative evidence are right behind free play as a vital component of developing coping strategies.

The development of an ability to tolerate feelings is never more important than in the area of aggression.

> When young humans, especially boys, play fight … they aren't just practising aggression, they are practising restraint and control as well.
>
> Cohen 2001, p.104

Research into the positive effects of parents and children having fun in R&T play is extensive. Research in animals around the later benefits of early peer and sibling play-fighting is also substantial. Early play experiences build brain pathways that say *"I've been here before"*. And more importantly say *"I can manage this"*.

'Tell me a story'

One of the ways play is a safe place to develop emotional regulation is through play's use of symbolism. Childhood stories are often metaphors for childhood experiences. Brain science confirms the wisdom of the storytelling tradition. We now know that metaphors, parables, stories and analogies are all essential for learning (Zull 2002, p.128):

> ... when someone is stuck in some way, a time honoured way to change
> the patterns in their mind is through telling stories, using metaphors and
> appropriate humour.   Griffin & Tyrrell 2003, p.204

The Gruffalo (Donaldson, 1999) is one of the most popular stories for young children. Through hearing the story the child can feel fear and manage the feeling. He or she can be brave in the safety of their mother's lap. In playground games the child can run for their life from the jaws of 'Mister Wolf', screaming and giggling at the same time. In the role-play area children can be heroes or villains, a baby or a parent. They can love or hate, be sad or happy, and even kill or be killed. The biggest of life's experiences, shrunk down into manageable 'doses' of fear, joy, despair and disgust. Without play experiences of facing life's challenges, the feelings on meeting the trials of real life are overwhelming. Sutton Smith (In Lester & Maudsley, 2007) likened play space to a circus:

> In a circus, the animals symbolise the possibility of danger, the clowns
> symbolise the disruption of conventions, while the acrobats symbolise the
> disruption of physical safety. Yet all of this takes place in a circus tent,
> where it is known that nothing really dangerous or disruptive will happen.
>
> Sutton-Smith 2002, p.19

So much of children's play is about 'naughtiness', danger and risk. *Goldilocks and the Three Bears* has it all. The child, whether listening to the story, or playing it out, identifies with Goldilocks, disobeying adult direction, feeling brave, naughty, big, scared and defiant. Then he or she identifies with the wolf - sneaky, cunning, dangerous, dishonest and powerful. At the end of the story the child can imagine they are the rescuer and feel the relief of being rescued. A world full of feelings, in teaspoon-size doses, contained safely on a page or in the imagination of the player.

Without an ability to regulate our emotions, we are lost. We become prey to any difficult feeling, with no belief that we can tolerate, survive, or bounce back. Our options then are back to basics: fight, flight or freeze. In play, feeling are managed because they are manageable, and this creates a template in the brain for managing feelings. A template we call on at the best and worst of times throughout our lives.

Motivation

> There is arguably no such thing as unmotivated behaviour. This is largely
> due to the fact that our brain is designed to seek pleasure and avoid
> displeasure. Sunderland 2006, p.169

Everything we do is motivated firstly by our animal instinct to survive; then secondly, to avoid pain wherever possible and seek out pleasure whenever we can. Educators theorise over motivation, as motivation really matters to their pedagogy of learning. Motivating children to learn is seen in terms of how a task fits with the level of ability of the targeted child or group. Weiner (2010, p.35) points out the uncertainties around this matching of task to pupil ability:

- *It may be that low expectancy of success or a difficult task generates most effort*

- *It may be that intermediate difficulty tasks are most motivating*

- *It may be that being close to a goal generates most motivation*

If the experts cannot agree on optimal conditions for motivating pupils, what chance is there for the teacher in the classroom? Elkind (2007) notes that when:

> … children were bored and unmotivated, it was *not* because they were lazy or lacked interest in learning. They were bored and unmotivated because they had been taught that their interests and passions were of little value.
>
> (p.59)

He believes that children are not 'naturally motivated' to learn through the taught curriculum, formal instruction and work. The brains of children are designed to learn through play (p.127). From birth, humans are motivated to learn. Getting better at surviving means learning what works. Relevant learning needs little motivation. Learning of no immediate relevance to the child needs more motivation, another reason for it to be of interest to the learner. 'If we want to help people learn *we must help them see how it matters in their lives'* (Zull 2002, p.52). Not everything has to 'matter' in a practical, survival, 'getting a job at the end of it' kind of way! Luckily being human is also about pushing ourselves; enjoying challenge, finding out for the sake of it, competing with others and being amazed and awed by the wonder of life. It is these areas of motivation that need educators' attention and understanding.

The way to create motivated pupils is to foster motivation through play. Watching children at play you can see how some struggle to start anything, while others are constantly driven to try, test, create and invent. As Elkind suggests, these children who appear unmotivated in play were once explorers and investigators of their world. But adults' disinterest may have de-motivated the little learners, and often worse, adults' derision, desire for control and lack of time for the learner have disinherited the children of their inborn drive and purpose.

> Because it is so serious, no outside influence or force can cause a brain to learn. It will decide that on its own. Thus, one important rule for helping people learn is *to help the learner feel she is in control*. This is probably the best trick that good teachers have.　　　　　　　　　　　Zull 2002, p.52

Another motivating factor of play is its healing quality. Play has the ability to make us feel whole, to make us feel better and to make us actually well. 'To play it out is the most natural self-healing measure childhood affords' (Erikson 1995, p.200). Children are motivated to play when things are getting them down. People are motivated to seek out reparative experiences. Just like our skin heals itself and our bones knit back together, so our minds are also 'designed to repair themselves' (Craig 2007, p.63). Our minds have age-old motivations: to be well, to do well and to feel well. Play is the answer to all of these in-built drives. Why do we play? Because 'something inside' just makes us! Intrinsic motivation: the strongest force on earth (well maybe not, but certainly in the classroom). Make it motivating? Make it playful!

Empathy

> When empathy occurs, we find ourselves experiencing it, rather than directly causing it to happen. This is the characteristic that makes the act of empathy unteachable.
>
> Davis 1990, p.707

Empathy is: 'the ability to appreciate the emotions and feelings of others with a minimal distinction between self and other' (Decety 2010, p.204). Not to be confused with 'sympathy': 'the feelings of concern about the welfare of others' (*ibid*). Put more simply,

> The essence of empathy is to stand in another's shoes, to feel what it is like to be there and to care about making it better if it hurts.
>
> Szalavitz & Perry 2010, p.12

We have an inbuilt capacity for recognising feelings in others. It is called the 'mirror neuron system' or MNS. The mirror neuron system works by noticing facial expressions of others and then making the same expression on the face of the observer - in miniature, with tiny muscle movements that tell us how we feel when we make that face. Sounds complicated? You see someone you know walking towards you and before you consciously know that you see they are frowning, your MNS has clocked it and made the muscles in your forehead frown ever so slightly. It is this tightening of your face that tells you the feeling your friend or colleague is expressing. In animal research Decety (2010, p.205) explains how our brains, or the neurons in our brains, react similarly whether we act ourselves, or see someone else doing the action.

> These neurons respond both when the monkey executes a particular action - for example, grasping, placing or manipulating - and when the monkey observes someone else performing that same action.   *ibid*

This 'embodied emotion perception' (Neal & Chartrand 2011), this physical information from our own body, about the body of another, as we copy their body language, goes on without us ever noticing. It is unconscious, unintentional and automatic.

> How do we recognize the emotions other people are feeling?   One source of information may be facial feedback signals generated when we automatically mimic the expressions displayed on others' faces.   p.1

And where do we see people making the most animated facial expressions? In play. Mothers and fathers playing with their babies, making surprised, scared, excited, or sad faces to 'tell' the baby 'this is what that feeling looks like'. The parent's face shows exaggerated concern, delight, disapproval and exasperation. They only have non-verbal communication available to talk to their child. *'Look, this is how that makes me feel'*. Playful faces create meaning. Playful faces share meaning. Playful faces appear to be universally intuitively used when talking to a baby. If the baby does not learn this language, the opportunity is lost. However, before we get too despondent, we can use similar interactions at other stages, and more and more we are finding experts believe the brain remains more able to change later into life than we used to think. In Chapter 16 we will think about how we can make up for some of this lost opportunity for social learning; and we will find new ways of harnessing this powerful way to communicate and relate to others, and use it in our interactions with pupils.

The 'listening', or 'taking in' of this emotional literacy happens in the first months of life. The 'speaking' or 'giving out' is practised in the Early Years settings, where child communicates to child *'Look at my face - it is saying I am pretending to be sad in this game'*; *'See these narrow eyes, and these pursed lips? I am not happy you knocked my bricks over'*. These communications really matter, if my face is to understand your face, and then tell my brain how you feel by letting me feel it a bit too.

Empathy cannot be taught. The importance of empathy; why we need to feel it, how it changes our actions and what happens without it can be explained, but it needs to be felt. It really can only be 'caught and not taught' (Gordon 2009). Gordon's 'Roots of Empathy' programme in the US, and B.A.S.E.®Babywatching (www.base-babywatching-uk.org) in Europe, including here in the UK, use the experience of literally seeing empathy in action by bringing parents and very young children into the classroom. The pupils see the faces of the baby and parent as they interact. They get to match facial expressions and tone of voice to the feelings exchanged between two people as they tune in to each other.

Without introducing new ideas or new people into classrooms the great news is that when our children and our school staff play together we learn about each other and we get to understand people more and to feel more compassion for them and their worlds.

Social skills

Through play children learn how to compete, share and collaborate. Jarvis et al (2014) believe these are the essential skills for later coping with 'all adult social arenas' (p.63).

Social skills is a very broad categorisation. What are these mythical skills that make us a social success? In order to be part of a social world we need to:

notice ◆ think ◆ act

When we can see and hear what others are feeling and doing we take in the information we need to inform our responses to others. Then our brain can mull it over: *'Which response does this other person need and what might their response to my response be?'* Then the social being has a repertoire of responses they can appropriately use to connect with people and to belong in a community.

How can children develop social skills in conditions that are 'anti'-social - meaning not supportive of the sorts of social experiences children need and want? In one survey of children (Gill 2011, p.12) nearly two thirds (over 60 per cent) said 'their favourite playmate was a friend of a similar age' but 'over a third (36 percent) only get to see their friends outside of school once every 2 weeks or less'.

Fear of people, fear of traffic, fear of gangs, fear of the unknown, fear of recriminations if anything happens to a child that is out and about, all mean children are playing out less. Managing children's free time and giving them lots of structured activities mean children have less time just to hang out with friends. On-tap entertainment at home, TV, video, computers and game consoles all mean children have things to do that do not need siblings or peers to be there. But social play is vital to many areas of development:

➡ communication skills
➡ relational skills
➡ emotional intelligence

As I discussed above, these skills cannot be taught but are developed through social interactions in childhood and adolescence.

Some avenues to social intelligence can be opened up to children by teaching them skills, but many can't. This is because the 'social dance' is very subtle and highly complex.   Sunderland 2006, p.218

Social skills help us to make and to maintain friendships, to get along with colleagues, and to navigate interactions in the wider world. They can also keep us safe in tricky situations, help us help others without causing offence or embarrassment and when we use our social skills to rescue ourselves or others from hurt or distress, they can be the cause of us being able to feel good about ourselves. These skills include:

➡ conflict resolution

➡ negotiation

➡ resisting peer pressure

➡ effective communication

➡ anger management

➡ social problem solving

Social skills also include our old friends empathy, self-awareness, and self-regulation, and so many other skills that are developed through play; like turn-taking and sharing. In order to develop skills for the trickier social encounters in life, we need to have play experiences where we learn to resist the pressure of our peers, to negotiate for what could best serve everyone and to walk away when to stay would be bad for us or bad for others.

In light of the things we have looked at in this chapter, I wonder if we think schools and society are creating conditions that are likely to support the development of social and emotional skills? Or, if we believe we could be playing more in order to understand more, and playing together more so we feel better and get better at connecting with others?

and so ...

Oftsed (2013, p.4) report that 'the quality of PSHE education is not yet good enough in a sizeable proportion of schools in England' and that when it is it is because the skills, rather than the knowledge, had been prioritised:

> Where learning was strongest, pupils developed good strategies to resist peer-pressure to make unhealthy or unsafe choices by, for example, practising using their knowledge and skills in role-play situations.
>
> *ibid* p.10

The report found that half of the schools in their survey needed to improve their PSHE provision. The findings included the fact that pupils had developed knowledge but not the skills needed to apply that knowledge. Jarvis et al (2014, p.55) note that possibly SEAL 'has had some impact on behaviours which occur directly under the adult eye.' So the teaching has brought about learning; but has it brought about real change? Children may have learned about teachers' beliefs and expectations but have not 'become' (Woolf 2013) skilled social participants and confident autonomous individuals. In order to be able to apply the knowledge they had been taught, Ofsted (2013 p.14) believes children need to:

- ➡ develop self-esteem and confidence
- ➡ develop ways to be assertive and to 'stand up for themselves'
- ➡ develop skills to 'negotiate their way through difficult situations'
- ➡ be given the opportunity to rehearse how to behave in unfamiliar, risky settings

In secondary schools, pupils need opportunities for putting things into practice and for 'rehearsing' for real life (some theorists believe this is the major reason play exists, as I discussed earlier). In primary schools, children need lots and lots of opportunities for social play. Timetabled PSHE sessions could be free, real play time in class.

The evidence that play promotes PSHE is already there. The evidence that *lack* of social play harms the development of *self-awareness, self-regulation, motivation, empathy* and *social skills* is also abundant. You can't plan for better provision than the natural benefits of play. That is, as long as we do not forget 'that if the behaviour is not play, 'any benefits that are said to come from playing, will not apply'! (Hughes 2012, p.78).

KEY POINTS

Play is the way children develop self-awareness and practice being different parts of that 'self'

Play is the way children develop self-regulation (managing feelings)

Play is the time children develop and are free to follow their own motivation

Play is the way children develop empathy and try out standing in someone else's shoes

Play is the way children develop social skills and where 'getting along' brings the vital reward - the play carries on.

Play and PSHE: *Where do we go from here?*

In order for changes in practice to take place, Play England believes that the following developments need to take place in government policy. It recommends:

Play is a principal and recognised part of Healthy School status. All Healthy School co-ordinators to promote the importance of play in children's health and wellbeing.   *from* Play England, 2008, *Play in Schools and Integrated Settings*: A position statement London: NCB

· ·

The play-full school would -

☺   Include a member of staff with Playworker qualification in their PSHE team

☺   Provide free play opportunities within their PSHE provision

· ·

If you want to know more, try reading

Appleton, L. (1910) *A Comparative Study of the Play Activities of Adult Savages and Civilized Children.* Chicago: University of Chicago Press.

Department for Education (DfE) (2011) Primary Social and Emotional Aspects of Learning: Small Group Work Evaluation Available at: education.gov. uk/publications/standard/ publicationDetail/ Page1/DCSF-RB064

Department for Education (DfE) (2013b) *Personal, Social, Health and Economic (PSHE) Education* Available at: education.gov.uk/schools/ teachingandlearning/curriculum/ b00223087/pshe

Department for Education (DfE) (2013c) *Spiritual, moral, social and cultural development.* Available at: education.gov.uk/schools/ teachingandlearning/curriculum/ a00199700/spiritual-and-moral

Department for Education (DfE) (2013d) *Consultation on PSHE Education: Summary report.* Department for Education. Available at: media.education. gov.uk/assets/files/pdf/p/pshe%20 cons%20report.pdf

Ofsted (2013) *Not Yet Good Enough: personal, social, health and economic education in schools Personal, social and health education in English schools in 2012.* Manchester: Ofsted

Sunderland, M. (2006) *The Science of Parenting* London: DK Publishing (also published as - *What Every Parent Needs to Know*)

Welsh Government (2011) Making a Difference on Behaviour and Attendance: An Action Plan for 2011-2013. Learning.Wales.Gov. Uk/Resources/Browse-All/ Attendance-Action-Plan/?Lang=En

Woolf, A. (2010) Better Playtimes: A school-based therapeutic play intervention for staff and children *in* Drewes, A & Schaefer, C. (eds.) *School-Based Play Therapy (2nd edition).* Hoboken, NJ: Wiley

If you want to understand more, try reading

de Saint-Exupery, A. (2002) *The Little Prince* London: Egmont

If you want a 15 minute group or individual training, try watching

Mihaly Csikszentmihalyi's 2008 TED talk on 'Flow, the secret to happiness' on the TED website, ted.com/talks, or on youtube. com

Chapter 13

Like stars on earth: every child is special (Disney 2010)

If you're so fond of racing, then breed racehorses … When will we learn that each child has his own abilities? Sooner or later all of them learn. Each has his own pace. Ram Shankar Nikumbh, Disney 2010

Each child has a pace, style, passion and dream of his own. Every child is special. And every child is unique. Some children have special or unique learning needs, others have emotional challenges that can set them apart, while others still have the human condition of being unique individuals. We have fought for 'education for the masses'. We prize our conviction of 'education for all'. But does that come at a price? Catering for everyone usually means finding a common ground that suits most people. Buying clothes, it often seems one size is too small, but the next size too big. Choosing from a menu, I often want one thing but with the sauce that comes on another dish. Caterers and providers have to have systems in place and ways of grouping things together. But if I can afford to have clothes 'tailor made' or food personally planned and prepared, I may get a perfect fit.

So how could we make pupils' schooling experience a 'good enough' (more achievable and actually better than perfect, because more like the life that awaits after school years are done) fit for all and for each? Some questions that politicians and philosophers have argued over include: how to 'group' pupils and the ideologies around inclusion and streaming; how to teach pupils, and the different methodologies preferred at different times and by different parties. These debates are easier to address for national or local provisions but harder to answer for Jacob or Meena who have unique strengths and difficulties in accessing learning. Every child is special, and if you have one or work with one you will know that!

In this chapter we will think about how we group our pupils and the systems we put in place to cater for our learners, and the part that play can have in children's experience of school.

THE QUESTIONS TO CONSIDER ARE:

MAKING IT PERSONAL

How can we make children's learning personal and relevant? How do we offer the appropriate balance of challenge and mastery for each child's needs on any given day?

LOOK AND LEARN

How can watching the child at play be a good start to understanding their 'baseline'? How can a child's play inform us on where to take them next?

PLAY FOR ALL

How can we be providers of play for each and every one so their experience becomes personal? Can we notice and respond to the messages we take from the play?

REASONS TO PLAY MORE

When can play help students with identified needs for specific, additional or alternative learning experiences? Who needs more play or different sorts of play? Can we follow the child's lead when it seems they know the play that they need?

SOMETHING AMAZING YOU MAYBE DIDN'T KNOW ABOUT PLAY

Did you know you don't have to be playing to get some of the benefits of play?

Welcome to a positive, and I am thinking probably new to you, way that play can help everyone - even those who don't or can't play!

THE LINK BETWEEN PLAY DEFICITS AND ENGAGEMENT IN LEARNING
What does the research tell us about why some children behave in the ways that they do? How can play be the answer that changes their ability to learn, helping them, their peers and us to become more productive and enjoy school more?

MAKING IT PERSONAL

Nicola Marshall (2014) has created five guiding principles for school staff supporting the attachment needs of pupils. The first two are:

- *Relationships over programmes*
- *Emotional age over chronological age*

In other words, know and relate to the uniqueness of the child. Notice what they need, and how they are, then think about appropriate expectations and relevant curriculum and environment. I have worked in schools where chronological age always dictates learning groups and a school where learning stage decides who the children are grouped with. I acknowledge the challenges of older children feeling embarrassed or being thought of as not being able to do what their friends may be doing but I think schools that believe in children and also believe in the choices they make about the best education for their pupils can overcome these natural difficulties. And I believe, I hope that you do to, that relationships matter more than structure and more than following the ways we have always done things.

In his inspirational 2013 TED talk, *How to get out of the educational 'death valley' we now face*, Sir Ken Robinson outlines how humans learn and the way schools can nurture or sometimes neglect this learning. His first observation on learning is on the diversity of learners, the uniqueness of every child. From this starting point, we are encouraged to look at every child and see their unique strengths and difficulties. Following the child's interests creates an individualised curriculum. Planning in time for freely-chosen play offers a window into the interests of the child. Play at a child's pace provides a unique response to the individual child's needs.

In the last chapter, we saw how the equation of work + play was helpful in consolidating, enriching, and applying learning. Now our equation of the taught element + individual discovery helps with *pacing* the learning (we started this chapter remembering how everyone will learn, but in their own time), exciting the learner and differentiating the experience. By now I hope you are seeing that better play in schools is *as well as*, not *instead of*, great teaching in schools.

Robinson (*ibid*) contrasts the nature of being human and unique with the aim of most education systems, which are designed to create standardisation and conformity. Boli, Ramirez & Meyer (1985) note two points shared by education systems across the world:

- *Mass education is institutionally chartered to be universal, standardized, and rationalised.*
- *Mass education is very highly institutionalised at a very general collective level.*

But these researchers also found that 'although education is supposed to be homogeneous and standardised, the formal values and rituals it promotes celebrate the competence, capacities, and responsibility of the individual member of society' (p.149). They were impressed and surprised how, despite the standardised and institutionalised nature of large education systems, the various cultures they studied all 'attempt to build collective society by enhancing individual development' (*ibid*).

For Robinson the logical and necessary way forward is to individualise all teaching and learning. This feels like a big ask and a logistical nightmare. But adding time to play onto the taught element means the *child* does all the differentiation and the tailoring to individual needs. Play *is* an individualised learning curriculum. It is developmentally and personally led, and nothing could offer a better fit for each child's growth.

By its very nature, play will always fulfil a personal need. It:

➡   builds on the knowledge and understanding the child already has

➡   provides challenge and success in the perfect balance for the child at
        that moment in time

➡   develops physical, cognitive and emotional skills

➡   has resonance and meaning for the child

➡   fills in unknown, unrecognised gaps in the child's understanding

➡   makes sense to the child (although not always to the observer)

So is intrinsically personal, inherently meaningful and innately appropriate to need at any given time for any given child. In other words - a great thing for everyone because it belongs to the player, and it matters to him or to her.

LOOK AND LEARN

In my experience, observing self-chosen play and social play is the most helpful assessment for an adult wishing to understand the unique child. Watching play:

➡   demonstrates the child's strengths

➡   highlights the child's own goals for development

➡   reveals the child's struggles and difficulties

Robinson's (2013) second principle of education is that 'Curiosity drives all learning'. He believes that humans are naturally curious and that our curiosity is hard to extinguish. Elkind however (2007, p.95), believes we frequently succeed in putting out the fire of a child's motivation to discover. Bruner (1974, p. 406) believed that when a child approaches learning as a task of discovery - 'finding out about', it is naturally self-rewarding and therefore motivating. Very different to the experience of being 'taught about' (*ibid*), which may be a trap we educators fall into when we hope to encourage a thirst for knowledge; unwittingly diminishing the very thing we are seeking to foster!

Both Robinson and Elkind recognise children's natural desire to find out and to learn. Panksepp calls this natural curiosity a 'Seeking' drive. He places it alongside the 'Play' drive as one of the fundamental animal and human life forces. Educators who combine the Seeking and Play urges of each child offer 'optimal opportunities to internalise joyful living and learning as life-long habits' (Panksepp 2007, p.64).

To sustain a child's natural human curiosity about the world, we need to find ways to follow each child's unique desire to find out. In order to allow the child to discover and to feel the excitement of being an archaeologist of knowledge, we need to provide for uncertainty and chance: 'Maybe we should give students more time for random actions.' (Zull 2002, p.217)

Teachers are facilitators of environments, resources, and possibilities. We are witnesses to wonder, invention, creativity and to the re-discovery of truths and natural laws. Learning without curiosity will not occur. And crucially, curiosity will not occur until secure relationships are in place in our schools, (*see* Chapter 14).

Like all teaching, education for pupils with alternative needs starts with the interests of the child and at the place where the child is; with the knowledge they already have as the foundation to be built on. 'Watching the learner is basic to effective instruction' (Elkind 2007, p.95), a truth that is even more imperative with pupils who are not able to communicate their needs. When a child cannot answer the question *"What do you already know about this?"* we have to watch their actions in order to understand where they are up to. Only once we 'establish a base-line' can we plan an intervention or launch into a lesson. No instruction can be effective without the pupil having a foundation in place for the learning to connect to.

Allowing a child to explore the environment (play), to create (play) and to problem-solve (play) gives an opportunity for the adult to observe:

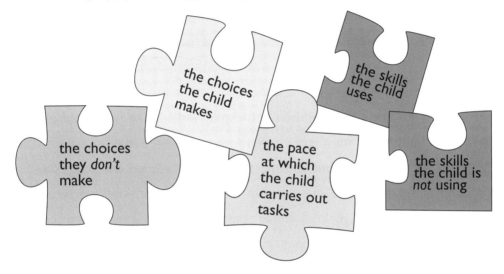

This is as true for the child who is doing well as it is for the child whose developmental pace is a lot slower. Observing play can give us a sensitive and nuanced picture of the child's unique developmental needs and abilities. This will lead us naturally to an understanding of 'where to go next'. Zull challenges us to trust the child to move towards growth and development. He believes that every child will 'learn by selecting the right neuronal networks from among those that already exist' (2002, p.122), if the environment allows them to do so.

PLAY FOR ALL

Providing an individualised play experience means:

> Knowing how to recognise both the verbal and non-verbal cues that children use to show how, what and where they want to play
>
> Knowing and being sensitive to the character, capabilities and communication preferences of all the children in the setting
>
> Knowing how to interpret children's needs and adapt a situation or environment in order to extend their play and their range of experiences.
>
> Play Wales 2007, p.3

School may be the first place children get to play outside the home and away from the immediate family. It may feel scary to be with new adults in a new situation where expectations are different and the intimate knowledge and understanding of a main carer is missing. It is also the start of a world of possibilities, a new social playground with often bigger and better resources than a family home could ever hope to offer. This new environment 'provides a wide range of sensory (and other) experiences, access to other children, and opportunities to extend capabilities and explore possibilities' (*ibid* p.4)

The natural and appropriate adult response to children is to take the role of caregiver, protector and helper. This is more important and needed for longer when the child has specific and individual requirements.

> When a child has a physical disability, playfulness can be diminished. Research suggests that young children with cerebral palsy are often limited in their expression of playfulness due, in part, to suboptimal interactions that take place with their caregivers.   Okimoto, Bundy & Hanzlik 2000, p.73

Okimoto et al. found that the way parents related to their child during play sessions had an impact on the playfulness the child developed. Less direction, more eye contact and better awareness for noticing the child's abilities increase the playfulness of the child. Standing or sitting back is hard when a child may be struggling; but children need to be in control of their play. A constant sensitivity to a child's need for adult direction and help, alongside a constant monitoring of the adult desire to help and to be 'teaching', allows for the moments of breakthrough in the child's developing repertoire of play skills and abilities.

REASONS TO PLAY MORE

Play is the way the young baby learns. As we discovered in Chapter 11, play is the way Nobel prize-winning scientists learn too. Play is the most appropriate way learning happens whatever the developmental age and stage of the learner. Play in settings for pupils with specific and alternative requirements is often more important for longer than in other classrooms. Children who find access to play more difficult will need lots of 'catch up' time.

> *"I want to find people who will take me ice skating, climbing and trampolining ... I am waiting to find such people and then I will take off and soar like a bird".*   Young person, *in* Murray 2002, pp.40-41

In our schools, children are not always able to find out about the external world, or to express the experience of their internal world, at an individual pace and level. In schools, our pupils and students are part of a learning community and of a broader educational system. How groups of pupils are organised varies according to cultural and/or political climate. Children and young people are grouped, placed, streamed or sorted according to age, ability, developmental level or specific identifiable needs. The streaming in schools is often 'Gifted and Talented', 'Average or Mainstream' and 'Special Educational Needs' (still true in England, as of 2016, however in Wales now described as ALN - Additional Learning Needs). Nearly a fifth of pupils in the United Kingdom are recorded as having Special Educational Needs (SEN) (Doherty 2007; DfE 2012). Those needs are variously described in four broad groups:

Cognitive and learning
Emotional, behavioural and social
Communication
Physical/sensory   Doherty 2007, p.202

Of the children with special needs, about 15% have a statement of their special educational needs. These named needs include such descriptions as:

- *Autistic Spectrum Disorder*
- *Moderate Learning Difficulties*
- *Severe Learning Difficulties*
- *Behavioural, Emotional and Social Difficulties*
- *Speech, Language and Communication Difficulties*

Many children with a requirement that has been identified through a process of assessments and diagnostics also have other struggles too. Sometimes the challenges a child faces physically, socially or cognitively lead on to them experiencing emotional or social consequences. Perceptions of children's difficulties or needs also changes over time. Different expectations at different ages and stages seem to impact on the 'label' given to pupils. In primary schools, just under 30% of statemented pupils are considered to have Speech, Language and Communication difficulties. The numbers seem to suggest this converts to a classification of Behavioural, Emotional and Social Difficulties on arrival at secondary school!

Children who are developing at a different pace need play opportunities that match that pace. They often need more play and different kinds of play to others at their age or stage.

One reception-aged child I have come across had been supervised to within an inch of his life in his nursery class! And meeting him for the first time it was easy to understand why. Having probably multi-layered difficulties, but certainly dyspraxia and developmental delay, his management of space and his ability to negotiate his physical environment was not the same as the others in his class. My philosophy that, given time and experience, every child will learn, at their own pace, was to be tested to the max. Provide sand, water, lots of sets of construction toys, cars and figures: stand back and let the fun begin.

Mason created the gloopiest gunge any child could wish for, that took weeks to dry out. He trod on the toys he left covering the floor space and appeared not to notice the chaos we were engulfed in. Simple and consistent rules about not breaking any toys and not getting sand or water (now gloop) on the carpet seemed impossible to stick to. Mason always returned to the same challenging activities, despite not being able to use them within the limits, and so having to leave the play time after time. But if ever a child knew what he needed to do it was Mason. And it worked for him. He did learn, eventually, to either walk very gingerly round the room threading in and out of the toys he had scattered on the floor, or to put things away and create open spaces. He also discovered that less water in the sand might not be so satisfying but it meant he could stay and play longer. Without experience, how can we learn? Mason's play changed and he made it different. Sometimes children need the very play experiences we feel most challenged by and least want to clear up after!

Children who experience set-backs in life, life experiences such as illness, trauma or loss, often need to re-visit play experiences - perhaps because they missed out because of time in bed, in hospital, or in care; or because they were protected or prevented from engaging in anything risky, as they already had so much other stuff to contend with that most of us don't. But we all need to play, especially when we are children and when we face the difficult things life can throw at us because:

➡ Play is the answer to uncertainty; and becomes much more important at times of change

➡ Play is the way we make sense of our world; and opportunities for playing with new ideas are vital to integrate them into existing understanding

➡ Play is the way we come to terms with events; and provides an ongoing space for adjustment to our experience of life

SOMETHING AMAZING YOU MAYBE DIDN'T KNOW ABOUT PLAY

Play is so important to development and wellbeing that it has some very powerful ways of getting its job done! For children who can't play or won't play, just being around play has been shown to have important benefits for cognitive learning and for emotional development. You don't need to be able to join in the play to get the benefits that play has to offer. Observing play allows the child to 'mentally join in,' while being physically outside of the play.

> ... when watching pretend play, observers automatically adopt the intentional stance necessary to understand what the actor is doing.
>
> Whitehead, Marchant, Craik & Frith 2009, p.370

It is 'as if' the observer feels what the player feels. Remember the 'as if' quality of play? Well, this seems to be the 'as if' quality of play observation.

Humans are programmed to feel what others feel. The mirror neurons in our brains respond by reflecting on what others are doing, feeling and thinking, as we saw in the last chapter. Remember the research and classroom practice on empathy? Although it may feel frustrating to be only able to observe others playing, it is still doing amazing things to the understanding of the bystander. Our anxiety that 'doing something' is so much more important than 'being there' often means we take children away from the side-lines of play and direct them to engage in something else. A new belief in the power of watching play changes classroom practice. Learning from others is an eternal human truth; there may be more to be learned by observing a rich, vibrant play activity of others, than by engaging in a stilted, fabricated 'play' activity of your own.

The way that we manage play provision in our classrooms depends on our knowledge and understanding of the nature of play. Our beliefs around play and the emotionally vulnerable or physically fragile children we work with have a big impact on the environments and opportunities we provide.

THE LINK BETWEEN PLAY DEFICITS AND ENGAGEMENT IN LEARNING

Jaak Panksepp (1998) is one of the foremost authorities on the emotional life of animals. His area of expertise in psychobiology and his research into the workings of the animal brain have led to new understanding about play and social relationships. Panksepp's work brings new insight into the way the brain works in disorders such as ADHD and Autism. He believes that one reason a child may develop Attention Deficit Hyperactivity Disorder (ADHD) is because of a lack of sufficient free play experiences. He makes a connection between the increase of ADHD across the population and the decrease in social play opportunities in early childhood, including at school.

Panksepp (2007, p.57) has a two-fold concern around our current wisdom on the treatment of ADHD. He believes that children would benefit from more play experiences rather than medication, and that the medication itself is known to decrease playfulness in those who are taking it. So in these instances, not only are we offering the potentially less appropriate of two possible prescriptions, but the medicine that we provide actually *decreases* the likelihood that the alternative therapy - more play experiences - can be taken up. He acknowledges that his theories have yet to be adequately tested:

> The idea that intensive social play interventions, throughout early childhood, may alleviate ADHD symptoms remains to be evaluated. As an alternative to the use of play-reducing psycho-stimulants, society could establish play 'sanctuaries' for at-risk children in order to facilitate frontal lobe maturation and the healthy development of pro-social minds.   *ibid*

The 'pro-social mind' he talks of is the brain's ability to regulate behaviour and emotion, the ability to 'stop, look, listen & feel' (*ibid* p.58). The brain needs play in order to develop the skill of self-regulation, and the ability to self-regulate increases our ability to play! Play and its benefits increase the likelihood a child can stay on task and be motivated to learn.

Starved of play, the brain seeks opportunities to do just that. Brown (2009, p.43) likens what he calls *play deficit* to sleep deficit. Our brains crave the experience of sleep or of play to make up the lack we experience. He calls the extra play that we need 'rebound', a need that once met gives us a chance to 'bounce back' (in Chapter 2 we learned about the ability of play to create bounce back-ability). Panksepp (2007) suggests that a play-starved child in a room full of peers feels like a hungry kid in a candyshop. 'All those resources for meeting my need for social play and just a teacher standing between us!' He believes that the child with ADHD is longing for play, particularly close physical interactive relationship play. All those 'readily available playmates', but the child's natural drive and biological need for 'rough-and-tumble' play is currently seen as, always and absolutely, 'not acceptable' (p.58).

Some schools make sure the over-tired, sleep-deprived pupil can have a 'catch-up' nap in order that the rest of the day can be optimised. Some schools provide ad-hoc snacks when a hungry child is unable to concentrate or engage in activities, believing that the mind and the body need fuel if the work is going to get done. Some schools give play-starved pupils time to run around, exercise or maybe even to draw or use the Lego before asking them to get back on task. Few schools feel able to offer social play experiences, because that means other pupils are disrupted, and I'm guessing hardly any (probably none) have a quick round of play wrestling before writing that essay! I'm not suggesting they should; (although in my perfect world they would, but then all children would be full to the brim of joyful play anyway!) but letting the play-starved child go hungry in a world where play could be plentiful for all is not the right answer either.

Writing this book is exciting for me, but it is also that ever-present mix of work and play. Sometimes the work part makes my brain feel tired, or full-up, or empty. A quick escape to rearrange some of my artefacts or totems (thank you Sigmund Freud and Carl Jung, for acknowledging I don't just have ornaments or trinkets - no, I have objects of deep symbolic meaning), to indulge my love of interior design confessed in Chapter 1; or a walk round the field with the dogs, watching the light on the crops or the clouds in the sky and letting my mind wander - these things feed me. I guess my brain gets to sleep (well the bit that is working on the facts stuff) and my brain gets to play.

Remember the lack of a vocabulary for the biological need for play? A child who has not slept communicates their need - *"I'm tired!"* The child who has not eaten communicates their need - *"I'm hungry!"* The child who has not played communicates their need: *"I'm ...?"* This all too easily leads to *"I don't know what to say, so I'll act it out instead!"* - thus increasing the likelihood of being kept behind at playtime and accruing further play deprivation.

There are many reasons why ADHD children may be play-deficient. The impulsive, socially inappropriate, and sometimes physically uncoordinated overtures of some children are not welcomed by peers, and provoke anxiety or impatience in adults. This leads to a complete and inescapable circuit of need, rejection or prohibition, unmet need, further need. Panksepp (2007) describes how some ADHD children may appear to avoid social play or can seem to choose to be solitary. But he suggests this may be due to previous experience of peers not accepting them into the play as their ways of joining in are 'too rough or primitive - too 'rude" (p.62). Panksepp's 'answer' to the condition of ADHD is for more play and less drugs. He believes that not only would this address the problem of ADHD, it also avoids the unwanted side-effects of medication and gives all the wider benefits of play to the child as well as addressing the specific biological need of the brain.

Understanding this has made me see the actions of the child walking the boundary of the playground alone, or not joining in when invited by a group, in a different way. Perhaps not as a child who chooses to be alone, or as a child who does not have the courage to try out their strategies for playing with peers. But maybe as a child who has learned that those strategies did not work, or that their brave attempts to join in with others led to rejection, ridicule or sanctions. But let's hold mind that whilst it is still just as possible the child *is* a rejected and dejected outcast, longing to be included and invited to become an insider, he might alternatively be one who chooses or needs to be alone. And whichever is the case, he or she can still be benefiting from the (amazing) learning of watching others play.

. . . .

and so ...

We now know: that the need for play is universal. It is a life-long developmental journey of discovery. And: that the nature of play is such that it always goes at the pace of the player, and starts at the point where the player is 'at'. Exploratory and sensory play underpins the curriculum in many alternative learning settings. For children with unique needs, the adults' knowledge and understanding of play is vital to the effective and appropriate provision for each child.

The adults' self-awareness of their own needs and their own anxieties are also crucial in what happens, and how it happens in play. Bearing in mind that risk assessment by staff is more complex in alternative provision, health and safety assessments include additional physical, developmental, cognitive, emotional and medical considerations. But challenge is still important for the child. And play entails risk. The play provider 'must balance risk with the developmental benefit and wellbeing of children' (Hughes 2012, p.69). Some pupils need staff to take a risk and to trust the child. But every child needs to be able to follow their own interests, to be who they feel they are and to have the dignity of choice - even when that includes the *dignity of risk* (Lehan, Morrison & Stanley 2004). Play always includes risk (Hughes 2012, *and see* Chapter 4): without risk there can be no sense of achievement, or sense of one's own effectiveness and impact on the world. That risk includes the risk to me as the adult - whether it is that the child may 'fail' and I will feel bad, or at the end, that the tidy-up job may be massive.

Everyone has the right to 'dare to dream'. In play the child can be anyone, do anything, imagine, pretend and believe. This is not escapism, it is an 'alternative reality'. In the moment of playing not only is anything possible, but in the play time and space the child is who they dare to dream to be. In play the child is him or herself, unique, and each of them special. We won't know what that dream might be unless we allow the children to play and observe the message their play may contain. Understanding our children, knowing what they need, means that we could truly provide appropriate education for each and for all.

KEY POINTS

Play is a universal need in childhood (and ever thereafter!)

Being given play opportunities is every child's right

Self-chosen play is always developmentally appropriate even when it does not appear age-appropriate.

Sometimes we prevent children playing because we struggle with our own need to protect (particularly if we think a child is vulnerable in some way).

*Play can often be the most appropriate prescription for meeting the needs of **all** children.*

Play and meeting the needs of every child:
Where do we go from here?

There are many sources of information and guidance on the current practice of meeting the needs of all children for play. They include:

Mythbusting: Busting the myths of inclusion (2011) London: KIDSNDD

Inclusive Play and Disability (2007) Cardiff: Play Wales

*I Want to Play Too: Developing inclusive play and leisure for children and young
    people* (2004) Ilford, Essex: Barnado's

· ·

A play-full school would -

☺   Have at least one member of staff with a Playwork qualification

☺   Provide a rich environment of play and an ethos of valuing play

☺   Assess, plan and deliver individual pupil programmes through play

☺   Develop the staff members' ability to finely attune to the needs of each
      pupil for support and for independence

· ·

If you want to know more, try reading:

Boli, J., Ramirez, F.O. & Meyer, J. (1985). Explaining the Origins and Expansion of Mass Education. In *Comparative Education Review* Vol. 29:2 pp.145–170.

Department for Education (DfE) (2012) Special Educational Needs In England, January 2012, Statistical First Release. London: Department for Education

Murray, P. (2002) *Hello! Are you listening? Disabled teenagers' experience of access to inclusive leisure.* Joseph Rowntree Foundation. York: YPS

Okimoto, A., Bundy, A. & Hanzlik, J. (2000) Playfulness in Children with and without Disability: Measurement and intervention. *American Journal of Occupational Therapy,* Vol. 54 pp.73–82.

Panksepp, J. (2007) Can PLAY Diminish ADHD and Facilitate the Construction of the Social Brain? *Journal of the Canadian Academy of Child and Adolescent Psychiatry.* Vol. 16:2 pp.57–66

Play Wales (2007) *Inclusive play and disability.* Cardiff: Play Wales

Whitehead, C., Marchant, J., Craik, D. & Frith, C. (2009) Neural Correlates of Observing Pretend Play in which one Object is Represented as Another. *Social Cognitive Affective Neuroscience.* Vol. 4:4 pp.369-378.

If you want to understand more, try reading:

Stockdale, S., Strick, A. & Asquith, R. (2013) *Max the Champion* London: Frances Lincoln Children's Books

If you want a 15 minute group or individual training, try watching:

The KaBOOM (kaboom.org) 2011 'Prescription for Play' video on youtube.com

Better play

SECTION 3 : SKILLS FOR BETTER PLAY

Chapter 14

Better equipped for play:
the importance of relationship

Now you've read Chapter 1 on the nature of play, and if you've been thinking about Chapter 2 and the importance of play whilst you've read through the rest of the book, you may have learned something new or have been reminded of something you knew before but had forgotten to remember!

Whenever we learn something new, or get to re-learn something again, our brains will change and we will be different. If we have understood something in a new way, we will have made new connections in our brains. So, if after reading the chapters that have gone before this one, and when you've found things making a new kind of sense, and fitting differently in your understanding of the world, you will have been changing neural networks and bridged previous gaps.

Maybe by now you have made new connections between your left brain and your right brain, and between the thinking and feeling areas of your brain. You will be different, see differently and understand more. You will already be providing better play in your school. You will be responding better to the play that you see without maybe even realising it. Without planning new initiatives, or attending additional training, your relationship with play has changed, and children playing in your presence will be feeling better.

In this section we are now ready to start to think about the application of the previous chapters to our work in schools. Knowing more about play, you are already a more skilled provider. If you believe new things about play and if you now feel you know play when you see it, your responses to play will be different. There are techniques you can use in play, times you can give over to play and spaces you can designate as play places; but your attitude to play and your knowledge of play are the real game changers.

Seems unlikely? These are certainly big claims - but I've seen it happen many times, and school staff have recognised how *knowing* more about play and *thinking* more about play can be life-changing. While skills and techniques can be used to support and deepen better play experiences, it is our *personal beliefs* and *understanding* that influence our way of working (and being) the most. When one of us notices that after learning more about play,

> *"I've also looked at my own feelings and reactions and have been really surprised at these."*   *feedback from a teacher in* Woolf 2010, p.19

… we most likely start to realise that the result is a change in those reactions and responses.

I know that once I learned that play is not necessarily a teaching tool; that it is not necessary that it is fun, and that just like life it can sometimes be messy, uncomfortable, challenging and unfair, then play in my classrooms opened up in new ways.

When Stacey's brother joined the army, and on the day he left home for the first time, her Mum came in to the Nursery to say Stacey had been really upset and could I make sure she was alright. I quickly removed the tub of soldiers from the shelves beside the sand tray. And later when I noticed Stacey had the set of animal babies lined up facing the family figures preparing to 'fight', I called over to her to put her apron on as it was nearly her turn to bake scones. I think I believed that Stacey would be more likely to be 'alright' through distraction from and disruption of her processing of this difficult and very new experience. Or maybe I needed to be alright too, and not have a child feel sad or confused or angry or scared?

Having learned more about play, I hope that now I would believe that Stacey could play what she needed to play, that I could cope with her emotions as they might have emerged as she played, and that I could have supported Mum as well: because of course, I would make sure that Stacey played within her 'window of tolerance' and that I allowed for any time or support needed to 'recover' from her play.

In this chapter we will think about how we can become Better Equipped for Play.

THE QUESTIONS TO CONSIDER ARE:

A WHOLE SCHOOL APPROACH

How important is it in changing our way of working or our attitude to new interventions?

IT'S THE RELATIONSHIP, STUPID!

How important is the relationship between individual members of staff and our pupils? How does it impact on how well children do in school, and on how happy they feel about schooling?

A WHOLE SCHOOL APPROACH

Including play opportunities as part of everything that happens in schools:

- gives pupils opportunities to process thoughts, express feelings and develop beliefs
- gives staff opportunities to develop a deeper understanding of their pupils' strengths and difficulties
- enhances relationships between adults and pupils

In order to provide better play throughout schools, whole staff groups need to want to engage with change. Most importantly school leaders need to develop:

- a new belief in the power of play
- a new attitude towards the role of play
- a new ethos of school as a place where work and play are equally valued media for developing the whole person and equipping young people for life

In short, school staff teams need to ask ourselves the questions -

… 'why learn through play?' and 'why play whilst learning?'

Rice 2009, p.96

When all members of the school team are comfortable and confident that the answer to both those questions is: because current knowledge about play and brain development demonstrates that play is:

- integral to developing cognitive understanding
- essential to developing social skills
- fundamental to developing emotional intelligence and wellbeing

… the magic can begin! Recognising the role and value of play in schools means that staff understand 'the dimensions of learning in play and the dimensions of play in learning' (Pramling Samuelsson & Johansson 2006, p.47). While the whole school commitment is important, so is the individual. Each member of the school team can influence how their school works and give a perspective on how it feels to be a learner there.

IT'S THE RELATIONSHIP, STUPID!

To coin, or paraphrase, Bill Clinton's 1992 presidential campaign slogan about how the economy is really all that matters to voters; it really is the relationships in school that matter most to pupils - to their experience of being there, as well as to the achievements they leave with at the end.

> Schools can no longer keep up the pretence that relationships do not affect performance, either academic or professional … some teachers claim that their prime task is to organise their students' intellectual development, whereas others argue that the major source of difficulty in their work is the problem of relating to their students and their colleagues, and that once this has been sorted out, the academic issues are relatively simple.
>
> Hall & Hall 1988, p.1

Training for staff in schools across the board, has rarely, if ever, included adequate training in theories of human relationships. Mine certainly did not. As we heard in Chapter 9, an understanding of attachment is key to the awareness of the ways we relate to others and others relate to us. My own schooling in attachment in my initial teacher training was a cursory nod to Bowlby and the theory of separation anxiety. I had no sense that initial relationships or attachments could influence later relationships and expectations of others, or of who and how we are.

Even as a nineteen year old just out of school myself, I don't think I needed training to understand that a new pupil in my nursery or reception class might struggle to separate from a parent or might be wary of me as a stranger in their life! I might have found it helpful to know that that child's earliest relationships had created a template, a pattern, an expectation and belief about relationships, which he or she would hold up against me and use as a guide to build our new pupil-teacher relationship.

Even more helpful would have been training on how unwittingly I was getting out my own set of 'patterns', choosing one that best fit the new people I met, and then failing to notice the differences and uniqueness between people. And most importantly of all would have been training that helped me to see the way I tended to be with others. The way I might indulge 'naughty' boys; encourage 'good girls'; or empathise with those who struggle with maths, while being impatient with those who found reading hard. How everything I was and all my own experiences clouded my vision of others.

I wish I had known more, but as with other areas of my training, I think I would have understood all these complicated human interactions better after I had had some experience in the job.

An introduction to theoretical models of relationships can help school staff to be more insightful into their own ways of being, as well as into the ways their pupils behave. Understanding the dynamics of human relationships also helps us to notice how some of the people we interact with make us feel. This understanding is so helpful in schools, as it can be used to inform strategies for how to relate to individual children and for how to take care of ourselves. Better relationships, based on better understanding of self and of how we relate to others is important for the all-round success of pupils in education.

> The quality of teacher-child relationships has taken on a new significance as a growing number of studies suggest their link with children's short- and long-term wellbeing.   Fumoto 2011, p.19

It is relationships in schools that change the people in schools. And that goes both ways! When we as staff suffer from *'Wemustimpartforyoutolearn-itus'* (Harris, 2012; already introduced in Chapter 9) we concentrate on me talking and ensuring they, the pupils, are listening. This might seem to work at the time, but in the long run children remember the bigger picture of their experience of school:

> *They may forget what you said, but they will never forget how you made them feel.*   (source unknown)

How *do* we 'make them feel? Do we know what children's experience of adult-pupil relationships in school is? A UNICEF poll (2001b) of over fifteen thousand children between nine and eighteen years of age, conducted between 1999 and 2001 in Europe and Central Asia, found that:

△   Nearly 70% of children report having good or very good relations
       with their teachers
△   About 3% say they have poor relations with teachers
       (teachers tell them off, are not fair and do not listen)
△   20% wanted better teacher-student relationships

So great news for two thirds of pupils: having good relationships with staff means not only will they enjoy school, they will also be much more likely to do well at school. Of the remaining third of pupils, many wish for better relationships with staff and a few feel we just do not listen to them. Sometimes it is certainly true that we do not listen. Sometimes we listen but do not hear. Sometimes we hear but then we are not able to convey our deep desire to understand or to help the child.

How can relationships in schools be improved? How can communication between pupils and adults be enhanced? We need to find a new space and a new medium to reach the third of pupils who currently feel we don't hear, or care. Play can be that new opportunity. Learning and wellbeing in schools are maximised when play becomes a part of everyday education, and that happens by 'using the playful interaction between children and teachers as a starting point' (Pramling Samuelsson & Johansson 2006, p.47).

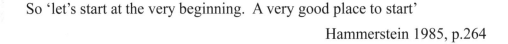

So 'let's start at the very beginning. A very good place to start'

Hammerstein 1985, p.264

and so ...

The beginning is always going to be you, and who and how you are. 'The Playful Teacher' is the heart and the foundation stone of better play in schools. So that is where we will start, in the first of the next four chapters. In the rest of this section of the book I'll be looking more at the ways we can support children at play in school by

△   Being playful

△   Using our communication skills to support play and to boost what
       play is doing for the player

△   Keeping the peace while not stifling the conflict when play breaks out

△   Equipping better play, but with the understanding that **you** remain the
       most important resource there is

KEY POINTS

In schools every adult can be an important relationship figure for children

The whole school approach is vital to the ethos - the 'feel'- of the place

Relationships matter more than anything else in creating happy schools

Relationships in school: *Where do we go from here?*

Training for school staff over-relies on curriculum and teaching and learning studies. Our current understanding from the study of attachment and neuroscience tells us training has to include more on relationships:

- △ We learn in relationships
- △ We learn when we feel safe
- △ We support learning when we understand ourselves better
- △ We support learning when we understand others better

The play-full school would -

- ☺ Believe that the quality of the relationships in schools matters more than anything else
- ☺ Value play experiences for their pupils and value playfulness in their staff
- ☺ Recognise the importance of creating a belief in the value of play across the whole staff group

If you want to know more, try reading:

Fumoto, H. (2011) Teacher-child Relationships and Early Childhood Practice. *Early Years* Vol. 31:1 pp.19-30

Hall, E. & Hall, C. (1988) *Human Relations in Education.* London: Routledge

Kohl, H., & Ayers, W., (2009) *The Herb Kohl Reader: Awakening the heart of teaching* New York: The New Press

Rice, L. (2009) Playful Learning. *Journal for Education in the Built Environment* Vol. 4:2 pp.94-108

UNICEF (2001b) *What Young People Think: Europe and central Asia.* Available at: unicef.org/polls/cee/school/index.html

If you want to understand more, try reading:

Brown, B. (2013) *Daring Greatly: How the courage to be vulnerable transforms the way we live, love, parent, and lead* London: Portfolio Penguin

If you want a top-up to remind you why you work in Education and why play matters, try watching:

School of Rock (2003) Paramount Pictures.

I know being playful is not all there is to being a teacher; and that lying about your CV is never OK: but a sprinkle of the magic of 'anything is possible' can go a long way!

Chapter 15

The playful teacher

It ain't what you do it's the way that you do it, and that's what gets results!

> *"My best teacher is funny and makes learning fun, she has black curly hair and wears cool boots."* English Teachers Network 1997

And on hearing that I want to be in her class too! In schools, relationships between staff and pupils are the most important part of the school's ethos. The staff members are the most important resource any school has. *You* are the most important resource school has.

> Throughout history teachers have played a role more profound and subtle than that of instruction … It is imperative that we never lose sight of the teacher in this personal, interfacing sense as the critical instrument in the educational process. Delors 1996, p.224

Nationally and internationally, the teacher, or the adult working in school, is placed at the heart of the child's experience of education, and is acknowledged (by those who understand!) as the foundation for learning, wellbeing and success. 'The powers that be' are all singing from the same hymn sheet.

> There is simply no way of generating educational improvement more effectively than by having the best qualified, most highly motivated and most talented teachers in the classroom. Everything should be driven by that.   Education Secretary Michael Gove *in* Bassett,
> Haldenby, Tanner & Trewhitt 2010, p.5

But maybe the movers and shakers in the legislative bodies understand the lyrics and the melody rather differently than the coal-face practitioners. What educational improvements does society hope for and value? More importantly for everyone who cares about education and about childhood: what are the qualifications, motivation and talents that are essential for staff in our schools?

> Given the significance of play in the lives of children, both from their own accounts and from the brain sciences, it would seem that it should, as a minimum, be part of the common core of knowledge that every adult needs when working with children.   Lester & Russell 2008, p.13

I absolutely agree. Much more theory on training courses about play and learning please, for those working with all ages. But more important than knowledge about play is an ability *to* play!

In this chapter we will think about how we can become more playful and how to observe children while being open to their playful communications.

THE QUESTIONS TO CONSIDER ARE:

GIVING OURSELVES TIME TO BE PLAYFUL

Some children (and many adults? Or adults at many times - the run-up to exams, the approach of an inspection, the day after an all-night marking marathon) find playfulness eludes them, so modelling our own playful ways of interacting can give others permission to be playful too. Can we allow our playfulness to become part of our educator selves?

OBSERVING PLAY:
LEARNING ABOUT THE INNER WORLD OF THE CHILD

When we want to understand more and we believe, as the last chapter hopefully demonstrated, that relationships matter more than anything, how will that alter our observations of play? Can we really listen, with open eyes, ears, minds and hearts? And will this make it more likely we will be able to develop positive relationships in schools?

FOR THE DAYS WHEN PLAYFULNESS ELUDES US

As it surely will; and for some of us that may feel like a pretty permanent state of affairs. Playfulness can be catching for those of us who have not yet caught it, or it can feel very much out of our comfort zone or completely false. So how can we develop our playfulness? Or find it again when it appears to have gone AWOL? How can we make sure that our playfulness is not at the expenses of anyone else's feelings?

GIVING OURSELVES TIME TO BE PLAYFUL

Play matters, and therefore so does being a playful adult: an adult able to support the development of playful skills and attitudes in the children we meet. Remember in Chapter 12 we thought about how the way we adults model behaviours and beliefs is an important element of teaching? And in Chapter 6, we learned how important play is for adult health and wellbeing. So being playful is good for us as well as being helpful in our work with children. Being playful, showing an on-going joy in the act of playing, is about giving pupils permission to be that way too. Sherman (2015, p.147) lists some great ways to practice being playful, among which are:

➡   being spontaneous

➡   telling jokes

➡   taking some small risks

➡   getting something wrong and seeing the funny side
        (risky stuff for some of us?)

She also suggests that allowing ourselves to feel our feelings as fully as we can, reminds us how children feel. Her final piece of advice on being playful? 'Ignore this list of activities because you are not interested in doing them!' (*ibid*). Because, as we know from Mark Twain (Chapter 1) the nature of play means it is only play if we choose to freely act that way.

The playfulness showed by an adult permits play in their presence, and lets pupils know that this teacher, dinner lady, caretaker and so on will be accepting of play when it appears in all of its guises (or most, anyway - there are times and places not for playing).

Do you remember a teacher who made lessons fun? Not just because they planned for lots of interesting and practical activities in sessions, but because he or she was fun to be with and could be spontaneous and demonstrated wit and good humour?

> *"My favourite teacher was my freshman math teacher. He was one of the goofiest people I ever knew ... I felt most comfortable in the environment he set up and it was fun every day."*   English Teachers Network 1997

The comments left by pupils on the 'Best Ever Teacher' page of the English Teachers

Network site seemed pretty much split 50:50 about what made a great teacher: their caring, and respect for pupils, and the passion for their subject were recognised, but so also were their humour and ability to make learning fun. The positive comments include how playful staff can create an inclusive, cohesive classroom team. And the science advocating for the positive brain-enhancing benefits of humour mean that including humour in the classroom is 'a no-brainer' (Cozolino 2014, p.81).

The charity Barnado's (2008) asked over 100 teenagers about how pupil-teacher relationships could be improved. 31% felt teachers could be more lively, and make lessons more interesting. A third of us need to liven ourselves up? Or maybe I need to liven myself up a third of the time? I guess I will not be all that I want to be all of the time. I recognise that some of the things I am timetabled to teach are not as inspiring or engaging to me as some others. When I'm not excited by something, I know I don't feel as good about the way I present it. That's when I 'sneak' in something I do find amusing or of interest, because as I have grown older it is easier to allow that 'Life is too short not to be having some fun'.

You've probably noticed that I offer you a story about Oz, or about some of the children I have known, when I get the sense that the words and the theory alone might start to befuddle your brain (because they certainly had mine). For me I find that watching others play, remembering when I played, or imagining how I could turn something on its head until it becomes absurd or ridiculous, can change my emotional and even physical state. As I write this what came to mind was that age-old custom of drawing a moustache on a serious picture; sometimes we feel an impulse to lighten the mood or to make ourselves smile. And the good thing is that once we reach early adolescence, we can complete anarchic and unacceptable actions in our minds without any of the probable external consequences but with some of the internal consequences of amusement, satisfaction and a sense that 'I am an outrageous devil-may-care rebel, albeit disguised as a responsible, serious educator!'

Another survey by the National Foundation for Educational Research (Chamberlain, George, Golden, Walker & Benton 2010) asked over 200,000 pupils about their experience of school. Overall less than half the pupils thought their teachers made lessons fun and interesting. They did not have Mr Herr as their teacher then:

> *"The best teacher I ever had was my eighth grade science teacher, Mr. Jack Herr. He was the funniest person I had ever known in my life, every class was fun and I actually learned stuff about science".*
>
> English Teachers Network 1997

Of course 'interesting' and 'playful' are not interchangeable words. But playful lessons are likely to be interesting, and playful teachers or adults most probably make the things they talk about interesting and fun, and help pupils 'actually learn.'

Hyvonen (2011) describes 'playful teaching' as a 'rich and comprehensive developmental' continuum for learning (p.77). In this model, the role of the adult moves from 'leading play', through 'allowing play', to 'affording play'. In other words the member of staff uses the appropriate level of play provision from a choice between:

➡ Choosing and/or initiating play (leading, teaching, skill-based)
➡ Letting play happen
      (allowing through a responsive, integrated approach to play and work)
➡ Providing rich opportunities for play
      (affording or making sure of play as the best way to learn)

The playful teacher harnesses the power of play when appropriate, and notices when a child is playing and how that play is complementing or guiding the learning.

Hyvonen believes that the children follow the lead of the adult. She observes that pupils will play when that is the task they are given, grab chances to play in between and alongside directed activities, and, when afforded opportunities to do so, they will wallow and immerse themselves in play. So simple things, like asking pupils to be playful by introducing fun activities or verbal interactions (teacher-led play), can increase the interest of the lesson. And allowing play to seep through the cracks can enliven the content, the learning, the learners and, importantly, the instructor! Remember how this *will* happen anyway, as we heard in Chapter 10? So why not acknowledge it, build it in and celebrate it? Or afford a bit of wallow time and let the children play, with ideas, possibilities, responses and alternatives.

A frequent play observer will notice how learning and lesson content seeps into play too and can transform or be transformed until it means something to the player and then, probably, gets a firmer grip in the memory and a better fit in the brain's structural organisation (*see* Chapter 12 again to refresh your memory on how play makes for neural re-organisation). Our inclusion of play opportunities matters for the child; but they also contribute towards better relationships in schools. Play is one of the major ways we build and maintain relationships. And, as we heard in the last chapter, relationships in school *really* matter.

Playful adults who join with children in playful interactions convey their acceptance of a child's right to play and of the value of play for children and young people. Adults who can play are accepted by children as someone who understands, and who has not forgotten that play matters more than anything! Playing alongside, without taking over, playful responses that are not sarcastic or unkind and hurtful, are ways we can demonstrate our interest in the world of our pupils and our efforts to understand them and to relate to them in their own natural, developmental language of play.

In a programme for student teachers, Bredikyte (2012) wanted to look at the experience of student teachers as they joined in a child's play. The students reflected on their experiences (of playing with children). The findings of the programme stressed the importance of the adult's 'active 'in role' participation' and 'emotional involvement'. This active, emotional engagement (playfulness), was coupled with the need for the adult to also be play-observer. The students described how they had to 'learn to be involved in play and to be able to observe the whole situation as if from the outside at the same time' (*ibid*). Their learning about the role of the adult in play included several important points, the understanding that playing with children:

➡ can be fun but can also be a 'challenge'
➡ means learning a whole new way of communicating
➡ demands that we take a risk and try out roles and pretences
➡ offers time to build relationships and to be equal partners in the play
➡ helps us to understand the child better

They also realised that:

➡ adults so often and easily change the play and how the child
     might behave in response
➡ children expect you to 'really' play "*not just 'pretend' that
     you are playing ...*"   (*summarised from Bredikyte 2012*)

The findings bring together the rewards for the children, the challenge for the staff and the benefits to the adult-child relationship. Not many interventions in schools recognise or value 'the development of all participants (both children and adults)' (*ibid*).

Whether watching play or being invited into the play, the adult can enhance or stifle the play, shorten or lengthen the time a child wants to stay at play, and make a child feel good or bad about themselves and their play. Observing play it is easier to stay in the role of 'witness' and 'bystander'. It does not mean you have to be 'neutral'; it is not the role of UN peacekeeper (it may involve that too - but that is not all there is to it). In your role as observer of play you can empathise with a child, root for a child, celebrate with a child and be surprised by the twists and turns of the unfolding play of a child. You just don't 'fix it', 'make it better', 'rescue' anyone or make it 'nice' for everyone (much more about the UN peacekeeping role and the 'play nicely' rule in Chapter 17, on creating safe play spaces).

When you are press-ganged into action as playmate your role is to play, follow the lead of the child, and have fun. For some of us that is hard, for others it is easier: but for quite a few of us it is such good fun we don't notice that we have actually taken over. Some children who are invited to join in a game are just like those of us who only want to play if we can be 'boss.' These children may be very skilled at taking over and so charismatic and socially adept that other children accept their megalomania. Other children do not have the charm, the cunning, the skills of successful leadership and inclusion to bring others along as they take over the play world. These children may find themselves ejected from the play group and excluded from returning.

As adults-in-charge it is harder for children to curb our enthusiasm and contain our advance on the goal of ultimate ownership of the play. Learning to play is a skill like any other. In social play the learning is fostered by the group: 'you need to be like this if you want to play in this group'. When an adult, and an adult normally in a position of authority, leadership, direction and power, enters the group, the dynamics are not the same. The adult has to monitor their own engagement in the play, both *stepping back* when taking over and *stepping up* when not engaging fully.

I think the reason this balance of genuinely joining in but not taking over is so often hard for me is because I really enjoy playing, and because I have lots of ideas about the world that I sometimes forget are not universally shared!

When Effie asked me to play in the cars and to take the role of the robber being chased by the police, I didn't know how fast to drive my yellow truck round the roadway she had set up on the carpet. My beliefs were that the police should catch my car and that 'good' would naturally triumph over 'bad'. But that meant I was talking the play literally - the robber was a robber and the police were the police: and I sided with the police as the good people.

In play the characters can symbolise other people. Maybe for Effie the police were any grown-ups who made all the rules and didn't seem to understand or care about those who got things 'wrong,' and the robber could be a child who made a mistake and is hoping to evade an unfair or unpleasant consequence (and that could mean that they actually stood in for her feelings about her and about me!). And for some of the children I have played with, the police have seemed like the 'bad' people who may have 'taken away' a member of the family, or been used as a threat by adults as people to be feared and the enforcers of punishment on children who dare to be 'naughty'.

So armed with my new understanding about Effie's play world I chose to drive neither too fast, so she couldn't catch me, nor too slow, so she couldn't fail to. When I did this I saw that Effie drove her police car slower than mine so I sped up a bit and so did she - whilst she still made sure she did not gain on my yellow truck. The faster I drove the more Effie started to giggle, giving me the red light to really join in. So the two of us chased our vehicles around and around until the police got a call to another emergency and the robber got to go home, where there was sausage and mash for tea. But the robber's Mum was cross because it got cold when the robber was late home for tea, so then she had to eat cold food and have her Mum tell her off. And the moral of that story is: for me? Join in - but maybe tentatively to start with, until the story becomes clear. And for Effie? Maybe that there are consequences and trouble for people who do things that are not OK - but that those consequences can be bearable and appropriate. I don't need to know what Effie learned about the world through this play, but I do like to think she enjoyed my joining in.

OBSERVING PLAY:
Learning about the inner world of the child

In Chapter 13 observing children and observing play was seen as crucial to good teaching and assessment (as well as for pupils who can't 'do,' for some reason, but who might be able to get involved through observing their peers). When we come back to ideas, it usually shows that it is something that really matters, and that it is worth more than one look.

> Optimally, play in educational situations not only provides a real medium for learning, but also enables discerning and knowledgeable adults to learn about children and their needs.   Moyles 1989, p.67

Observing play and playing with players are unique opportunities for listening to the child. When we know children better, when we learn things about them, it helps us in all sorts of ways. When we understand a child, when we see them in their natural environment of play, it can change how we feel about them. When we see a child choose their own challenges, face their own fears and solve their own problems in play, it can change what we know about them.

When I played with Effie I understood that she was thinking about the big choices in life, the internal conflicts about good and bad and possibly her personal anxieties about being in trouble. Once I had noticed this I saw how she 'played' with these ideas in imaginative role-play with peers, and how the ideas were often reflected in the stories she chose to look at.

Several weeks later I overheard Effie and Robert arguing about how their game should develop. Effie wanted Robert to be the Headmaster while she was the girl who broke his window; and she wanted Robert to keep her behind after school. But Robert wanted to break the window and for Effie to be the one the Headmaster punished while Robert got away. They agreed to both break the window and Robert to get away while Effie took all the blame (thank goodness I had not intervened and told them they could take turns to each have their story acted out - what amazing problem-solvers children can be!). I think I was witnessing Effie facing her own fears and working out solutions through an ongoing process of play.

When children are independently involved in play, it often goes unnoticed by teachers who use this time for other pressing needs in their job … Yet observation of children at play is sure to bring teachers delight as well as insight.   Carter 1993, p.38

This was certainly true for me with Effie. I had not realised her struggles around actions and consequences and was only able to have the time to notice this through her invitation to me to play, followed by glimpses of her engaging in classroom activities. I was then able to experience that 'delight' in seeing the amazingness of us humans in our willingness to take on a challenge and solve our own problems.

Just like the students in Bredikyte's (2012) research, other staff also discover the relationship between the development of the child and the development of the adult when they get to play together. 'Better understanding on the part of staff lead(s) to pupils feeling heard, while pupils [are] more able to communicate and thus help staff to better understand the world of the child' (Woolf 2008, p.58). Staff observing, or joining play, feel more positive about their pupils. They are more positive about the child's 'ability to work through conflicts and communicate their struggles' and they find that their own 'depth of understanding' of a child increases (*ibid*).

Play opens up a new window into the lives of our pupils. Play opens up a new way for children to see us too;

Letting on we are human, allowing children to enjoy a bit of role-reversal sometimes, does not mean loss of respect for the role of the educator; or a slippery slope to losing control in the classroom. It can mean improved relationships leading to less conflict and more cooperation. Better play in schools leads to better relationships, which is the foundation for creating better schools.

FOR THE DAYS WHEN PLAYFULNESS ELUDES US

How playful are you? Even more important, what do you think that 'playful' means? I imagine we have different ideas about an exact definition, but we might mostly agree that 'light-hearted' and 'not serious' are in there somewhere. *Play* might be a thing that you do while *playful* might be an attitude or a characteristic that you have. Because of the nature of play (discussed at some length in Section 1) you cannot *make* someone play. The 'making' means the activity ceases to be play. You can't make someone playful, and also you cannot make someone *stop* being playful! Before we think about ways we can maybe nurture our inner playfulness, let's take a moment to think about some ways we can be playful and maybe a couple of ways to avoid doing it at anyone else's expense.

I know lots of playful people and I think sometimes some people's playfulness can feel uncomfortable. Particularly if I don't know them yet. I think I 'read' their playfulness and come to some conclusions - I could suspect they are being playful at mine, or someone else's expense. Often people are playful at their own expense, from those who we often appreciate as someone who 'doesn't take herself too seriously' to someone who seems constantly self-deprecating. However I think a caution against being *too* self-deprecating in playful words is worth considering. We can be powerful role models for children, and putting myself down sometimes in playful ways demonstrates my ability to not take myself too seriously; but I think constantly, albeit playfully, 'rubbishing' myself is not how I want a child to learn how to be.

That said, the main thing to be mindful of is of not belittling, making fun of, criticising or offending others by our 'playful' interactions. Words or actions can only be playful if the person receiving the 'playful' communication feels it is playful too! I might affectionately tease a friend or lovingly draw attention to the inconsistency of a family member. Playfulness within safe relationships and between equal holders of power has fewer constraints than playfulness with people outside our closest circle and most certainly with those over whom we hold power. I might feel differently when the person I sit next to in the office playfully mentions that my hair looks like I've been dragged through a hedge backwards, than when my boss walks in and says almost exactly the same thing.

When being playful we need to remember to remain kind and choose our words wisely. Keep in mind that we never want a child to feel 'stupid' or small but rather to feel valued and liked (more on this in Chapter 17 when we look at how to give limits: the things to remember that we look at there are true for us here too). As long as we use playfulness to *enhance* relationships and not to corrode them, most of those we are communicating with have the tolerance to forgive us when we occasionally get it slightly wrong.

A lot of what we learn is 'caught' from our first teachers - our family and their friends. If we had a playful role model early on, chances are we have playfulness as one of our tools in our relationship toolbox. But how do we learn something we don't yet know how to do? You could visit the library and get out a book on it - or more likely do a web search on it and read self-help articles all about it. Or you could spend time with playful people. In other words - children. Most children are playful, most young of mammalian species are playful, so pets are another good place to start. As adults we often feel more comfortable trying out new skills with others who are new to things too. Think how you would describe your current state of playfulness, and then notice that any growth in your use of playfulness or in your comfort around others being playful with you will extend your 'use' of playfulness as an important part of your approach to the children and adolescents you work with.

The same goes for those of us who forgot how to be playful, or who had things happen that buried our sense of playfulness. Try reading some playful books - for adults, or written for children. The *Dr Seuss* books by Theodor Seuss Geisel always do it for me: as a lover of words I find his ability to play with them mesmerising. Or watch a playful film, and try dancing when no-one is watching. Because play is personal, and as adults we may have different play 'types' (described in a list from Stuart Brown in Chapter 6), the best way to practice being playful is to start to notice anytime something inside seems to be suggesting you take a risk or do something pointless or change how you act (and have always acted) when carrying out an everyday task. Try embracing 'daft'; own 'silly'; and wallow in 'indulgent'! Allow yourself to challenge your status quo; accept your own inner voice's challenge - 'Go on I dare you' - and give something different a go. And once you have tried that a few times you might find you are relaxing and doing those small changes more playfully.

So this chapter has taken us from *how to be* in play with a child to *how to be playful* ourselves, and included thoughts about observing and noticing how play can change things for the player when it seems to be about some real-life experience. Before we move forward, let's have a quick recap of things we have learned:

and so ...

Being with the child at play is a personal skill; it is about 'who you can be' and 'how you can be'. There are also techniques that can be added to play opportunities to support the play and also develop language skills, emotional intelligence and social competencies. In the following chapters we will look at how the things we say and the way that we say them can have a powerful impact on the experience of the child and on the relationship we have with them. And how adding some new ways of interacting to the good things we are already doing gives us more tools in our educators' toolbox.

KEY POINTS

Find times to 'witness' play: listen and empathise, don't teach or sympathise

Notice the strengths and difficulties being explored or resolved by the child through her play

Be playful

Be fun to be with

The Playful Teacher: *Where do we go from here?*

We could follow the example of the Northern Ireland Council for the Curriculum, Examinations and Assessment Early Years Enriched Curriculum Evaluation Project, in association with Queen's University, Belfast, who developed the 'Playful Structure' model of education.

△ 'Infuse' our schools with playfulness
△ Enjoy playful interactions
△ Create playful opportunities
△ Allow for spontaneity

From Walsh, G., Sproule, L., McGuinness, C. & Trew, K. (2011) Playful Structure: A novel image of early years pedagogy for primary school classrooms *in* Early Years Vol 31, Issue 2, 2011

The play-full school would -

☺   Embed playfulness into all areas of provision

☺   Support staff in finding their own playful ways of being in the classroom

☺   Include playful in-service training opportunities

☺   Play out together

. . . .

If you want to know more, try reading

The Walsh, Sproule, McGuinness and Trew article (see above) on the Playful Structure way of working

Barnado's (2008) *Don't give up on us: Survey of Barnardo's young people.* Available at: barnardos. org.uk/resources/resources_ students_advertising/dont_give_ up_on_us_childrens_survey.pdf

'Best Ever Teacher' at: English Teachers Network (1997) ETNI etni.org.il/bestteacherever.htm

Bassett, D., Haldenby, A., Tanner, W. & Trewhitt, K. (2010) *Every Teacher Matters* London: Reform Research Trust

Carter, M (1993) Catching the Spirit: Training teachers to be playful *in, Child Care Information Exchange* Vol. 87 pp.37-39

Chamberlain, T., George, N., Golden, S., Walker, F. & Benton, T. (2010). Tellus4 National Report (DCSF Research Report 218). London: DCSF. Available at: nfer.ac.uk/publications/TEL01/

Sherman, L. (2015) *Skills in Counselling and Psychotherapy with Children and Young People.* London: Sage

If you want to understand more, try reading

Anything that makes you smile even though it is daft, silly and doesn't make an awful lot of sense! Then hold onto that feeling.

If you want a 15 minute group or individual training

Seek out playful people and 'catch' their playful ways of being. Maybe it cannot be taught, but playfulness can be caught!

Chapter 16

Communication skills

It is a very sad fact that 33% of children arrive at school without the requisite communication and language skills to take part in school education.

Elizabeth Truss, Education Minister, 2013

Many children need additional support to develop communication skills after they start school. Play is the way children learn both the 'rules' of communication and the nuts and bolts of language skills. It is the relationship in play that develops language skills. *"Your turn and my turn"*: *"You throw and I catch"*; play between pairs or more involves a give-and-take, action-and-response relationship. Just as communication is about both being able to speak, show or tell, and an ability to take in or listen. Play is often the way children communicate, but whether a child is at play, or an adolescent is talking about their experiences or feelings, the way we *listen* to the things they are telling us is the part that matters most. The way you listen and convey that listening - that's what gets results.

In this chapter we will think about how to listen and how to let the child know that you have heard.

THE QUESTIONS TO CONSIDER ARE:

LISTENING SKILLS
WHAT MAKES A GOOD LISTENER?

And what can it do for a child who feels truly listened to? What do children say about our listening in schools? And would they like us to be different?

LISTENING TO A CHILD'S PLAY
DO WE ONLY LISTEN WITH OUR EARS?

Or is there much more to it than that? Can we listen more in order to better understand? How can we give children the message we are really listening?

LISTENING TO A TEENAGER'S STORY

How good are we at listening and not jumping in or diverting the conversation?

When we really listen to understand, how do we relay back to the speaker that we have taken on board what was said?

Listening is one side of communication - responding is the other. Why does our training as educators to question and 'draw out' more information sometimes actually shut down the conversation and the imagination? How do informed responses affirm the child?

QUESTIONS, QUESTIONS, QUESTIONS?

Questions may help children who are working, but are they as important when they are playing? Are some questions about play just too hard to answer?

STATEMENTS, STATEMENTS, STATEMENTS!

Can statements convey interest without breaking the spell? Are there 'techniques' for adding language to the play of a child? Are the ways we speak to babies sometimes powerful ways of communicating with older children too?

LISTENING SKILLS

When I ask you to listen to me and you start giving advice,
you have not done what I asked.
When I ask you to listen to me and you begin to tell me why I shouldn't feel
that way, you are trampling on my feelings.
When I ask you to listen to me and you feel you have to do something to
solve my problem, you have failed me, strange as that may seem.
Listen! All I asked, was that you listen not talk or do - just hear me.

When I Ask You to Listen by Anonymous,

in Bailey & Bailey 1993, p.iv

Listening acts like a thermostat for the child, warming up the most reticent of pupils and cooling down even the most verbose. Feeling heard, or as Siegel (1999, p.89) describes, 'feeling felt,' is the most comforting, reassuring and affirming experience we can offer. Sometimes children feel that they have to make sure they are heard or 'felt' by us through increasing the volume or 'upping the ante'.

But, when you accept as a simple fact that I do feel what I feel, no matter
how irrational, then I can quit trying to convince you and can get about the
business of understanding what's behind this irrational feeling.

Bailey & Bailey 1993, p.iv

Listening skills are important to any relational tasks - teaching included. Teaching has moved on a long way since the days of *"I'll talk and you listen"*. But communication skills still underpin everything in education and in how schools operate. Speaking and listening is the first key skills area in the Early Years/Foundation Stage curriculum and is also the key skill set for effective teaching. Teachers have always been expected to be effective communicators; but often the emphasis has been on the efficacy of the *giving* part of communication rather than on the *receiving*.

Remember the 100 teenagers (Barnados 2008) who were asked: *What could improve your relationship with teachers?* (p.315) 60% felt that teachers could:

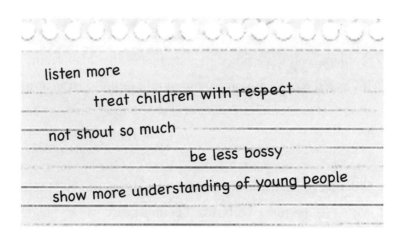

listen more

treat children with respect

not shout so much

be less bossy

show more understanding of young people

Both better listening, and the implicit message better listening conveys (that the speaker matters and that what they have to say is worth hearing), are really important to pupils. Many members of staff in school have a natural talent for relating to people. They really 'listen' to pupils and to their colleagues as well. Others may have had some training in the use of 'counselling skills' such as 'listening in a non-judgemental way' (Welsh Assembly Government 2008, p.8). Whether we are natural listeners or have to practise and focus on the role of listener, listening is the foundation of understanding.

Counselling skills are adopted by many professionals in other settings, because they work! Listening to others helps any group to get along. The skills of better listening are described in a variety of ways:

Reflective listening	Fischer 1981
Active listening	Geldard & Geldard 1997
Empathic listening	VanFleet 2000
Mindful listening	Shafir 2010

The various descriptive terms add up to a complete picture of the better listener. The use of all these skills means that the adult is:

| Really listening - to the feelings as well as the words | Delaney 2009 |
| Listening to understand | Blackard 2012 |

Really listening means the adult listens more than speaks, but also engages actively in the listening so the child knows the adult is truly present. *Listening to better understand* the world of the child means nor deflecting or distracting from the things the child is trying to convey. Accepting the child's feelings and beliefs does not mean you agree and hold those same beliefs; or that you agree those feelings are right for the experience the child is communicating. It *does* mean that the adult accepts and acknowledges that the child believes and feels the way they do.

Kohl (2009, p.302) talks about the 'nuances' of language, and recognises how the 'inflection, tone, modulation and vocabulary' we use influence the pupil-teacher relationship. He sees that for some pupils, school has many negative associations, and thinks that our ability to tune into our pupils and their perspective is central to our supporting their learning and wellbeing. This 'tuning in' involves:

Language	Intuition	
Patience	Intelligence	
Visceral perception	Compassion	*ibid* p.303

Better listening includes how we use these complex skills and how good we are at noticing the 'nuances' in other people's communications; watching body language and facial expressions and noticing the tone, volume and energy in the voice.

LISTENING TO A CHILD'S PLAY

Carla asked a group if she could join them in the home corner playing a shop game. Two of the group said no, they did not want Carla to play. She approached one of the members of staff, standing by her for a moment watching the group, then turned to Miss Jenkins and initiated her own play.

Carla	*We're going on a bear hunt!* (looking conspiratorial, on tiptoes, leaning in towards Miss Jenkins)
Miss Jenkins	*A bear hunt!* (leaning in towards Carla, tensing shoulders and looking around to confirm the 'just us-ness' of Carla's invitation)
Carla	*Stay behind me, don't make any noise* (finger to lips, then pointing to a space behind her)
Miss Jenkins	*Shhhh* (whispering, copying finger to lips, stepping in behind Carla)
Carla	*I'm going into the cave - you stay here and don't make a noise* (pointing where Miss Jenkins was to stand, giving loud instructions indicating their importance)
Miss Jenkins	*You're feeling brave* (sounding impressed in her role as co-hunter) *Reminding me I must be quiet* (whispering the

	last word to convey she understood the instruction)
Carla	*He's out - no-one there* (looking disappointed). *Let's go home* (Carla seemed to find a new focus - again leading with confidence)
Miss Jenkins	*Ah! No-one in,* (reflecting disappointment) *we're going home now.* (reflecting new purposefulness)
Carla	*I'll be back!* (a final warning to the bear, then flashes a smile at Miss Jenkins, and runs off to join a new group in the sand pit)
Miss Jenkins	(smiles back)

Sometimes a child can use an adult as a playmate who 'just is' (not 'just' at all really: there is no "It's not a big deal" about being able to be with, or about being what another person can use in that moment to move forward, or to move forward in life!) to re-group, to play out a fleeting disappointment, or to regain confidence after one of life's everyday knock-backs. Miss Jenkins allowed for Carla's play when her peers had rejected her as playmate. Miss Jenkins did not soothe Carla's feelings, boost Carla's confidence or re-direct Carla with other possibilities. Carla did all of that. While Miss Jenkins listened, waited, followed and trusted Carla to know what to do in her play.

'Mirroring' the non-verbal cues of the child conveys understanding too (Miss Jenkins' tone of voice and her facial expressions mirrored Carla's feelings). Matching the tone and the pace of the communication tells the child that however they are feeling you can manage those feelings with them. You are not there to cheer them up, you are just there to listen in order to understand. Action comes later when the child has been heard.

As the White Rabbit commanded in Alice in Wonderland (Disney 1951) - "Don't just do something! Stand there (and listen)". First listen - maybe later 'do'. As Donald Winnicott (1974) explains: Being always comes before Doing. Knowing how to 'Be' is important if 'Doing' is ever going to helpful or healthful.

LISTENING TO A TEENAGER'S STORY

Mr Okoye walked past the sport's notice board and saw Gethin reading the latest bulletin for the school football team. He stopped because he noticed Gethin looked unhappy and he waited to see if Gethin wanted to talk.

Gethin	*I'm useless* (looking down at the floor, hands in pockets, sounding flat)
Mr Okoye	(looking at Gethin, staying with the flat feeling, choosing to wait for Gethin to say more)
Gethin	*Mum said I'll never make the team and I should 'get over it'. What does she know! She never even came to watch when I was in the under 11's* (now sounding more emotional, maybe anger and frustration, now looking at Mr Okoye)
Mr Okoye	*You don't feel that your mum understands* (reflecting back what he hears)
Gethin	*It's not fair - I don't see why Josh is still playing. He never scores and he can't even run. There's others in the*

	team that aren't any good. Ben misses practice but still keeps his place. Mr Fossey just doesn't like me (more and more animated, frustrated)
Mr Okoye	*You're frustrated. You feel that there may be other reasons you're not getting picked and it feels unfair others are not as keen as you but get in the team anyway* (naming the feeling he hears and sees from Gethin)
Gethin	*It's true! I'm just as good as Rollo and Gary* (now sounding more confident, less frustrated, more reflective, looking into the distance)
Mr Okoye	(looking at Gethin, again choosing to wait for Gethin to say more as he seems to be thinking about something and not looking at Mr Okoye for any affirmation)
Gethin	*I'm going to ask Tony to take me to Parkside and see if I can join the 5-a-side club.*

Mr Okoye did not know Gethin very well: he had him in lessons but was not a tutor in his year group. Mr Okoye did not know anything about Gethin's family or his football ability. What he did know was how to just be with someone, to listen, to communicate that he was listening in order to understand. And he knew how to give someone space to think and time to reflect. Mr Okoye gave Gethin the sense that what he thought, felt and said were worth listening to and worth caring about.

He also gave himself time to reflect on what he might later 'do', if anything, about Gethin's story (remember safeguarding, highlighted on p.X). Mr Okoye did not try and reassure Gethin, solve his problems, boost his feelings of self-worth or make promises about the future that might have been unrealistic. Now he has an opportunity to choose whether to seek Gethin out again to follow up, and to discuss with him if involving his form tutor might help: or to trust that Gethin has someone he could use for support, or that he could carry though his own plan himself. Or, as Mr Okoye was wise enough to know, sometimes it is enough to voice our frustrations out loud and to have felt heard, for us to accept life's challenges and disappointments and move on!

Listening is one side of communication - responding is the other

In my view, the need to acknowledge and understand children's communications is crucial in providing a school environment that is safe enough in which to learn,   Watt 2000, p.67

Communication is about a 'to and fro', a 'back and forth' exchange. It does not have to be words, but acknowledging what you hear is part of the communication process.

The listener's active role in encouraging the speaker means demonstrating the desire to concentrate on the conversation. Giving full attention and not getting distracted may be a big ask in school. Returning to your best ever listening whenever you have had to break off may mean giving an apology, running through a quick recap or just offering an inclusive *"Now, where were we?"*. It is about conveying a genuine interest in listening in order to understand. Delaney (2009, p.160) also anticipates the practical school-specific dilemmas we may encounter when we are attempting to be amazing listeners. Our educator hat means we need to get the pupil 'back on track' as soon as possible. But active listening, being mindful of the child's needs and offering empathy with their feelings and reflection on their words really can 'make a big difference in a busy school' (*ibid*).

QUESTIONS, QUESTIONS, QUESTIONS?

Talking to children who are playing is not the same as talking to children who are working. When a child plays, he or she doesn't need to know the whys and wherefores. When an adult observes play or talks to a child at play, he or she does not need to know why, how, what or when either. And boy, is that hard! Us adults letting go of 'reason' and going with the flow!

> *Sam and Daniel were building a train track. At year 6, it was interesting to see how passionately involved they were in the project. They spoke occasionally but watching them I could not understand why each of them kept taking out the pieces the other had put in and replacing them with different directions of curved track and alternative lengths of pieces. I was also dying to know why neither of them mentioned that this was going on! For 20 minutes Sam and Daniel were engrossed in their play. It was progressing more slowly than it could have done because it was being re-built continually; as fast as a piece of track was going down, it was up, away, replaced and down again. I don't know why they did it that way. I don't know why they did not talk about it, and I don't know if they knew either! I never asked (despite my desire to). Without this seemingly pointless re-arrangement, it could have been built faster, bigger and, hard for me not to assume, better.*
>
> *But the thing is - it does not matter. It was what it was. Purposeful. Satisfying. Sustained. Quirky (like my magic carpet in Chapter 12) and playful.*

In a maths lesson it might be important for both adult and pupil to think about the question: *"Why did you put that decimal point there?"* In free play time, the question *"Why did you put that lion under that bucket?"* only disrupts the child's unfolding story.

Asking lots of questions may convey interest but it can convey a lack of understanding too. Feeling that another person wants to understand you, or is really listening to you does not mean you want to be asked a barrage of questions. Questions make us follow someone else's train of thought, rather than our own. Questions, by their very nature, suggest there must be an answer. Then we get into all the anxieties about the expectations of the person asking those questions. *"What answers are they looking for?"; "Will my answer be good enough?"; "Is this a trap?"*. And questions like:

- can suggest to the child that the right words are available to unlock their feelings or convey their thoughts. And that I expect them to find them and to give them to me. I know I often cannot put into words how I feel or what I think. I think it is because sometimes there *are* no words, and sometimes it is because my mind is not yet clear enough to match words to my experience. So I don't want to convey to others that if they can't tell me, or can't tell me yet, it's because they are too dumb to find the right words. Questions like:

- may mean - *"I'm interested in the choices you make and I would love to understand more as you are so inventive, creative and clever"*. But they may sound to the child as if you find their ideas baffling, unsuitable or just plain wrong. The child may actually hear -

If I ask questions I notice it can make children feel 'interrogated', 'compelled to perform' and 'defensive' (Lathey & Blake 2013). Questions put the onus on the child to help the adult to understand. If our understanding is the child's responsibility, then when we do not, or cannot understand, the child has 'failed'.

So how do we demonstrate interest and show our understanding to the child? Speech therapists, occupational therapists, play therapists, and parenting coaches all use the same technique that parents and grandparents intuitively employ: they 'Say What You See'. *Providing a commentary* (Delaney 2009, p.158) as the child plays, not only conveys our understanding to the player, but builds the structures of understanding in the child's brain.

This way of 'attuning' to someone lowers levels of the stress hormone cortisol (this chemical is part of our 'fight or flight' mechanism, and prepares our bodies to get away or to hit out). At the same time, it raises levels of oxytocin. Oxytocin creates the opposite feelings to cortisol; it is a chemical that supports our 'calm and connection response' (Moberg 2003, p.23), meaning we feel we can stay around and be close to others. Now that I know that giving language to children helps them process what just happened, I understand more why giving 'supportive and friendly psychological feedback' (*ibid* p.126) is such a great idea. It is a bit of an aside here, but Moberg also assures us that oxytocin is released when we experience fun too!

Lathey & Blake's *Small Talk* book (2013) is about encouraging language development in very young children. It formalises the interactions we see all around us wherever babies and adults are present. Rather than leaning into the pram and asking the baby, *"Why have you pulled off your mitten?"* most of us, without plan or forethought, say *"Look at you! You pulled off your mitten!"* Simply, and naturally, we *'Say What We See'*.

STATEMENTS, STATEMENTS, STATEMENTS

Written by a speech and language therapist, the *Small Talk* book is about improving early language development. This may feel outside our remit in schools. Increasingly, however, Early Years staff are finding that children arriving at school lack basic skills in communication, as the quote from Elizabeth Truss indicates on p.329. The *Small Talk* 'Say What You See' technique relies on:

Play	language is developed naturally and developmentally through play
Language	giving words to the child (rather than asking them to give you words) puts the child's thoughts into words as they play

Alongside Delaney in the UK and elsewhere (*see above*), Chaloner (2001, 2005, 2006) uses the same technique in schools in the US. He trains school staff to support children as they play by giving language to what they see. As well as 'Saying What You See' when talking to the child about actions as they play, Chaloner (2001, pp.373-4) encourages school staff to talk to children about their feelings, needs and beliefs. He explains that giving the child language as they play helps the child to process their experience:

> When teachers model this process by giving language, they literally loan
> their brain's language and cause-effect thinking centres to the child. This
> builds connections between the child's feeling and thinking centres in the
> brain critical to impulse control. Chaloner 2005, p.2

'Loaning your brain' is a great way to think about what we're doing when we add language and adult processing skill to the play of the child.

As parents and carers, we 'loan our brains' to babies and toddlers as we describe what a child is doing and how the child is feeling. We also exaggerate our facial feedback to help the child learn about feelings, and to communicate our understanding of the child. We accompany *"That surprised you!"* with wide eyes, raised eyebrows and an open mouth. We let the child *feel felt* - *"Look and Listen - my words and face are saying this is what that feeling is"*. Then our face relaxes into a reassuring smile. Our message is: *"We managed that feeling …"*: *"Together we got through"*: *"It's OK now, look how I'm smiling."*

All of this wonderful stuff is going on in homes all over the world, but maybe not so much in classrooms or playgrounds across the UK! But if this 'brain loaning' and non-verbal feedback support of early learning does *not* happen for any reason in the home, or if there was not quite enough of it, or the child needed more than most children do, then a huge opportunity for development has been missed, and school becomes even more critical as a place where the child can have a second chance (Bombèr 2007).

We are discovering that relationships in schools are so important in offering catch-up, top-up and make-up time and experiences to pupils who need new or more opportunities for achieving the positive outcomes of empathic early relationships. We can provide attachment relationships, and we can allow time for play, and we can use our listening skills as we work with children in our schools. Once you've used them a few times, you'll find that verbal commentary, feeding back emotions and loaning your brain's ability to process life become part of the toolbox that you use naturally in your everyday interactions in school.

Parenting-like ways of supporting emotional development come more naturally to some than to others. I chose Early Years as my 'born to do this' place of work (or did it choose me?). Nurture in the nursery is a given, I think: but in year 11 with sixteen year-olds? Maybe not so much - but it's still so important. I find 'Say What You See', *name the feeling* and *mirror that look* all feel comfortable and natural with littlies but take longer to find a natural ease with when I'm working with older children. But it is never too late to respond to children in these ways at any age, and more of the good stuff won't do any child - or young person - any harm. It's a bit like the government's initiative on free school dinners which I mentioned in Chapter 2: if we give every child a nurturing, healthy meal of understanding and wisdom, then we will catch those that need it most by including every child in our safety net.

> [*Saying What You See is*] a simple, powerful way of working with children that's as applicable to the challenges of adolescents as it is to the challenges of infants.   Teacher, USA, *in* Blackard, 2012 (*my parantheses*)

In Blackard's (2012) manual for parents and teachers, the 'Say What You See' technique is used as a parent or teacher coaching tool. Blackard's background is in play therapy, and like other play therapists, she adapts the 'Filial Therapy' model of family play therapy work (Van Fleet 2000; Landreth & Bratton 2006) for use in schools. Filial Therapy is an attachment based 'psycho-educational' programme (therapeutic & educational), where play, empathic listening skills, and consistent structures and boundaries are used by parents in individual weekly therapeutic play sessions with their child. Filial Therapy has been adapted for school-based programmes; models such as Kinder Training (White, Draper & Flynt 2003), and Better Playtimes (Woolf 2008) to train school staff to use the same skills that helps parents 'tune in' to their child to develop new skills for use in the classroom. Blackard explains how an 'understood child' not only feels felt, but also feels connected - one of our basic human needs, and critical for learning.

> Everything children *do* and *say* is a communication from their world to ours. From what they do and say, we can understand what they *think* and *feel*. Children love to be understood; even children who want to be a mystery feel connected when you say, *"You're just a mystery to me!"*
>
> Blackard 2012, pp.13-14

and so ...

These responses to play may seem very different to our usual responses at work. But once staff have used the communication skills in play, they usually find they add them to all the skills they already use to communicate in formal teaching times.

KEY POINTS

*Don't just do something - stand there **and listen***

*Listen and **accept** the communication: it has meaning to the child*

***Say what you see**: it's all that we can say for certain and asks for no answer*

***Loan your brain** by naming feelings and noticing relationships*

Communication skills: *Where do we go from here?*

We could read and take on board some of the messages from *Children, Their Voices and Their Experiences of School: What Does the Evidence Tell Us?* (Robinson, C. (2014) York: Cambridge Primary Review Trust).

> Teachers have a responsibility towards making decisions that are in children's best interests: they also have a responsibility to respect children's rights and to listen to, and acknowledge, their opinions and perspectives.
>
> (p.18)

> Schools need to provide ways of listening to pupils about matters important to the pupils themselves, and not just about issues which adults in the school consider to be important. (p.23)

> A school's listening culture should be based around respecting the views of the whole school community and ways of actively listening to staff and pupils, including those with limited communication skills and those who may not agree with the dominant cultural norms of the school. (p.23)

The play-full school would -

☺ Recognise that play can be a form of communication

☺ Have staff who really listen to children when they play

☺ Have managers who really listen to their staff

☺ Ensure all staff have access to training in active listening skills

If you want to know more, try reading

Blackard, S., (2012) *Say What You See For Parents and Teachers: More hugs. More respect. Elegantly simple* US: Language of Listening

Chaloner, W. B. (2001) Counselors Coaching Teachers to Use Play Therapy in Classrooms: The Play and Language to Succeed (PALS) early, school-based intervention for behaviourally at-risk children. *in* Drewes, A., Carey, L. & Schaefer, C. (Eds.) *School-based Play Therapy.* New York: John Wiley & Sons.

Chaloner, W. B. (2005) *Play Therapy in US Elementary and Preschools: Traditional and New Applications for Counselor and Teacher Use.* Available at: frontier. net/~barrychaloner/downloads/ play_therapy_us_9-21-05.pdf

Chaloner, W. B. (2006). *One Therapist's Journey Integrating Child-Centered with Attachment-Based Approaches to Play Therapy with At-Risk Children.* Available at: pals4schools.com/downloads/ therapist_journey_1-19-06.pdf

Truss, E. (2013) *A third of pupils 'can hardly communicate' when they start school: Education minister risks fresh clash with nursery chiefs.* In The Daily Mail, by James Chapman. published: 23:46, 22 April 2013. Available at: dailymail. co.uk/news/article-2313214/ Education-minister-Elizabeth-Truss-attacks-nurseries-A-hardly-communicate-start-school. html#ixzz2duiQ2gXo

When I Ask You to Listen *in*: Bailey, D. S. & Bailey, D. R. (1993) *Therapeutic approaches to the Care of the Mentally Ill* (Edition 3). Philadelphia: F. A. Davis Company

If you want to understand more, try reading

McKee, D. (2015) *Not Now Bernard* London: Andersen Press

If you want a 15 minute group or individual training, try watching

Julian Treasure's TED 2011 talk '5 Ways to Listen Better' on the TED website, ted.com/talks or on youtube.com

Chapter 17

Keeping play safe: thinking about limits

So far we have reflected on our adult role in play, and the balance we need in order to keep the play safe for everyone; while not over-regulating it, or making it sterile. A lot of what I have been saying throughout the book has suggested an 'Adults Keep Out!' sign on the doorway to play. Then other times I have been advocating that we jump in with enthusiasm, lean in and listen, or join the ranks as a foot soldier. And I have extolled the virtue of adult play, and playful adults.

I hope you have followed the magical mystery tour into the nature and importance of play, and are with me here in seeing that all of these different things can be true. I would like to imagine that the sign might look more like, 'Adults welcome, but Keep your agenda Out'? For me, as a therapist or as a teacher (or as a family member or friend), I have to hold in my mind as the adult playing or observing play that I 'keep out' unless and until my adult brain, or my professional responsibility, tell me to limit the play in order to keep everyone safe.

I won't always get this right. My brain will miss things; my ability to see ahead will fall short. I will feel overly-protective, my fear will sometimes cloud my judgement.

In my work life if I sometimes err on the side of caution, I feel fine about not being perfect, or not being the best play provider in the world. I am excited though by the way I have learned over time to extend my understanding about play, and, by knowing more, have challenged myself to notice my discomfort, assumptions and anxieties: and, by doing so, have created more space for children to play and to be safe. It feels good to believe that I am better now *at* playing, and better at *allowing for* play. Better play can happen when I'm around, and I can still be the limit setter and the safety officer, the peacekeeper and the mopper-upper of the spills and the tears.

I sometimes admit to my tendency to be 'bossy'. And if *I* call *myself* bossy, it saves my friends and family from having to do so! I know that one of the things I enjoyed about being in charge of a bunch of three- and four-year-olds at play was just that: being in charge. I like rules and I feel more comfortable when I know what those rules are. Whether I'm giving rules or being given rules I think I have a brain that finds it relaxing to have order and structure. But before I ever thought about play outside of a way to blow off steam and a way to teach Early Years curriculum, I had an in-born sense about the value of play. I thrive within structures, follow policies and procedures and I am very task-focussed and outcome driven in real life. Very! But in play, I am comfortable with being uncertain and aimless. More than comfortable; my play life is that other world where I can just be me and it has to be aimless, or to have a fantastical, useless and gloriously ridiculous aim; or it won't be play.

But enough about me! How about you? Before looking at what others have to say about limits, just take some time to reflect on your feelings about the giving and the being given limits.

In this chapter we will think about ways of keeping play safe that change the messages we sometimes unintentionally give about how we value play and what we believe about the play of our children.

TALES FROM OZ 🐾

'No Oz- it's not for you!'

This is something that proves to be an on-going challenge for me with Oz. Apologies that this example from my canine experience is clearly not the same as my supervision of young humans: but it does help me to see how I am in possibly 'risky' situations, and how that impacts on the subject of my anticipatory fear! As I am often reminded, 'Your anxiety travels down the lead!'

On meeting new dogs, I anticipate Oz will invite them to play in an overly dominant and boisterous way, because that was what he did when I first got him. I become tense, hold the lead more tightly and try to avoid the many situations that are most likely to be the very practice Oz needs to try out better strategies. This, I know, makes Oz tense. I can see his brain whirring: "She's seen danger - where is it? What does she see in this that I'm somehow missing? Oh well - better be on full alert." This of course makes Oz more likely to try and dominate and make sure he keeps us both safe. Worst of all is my inability to wait until a limit is required. Without reason or rhyme I hear myself say: "No Oz", or my favourite doggy limit "Not for you!" Clearly that suggests I assume Oz is going to break a limit. But I don't wait for evidence that he is. My evidence is my fantasy of possible (negative) imminent events!

Others who walk Oz tell me how good he is meeting new dogs, how much he has changed and how chilled out he is. How do I not notice he is older and wiser and more able to tackle 'risky' situations without his human holding him back? Says maybe more about me than it does about Oz or about the situations we are in?

THE QUESTIONS TO CONSIDER ARE:

WHY LIMIT THE USE OF LIMITS?

Why and when do we need limits? What is the problem with giving too many rules?

PROVIDING LIMITS

Which boundaries can we create that will keep a space safe for play, while also keeping it open enough to allow for play and the risks and challenges that it inherently brings?

AN IMPORTANT DETOUR

In this chapter we will take a detour (we are still on our magical playbus excursion), where we find out about one useful model of considering the basic needs of children (of humans at all ages too, in truth). This is helpful here because when we can hold in our minds (and hearts) the things children need and how they may be communicating those needs, we are more able to be sensitive to those needs when we have to limit the way the needs are being expressed. Then we will get back to the matter of limit setting.

THEM'S THE RULES

Are there ways we can give limits that make the limits clearer? Can this help children to feel safe?

THEM'S THE RULES - BUT I GET HOW YOU FEEL

Are there ways of giving limits that help children feel understood and valued? How does validating a child's feelings but still keeping your limits help build your relationship with the child?

AND THIS IS HOW IT'S GOING TO BE

Are there models out there we can learn from on how to be an effective limit setter? Happily there are - and we can look at ways of giving limits and rules to players that can really change how the child may feel about being sanctioned or being disrupted during such an important activity as play. What happens when we are wise and kind in our management of limits?

COMPETING NEEDS AND INCLUSIVE PLAY

What happens when we have more than one playing child? How do we provide limits to keep a group of children safe while still allowing for some tension and conflict to exist? And why does this matter?

So, on with the show ... or rather, take your seats: the bus is leaving for the next stop on the tour.

WHY LIMIT THE USE OF LIMITS?

Every limit or rule is one less thing for a child to find out for himself. Too many adult imposed rules stop children deciding on their own rules. Play is all about finding out; sometimes play, like life, is a place where we may have to learn a painful lesson. It really hurt when I hit my head on the concrete floor of our coal bunker (*as mentioned already in* Chapter 4), and what I learned was that concrete, gymnastics and me adds up to 'accident waiting to happen'! Keeley (2009), talking about life in general, suggests that we all need 'that which keeps us safe (physically, emotionally, psychologically and spiritually)' (p.2) and also -

> ... a space which by its nature is open to exploration, possibility, learning and energy ... in which of course, we might also experience the very natural exploratory discomfort.   *ibid*

In other words - we all need a play space for experiencing and exploring 'safe uncertainty'. 'Best Play' (NPFA, CPC & PLAYLINK 2000), The National Playing Fields Association charter, offers a set of guidelines for quality play provision. Two of their points concern the need for a balance between safety and uncertainty:

● *The provision recognises the child's need to test boundaries and responds positively to that need*

● *The provision manages the balance between the need to offer risk and the need to keep children safe from harm*

Like the 'Best Play' guidelines, the 'Playwork Principles' (Playwork Principles Scrutiny Group 2005) include advice about safe provision and the role of the adult.

> Playworkers choose an intervention style that enables children and young people to extend their play. All playworker interventions must balance risk with the developmental benefit and wellbeing of children.

Taking care of play is all about balancing the needs of the children, their need for a safe environment, against their developmental, social, physical, spiritual and psychological need for play. Play is a place for experiencing fear, failure, fall-outs, flops and fiascos in a way that would be far more painful to body and soul in the real world. But where the boundaries of the opportunity for risk and challenge are is up to the adults.

PROVIDING LIMITS

Limits are there to ensure safety - safe bodies, safe relationships, safe feelings, safe environment and safe resources. Everyone, players and observers, need to know they are safe, and that they are comfortable enough to carry on. The 'window of tolerance' needs to be extended, but not breached. In play times, we can set different limits from those we set in work times (or in the supermarket, choir rehearsal, great-grandma's house and so on). Maybe you never thought about that before. Can you imagine that different rules for *play* and for *not play* works? I know it took me some time to agree with some rules being different. 'No cheating' is an important rule for work, but for play it might not be so important and might put an end to fun and finding out.

How much can or should adults legitimately intervene in children's play? My judgement would suggest a sliding scale from 'not at all' to 'as little as necessary'.   Hughes 2012, p.126

In play, children experience 'natural and logical consequences' (Dreikurs, Grunwald & Pepper 1971, p.80). Through this connection of action with outcome or sanction -

> the child experiences the consequences of his own behaviour in such a way that he will relate pleasure and pain only to his behaviour and not to the intervention of anyone else.   *ibid*

We reflected on the natural sequence of action and outcome in Chapter 3, where the literature confirmed what we already knew from our classrooms and playgrounds; that if children don't 'play nicely', other children don't play with them anymore. The 'social order' is the policeman of peer play. Dreikurs at el believe that 'only in moments of real danger is it necessary to protect the child from the natural consequences of his ... behaviour' (*ibid*).

AN IMPORTANT DETOUR

Maintaining Sanity in the Classroom (Dreikurs et al 1971) describes techniques for everyday use to improve relationships in schools. The book is certainly not a recent contribution to the debate on behaviour management, but the principles of matching adult responses to the underlying motivation of the pupils is still a relevant and powerful way of working. Dreikurs et al believe that if we understand the *reasons* why a child just said or did something unacceptable, then our response will be more in tune with the child's needs. Like the *'Say What You See'* technique, the *'Respond to the Need'* technique helps children feel understood.

Children's needs are complex and unique, and they depend on the context and the relationship. The framework that Dreikurs et al use is similar to 'The Crucial Cs' (Bettner & Lew, 1990). Their 'C's are four essential areas that children need in order to survive and thrive:

Courage	I can handle what comes
Connect	I belong
Capable	I can do it
Count	I matter

Everyone needs to feel brave, able, of value and that they belong.

➡   Knowing we have *courage* helps us to face life's challenges, to be optimistic about our chances and to feel good about ourselves.

➡   Knowing we are *connected* means we know there are others who care and who can help. We believe we have friends and this means we must be likable.

➡   Knowing we are *capable* makes us feel good about ourselves. It makes us feel independent and also able to be of use to others. It is the basis of self-belief.

➡   Knowing we *count* makes life feel worthwhile. It means we feel recognised as unique and valuable. If we count in the world, we know that we matter and that we would be missed.

Let's remember that everything a child says and does is a communication about his or her thoughts feelings, beliefs and needs. Having a framework to guide our understanding of the beliefs and needs behind the behaviours can be really helpful.

If the behaviour or words suggest that the child needs to feel that they count or that they have courage, we can respond to that need rather than to the specific thing the child has said or done.

In play, we adults have time to reflect on things as they happen. We don't need to have an agenda for outcomes, or to get somewhere that is defined from the start. We are not in the driving seat, following a route or needing to be somewhere. We are passengers, along for the ride, noticing the view and wondering where the player is going. In a lesson when a child says *"I just can't do this,"* I know without thinking that at different times I will have said things like:

    (a)   *Well, you could do it yesterday*

    (b)   *I'll help you*

    (c)   *Leave that one out and go onto the next one*

I might respond unhelpfully (a) or helpfully (b). *"I'll help you"* might be the very right answer sometimes for some children. Other times it might be the answer I know best (remember the need I might have of finding a learner so I can be a teacher described in Chapter 9?). This answer could in some cases reinforce a (misplaced) belief a pupil has that they are not able. Or, I might respond in a positive way that addresses the practical difficulty (c); but this still doesn't quite 'touch the spot', because it doesn't address how the child might be feeling or offer the opportunity for the child to know I believe in him and his internal capacity to struggle for a bit longer than he thinks. In play I have learned with time and practice to say something more reflective:

    (d)   *You think you're no good at doing these*

    (e)   *You feel fed up it's not working for you*

    (f)   *You believe that is too hard for you*

These are responses that process the child's experience and acknowledge it for what it is *in that moment*. Responses that help the child be in touch with their needs, feelings, and beliefs (Chaloner 2001) and let the child know I understand, care about, or am listening in order to understand them.

In work time we often respond to practical, adult-led expectations. In play we can reflect on the thoughts, feelings, and beliefs of the child. The communication in this case is about the child's need to feel capable, and the pain of feeling a failure. In work time, we have goals which need achieving, so when a child says *"I'm not doing it anymore! - I'm giving up"*, I might have my sights set on *my* needs for the end of the lesson (the school targets, external expectations and so on and so on) and respond:

(g)   *I know you can do this*

(h)   *I need all twenty done by the end of this lesson*

Sometimes my needs and the needs of the child can coincide (g). I get my lesson outcome and she gets to succeed after hearing I believe in her. Sometimes my needs feel pressing and I rely on our relationship to encourage compliance (h). But read with a different tone of voice, response (h) can sound more like *"I don't care about you and I'm not listening to what you are saying."* 'It's not what you say it's the way that you say it' (like 'doing' in Chapter 16) is so very true.

TALES FROM OZ 🐾

Oz (my lurcher) doesn't care if I am saying "You, bad, bad dog" or saying "You beautiful, bestest, most wonderful of dogs". He cares about the tone of my voice and any other non-verbal clues I am giving him. The way I say "No" can have very different results. I have to really mean "No" for Oz to take "No" for an answer. The way I say "In your bed" can mean "You outrageous hound you are so, so cheeky". This 'in your bed' command has Oz running to his bed, sitting for a second then running straight back to me or to whoever he can see that might pat or tickle him. The 'in your bed' that means "You're covered in mud and until you are dry you must stay in your bed" sounds very different, because my tone of voice really means it. And Oz gets the message.

So yes, sometimes *I* need to maintain order rather than 'sanity in the classroom', so that necessary things can be done; and at such times, I may respond to a child thus:

(i)   *Any you don't do now you'll be doing at break when the others are outside*

In schools a child can sometimes get the message: *"This is all about the adults' needs and this is what we do here to make sure it happens."* Just as we can sometimes feel education is all about society's needs, and that things are put in place by 'the powers that be' to make sure they happen! In times when play is the activity however, our goal is to convey our understanding to the child, and the responses might be:

(j)   *You just don't need any more disappointments - you're giving yourself a break*

(k)   *You're stopping right now, you've had enough and you're sitting on your hands to make it absolutely clear*

In play, ideally, we are able to give the child the message: *"This is all about your needs and you know what you need, and that is OK."* And when we start speaking in new and effective ways we can't help ourselves doing it outside play situations as well. *'Say What You See'* and *'Respond to the Need'* communications convey the adult's trust in the child to work out what they need to do through play.

Back to the matter of limit setting

The best way to make sure limits are kept by children is for adults to keep limits consistent. That doesn't mean limits don't have context - 'never on Sundays' or 'only after dinner' are clear, consistent rules. Rules that are different because you are feeling different - *"Not now, I'm feeling fed up,"* or *"Today I'm so happy I don't care if you do"* make life very confusing for a child, and ultimately more difficult for us adults. 'The majority of children respond well to consistency, clear rules, boundaries and fairness' (Delaney 2009, p.9). It is the natural order of social society; those who do not respond readily to fair and clear limits often have developmental and/or emotional needs that can be addressed through the two strands of teaching and play.

'Effective rules are like walls', (Blackard 2012, p.45). A wall is always there to block any movement outside of the space. Doors are not as predictable. Doors are sometimes wide open, sometimes shut and sometimes not quite shut and can be opened by a bit of pushing. Anyone with a child (or a dog) will know that. Blackard recommends that a limit be like a wall - 'walls just are' (*ibid*); if you come up against a wall, and recognise that it is a wall, you don't try and go through it. If you see a door, although it might be shut, or even if it is locked, there is always a chance the door could be opened.

The way that limits are stated can make them sound like a wall or appear to be more like a wide open door, or even a window! Another image of limits that enclose a play space is the netting around a trampoline. As well as keeping players safe, the netting gives freedom for children and freedom for adults. Without the net, the play needs a series of rules and an adult close enough to catch a child in danger of falling. With the net, we can stand back and watch the bigger picture of the play, without the worry of the danger. With the net the children don't have to remember a list of 'do not's, and can jump and bounce and test themselves, and find out what their bodies can do and how courageous they can be.

THEM'S THE RULES!

Another of Blackard's (2012) recommendations is that:

> When you make a rule, omit the reasons. Explaining why to gain children's cooperation often backfires. Reasons create an opening for debate and manipulation.   p.47

This is going back to the analogy of the door: *"Is there a chink in your reasoning on this rule? If there is I can get round it."* *"Don't throw that ball in the classroom, you could break a window"* means, *"If I don't break a window, I can throw the ball"*. This leads to bargaining:

Bratton et al (2006, p.42) ask parents to consider what messages children may get from the way that adults phrase a limit they are setting. The example they give is of telling a child that painting a wall is outside a limit. The way the limit could be phrased includes:

(i)   *It's probably not a good idea to paint the wall.*

(ii)   *I can't let you paint the wall.*

(iii) *Maybe you could paint something else other than the wall*

(iv)   *The wall is not for painting on*

In response, the child may feel that the adult is:

(i)   Unsure

(ii)   Apologetic

(iii) Ready to engage in negotiation

(iv)   Certain, secure in their decision and not willing to negotiate

THEM'S THE RULES: but I get how you feel

As well as being clear and consistent when setting limits, *'Responding to the Need'* changes how the *"No"* feels for the child. Limits are a powerful battleground for adults and children, in my experience anyway - and maybe in yours? It is the area where the power differential can feel most threatening, unfair and persecutory to the child (I remember it well, which shows how enduring the impact of limit-setting can be) and most difficult to manage fairly and dispassionately for us (a work in progress for me, with many a slip-up along the way! How's it going for you?). If our aim is to lower the temperature in conflicts over limits, understanding and acknowledging the needs or feelings of the child 'acts like a fire extinguisher' (Blackard 2012, p.15).

Acknowledging a feeling, letting the child know you understand, when added to the *"No"* changes how the message is received by the child.

You really want to pour water into that sand tray; but that tray is for dry sand

You really don't want to stop playing yet; but time for play is over

You want everyone to listen; but playtime inside is not for shouting

Blackard recommends not explaining reasons for limits and VanFleet (2000) recommends not reeling off a list of limits before children start to play. Anyone who works with children understands that telling children what they can't do makes some children absolutely guaranteed to try out what happens when they do! Giving several rules means some children will then worry about forgetting them, or feel unsure of how far down a line the limit will kick in. These anxieties or uncertainties mean children stop exploring and finding out in order to be 'good'.

AND THIS IS HOW IT'S GOING TO BE

In Filial Therapy (parent-child play sessions, described briefly in the previous chapter) VanFleet (2000, p.27) teaches parents a three-step limit setting sequence, a *three strikes and you're out* model:

- **State the limit** *only after the child breaks a limit or is obviously about to do so for the first time. VanFleet includes an acknowledgment of the child's feelings in this first step*
- **Give a warning** *after a second time of breaking, or being about to break the same limit, tell the child what consequence will be given if it happens again*
- **Enforce the consequence** *on the third break of the same limit*

In play, the natural consequence is removal of the possibility of that limit being broken again. It might be removal of the resource causing the problem, or removal of the child from the area of play, or it may mean the end of that particular time of play for that child. So here's an example of how I would use the three 'strikes' in action:

You want to bury the doll but the doll is not to go in the sand tray.

The doll is not to go in the sand tray and if you put her in there again you will have to put the doll away

The doll is not to go in the sand tray. You have to put her away now and choose something else.

Bratton & Landreth also describe a three step limit-setting process with a memorable acronym - ACT:

(A) *Acknowledge* the child's feelings

(C) *Communicate* the limit

(T) *Target* an acceptable alternative   Landreth & Bratton 2006, p.227

So, these steps might be conveyed in comments such as -

(A) *You really want to bury the doll*

(C) *The doll is not to go in the sand tray*

(T) *You could use the blankets*

VanFleet and Landreth & Bratton diverge on the need to offer an acceptable alternative. VanFleet allows the child to continue exploring the play and to learn by trial and error if there is a way to accomplish their wish but still stay within limits. She trusts and believes in the ability of the child to problem-solve for themselves. Landreth & Bratton feel that telling the child *"You can't do that but you can do this"* or *"You can't use that but you can use this"* helps the child to stay within the limits, and demonstrates the adult's feelings about the child. The adult's response gives the message:

I am not cross, I don't think you are bad, I'm not disgusted, displeased or disappointed with you - you can have that feeling or need, it's just that you can't do it in that way.

I feel that the two strategies are useful along a developmental continuum. I might say to a three-year-old, *"You can't get in the sand pit with your shoes on, but you can take your shoes and socks off and then get in."* I am sure we are always judging, without realising that is what we are doing, 'What can I expect of this child's reasoning skills?' I think I unconsciously now consider, 'How can I give this child a limit that is understood but that is the least directive or limiting it can be?' I would give a sixteen year old the limit *"You can't get in the sand pit with your shoes on"* and not offer him or her an acceptable alternative. They can find that out for themselves! If children are able to do things for themselves, to be creative and resourceful, then we can allow for that. If children don't yet have the cognitive or emotional capacity to manage, then we can support them until they do.

Wise and compassionate people are great limit setters

Marvin et al (1998) have a great slogan for parent coaching: *(Almost) Everything I Need to Know About Being a Parent in 25 Words or Less.* They see four essential qualities for great parenting of a child: being Bigger, Stronger, Wiser and Kind. In limit-setting I have taken these parenting strengths and considered how to demonstrate them in the way we set limits:

△ You are *big enough* and *strong enough* not to need to make the
   child feel small

△ You are *wise enough* not to need to make the child feel stupid

△ You are *kind enough* to want the child to always feel he is liked

COMPETING NEEDS AND INCLUSIVE PLAY

In social play the challenge of limit-setting becomes more complex, more important and more frequent. One child's needs cannot override the comfort (comfortable enough to carry on) or safety of peers. In her enchanting book *You Can't Say You Can't Play* (1992), Vivian Gussin Paley devotes the entire text to her dilemma around the introduction of the rule given in the title into her Kindergarten class. The balance of needs is excruciating to contemplate. Paley asks the older class groups how they feel about the possible new rule: the children are perceptive about the difficulties ahead. Anyone who remembers the importance of play will absolutely understand Lisa's response (p.20) on being forced to let anyone and everyone join in her game:

"But then what's the whole point of playing?"

This one example of adult intervention in limiting the play autonomy of children illustrates the kinds of considerations we have to weigh up and then balance when making rules for emotional safety in play. Often one person's gain may be another person's pain. The children from the classes in Paley's Elementary school came up with many difficulties around imposing the *'You Can't Say You Can't Play'* rule. Their thoughts included:

The rule will be fought over. 'There could be more fights, not less'	(p.35)
Too many children may join in, making play impossible	(p.35)
It would be fairer 'but it would be impossible to have any fun'	(p.46)
It's fair but 'friendship comes first'	(p.57)
'It's a good rule but it could spoil a game'	(p.60)
It takes away choice, privacy, special moments	(p.99)

Emotional safety in play is important but very, very hard not only to enforce, but also to see or judge from the outside.

Making children play together can be as hurtful as allowing children to exclude peers or reject others. One child reflected on Paley's new rule:

"It hurts more if the teacher forces people to play with you."

5th Grade boy, p.101

Children want to be wanted by the other players, maybe more than they want to be allowed to join in play. They are well aware of the different feelings of being invited to play, welcomed into play and being suffered as an intruder into someone else's play space.

The issues of denying the players opportunities for showing favour, or for being kind, or for negotiating the way to resolve the differing desires were raised by Paley's older children. They were unanimous in recognising it was a 'nice' rule, and a fair rule. They were also unanimous in adding a decisive, *"But ..."* The 'but' was often followed by 'not for us', and 'as long as we don't have to do it'! Several children felt that Kindergarten pupils needed the rule because of their age and their developmental needs, but that older children could sort the problems out for themselves, and were also robust enough to manage their feelings when rejection and disappointment occurred. They recognised that it would happen in life out in the 'real' world, and that experiencing it in play helped them prepare for adult life.

Limits in play need to be appropriate to the age and the stage of the players. They need to consider the context of the play. Intervening in play as 'little as necessary' (Hughes 2012, p.126) and giving 'as few limits as possible but as many as necessary' (PTUK 2011) will mean different things to everyone. The culture and ethos of the school set the tone for everything that happens there. Context, age, ability, time, space, resources, and our tolerance as the adult are the parameters in which play in schools occurs. But when social play becomes dangerous play, an adult always steps in. Jarvis (2009, p.191) gives a framework for adult-led, but collaborative, conflict resolution:

- *Approach calmly, stopping any hurtful actions or language*
- *Acknowledge feelings*
- *Gather information*
- *Re-state the problem*
- *Ask for ideas for solutions and choose one together*
- *Give follow-up support as needed*

Being the safety net around the trampoline (play space) is our adult role in play. When children are 'on the bounce' and in danger of launching into a dangerous place, we need to move into a fielding position, to catch them before they fall. When it is appropriate or possible, I believe that the play must belong to the children. Whenever we can, let's give *"You can't ..."* as careful consideration as Paley (1992) gives it in her book. Grab the opportunity when 'Stand well back' best meets the needs of the child at play.

> We must exercise caution and not make play too much an object of adult gaze. Children's play belongs to children; adults should tread lightly when considering their responsibilities in this regard, being careful not to colonise or destroy children's own places for play through insensitive planning or the pursuit of other adult agendas.   Lester & Russell 2010, p.46

and so ...

As keepers of safe spaces for play, and as carers who see the underlying needs behind testing behaviours, we have choices to make. When we put limits in place to keep children safe we have ways of communicating them that ensure our relationships stay safe too. Limits are necessary, and confident communication of rules helps players feel safe (and me as observer, or as adult in charge, feel safe too). If there are limits there need to be consequences, and these consequences need to make sense because they 'fit' with the limit that has been broken. We enjoy play most when we feel safe. So keep play safe but keep it vital (*remember the definition in* Chapter 1?). Safe limits don't mean no spontaneity, uncertainty or risk: they just mean all the good things play offers while keeping everyone safe enough to carry on. And there are so many benefits to getting limit setting right:

> The therapeutic experience of effective limit setting also seems to enhance children's ability to find acceptable ways to channel feelings, take responsibility for their actions, and enhance their self-control and regulatory capacity beyond the playroom.   O'Sullivan & Ryan 2009, p.226

While O'Sullivan and Ryan are talking about play in therapy, they acknowledge it is the same in parent-child relationships too: and I know it is true for us in the classroom as well as in the playroom.

KEY POINTS

Play is just that - play. Pretend behaviour does not obey the same rules as behaviour at other times

Less is more; allow for children to develop their own limits in play

Understand the emotion behind the behaviour and respond accordingly

Be clear and consistent in setting limits and always give logical consequences

Set limits with strength, wisdom and kindness

Keeping play safe: *Where do we go from here?*

In order for changes in practice to take place in the way we decide what limits we need, how we communicate them and what the consequences are for limits that are broken, the language of Government guidance needs to be amended. Currently the UK Government (2015) offers the following guidelines. It states:

> Every school has a behaviour policy, which lists the rules of conduct
>   for pupils before and after school as well as during the school day
> Schools can punish pupils if they behave badly

Can we exchange 'rules' for 'expectations'? And even 'list' for 'set out'? And 'punishment' for 'consequence'? Or any other wording you choose that will keep our schools safe, happy, welcoming and inclusive places to be. And we will *all* do that by creating boundaries to behaviour that are wisely chosen, communicated kindly and firmly kept.

The play-full school would -

☺   Have limits for play that are appropriate to the need for
     freedom and choice

☺   *When appropriate,* communicate expectations playfully

☺   Notice how hard children try to keep limits when they play

☺   Celebrate how children find ways to be creative around limits in play;
     and discover acceptable alternatives for themselves

If you want to know more, try reading

Marvin, R., Cooper, G., Hoffman, K. & Powell, B. (2002) The Circle of Security project: Attachment-based intervention with caregiver–pre-school child dyads. *Attachment & Human Development* Vol 4:1 pp.107-124 Brunner Routledge

NPFA, CPC and PLAYLINK (2000) *Best Play - What play provision can do for children.* London: National Playing Fields Association.

O'Sullivan, L., & Ryan, V., (2009) Therapeutic limits from an attachment perspective *in Clinical Child Psychology & Psychiatry.* Apr; 14(2):215-35

Playwork Principles Scrutiny Group (2005) *Playwork Principles.* Cardiff 2005. Available at: skillsactive.com/our-sectors/playwork/playwork-principles

If you want to understand more, try reading

Shannon, D. (2003) *No David!* London: Scholastic

If you want a 15 minute group or individual training, try watching

Any video of children at play, but the more rambunctious the better! As you watch reflect on how the behaviours make you feel. Can you separate things you find discomforting from things that might hurt a child (body or feelings)? Practice how you might give a limit in new ways. Try the Three Step approaches. Try adding an acknowledgment of the feeling or the wish to the limit and see how that is for you. Like all the practice skills in the last section of this book - practice increases effective and easy use.

Chapter 18

Providing resources

> *"Loads of people in the world don't have toys and they find other ways
> of playing."*   10-year-old boy, IPA Scotland 2011, p.29

As you have probably seen time and time again, one child finding another child leads to play. So children are one critical ingredient of play but I would argue that *you* are the most important resource for play. Your attitude to play, your belief in play and your playfulness are the resources that lead to play happening. Happening in homes, on streets, and in communities as well as in our schools. For most children, *other children* are also important resources for play, and only then in priority come *the things* that can be used in the play. We adults, (parents, school staff and whole communities) provide resources for play by allowing places to be used for, and time to be given over to, play. 'Things' may not be essential, and are sometimes not important, but other times they are very much appreciated.

This chapter on resources feels like it could be an Appendix to the book, as in, a *list of useful resources.* But as we found in the opening chapter, the things are not necessarily the things we might think, and are often not called 'toys'. Much of play is about imagination, pretence or make believe - no props required. Other players pretend things are there when they are not, and substitute what is at hand for missing objects or the things that don't actually exist (or don't exist yet? Perhaps play is the place new things are first imagined?). But now let's look at tangible things.

THE QUESTIONS TO CONSIDER ARE:

OUTDOOR PLAY EQUIPMENT
Have our concerns over risk and the lack of clarity over Health and Safety guidance led to impoverished outdoor play in schools? Why are some resources for play outdoors important (not essential, but often much appreciated)? How can everyday, disposable materials support play on the playground and in other outdoor spaces?

DO WE NEED A TOY TO MAKE A STORY?
Can we play without resources? What is the child's point of view about that? Do we make assumptions about which resources suit which children best? Can some toys limit play rather than encourage it?

OUTDOOR PLAY EQUIPMENT

In England not only have conkers, and famously yo-yos, been banned from schools, but other playtime bans have included any touch, hide and seek and having best friends (Gill 2012).

With options removed for competitive, social and physical play, children spend their time 'mooching' (Thomson 2003). Now 'mooching' definitely has its place - on the days you feel like mooching. But when children are wandering aimlessly around because they are not allowed to run, chase, or hide; then their natural exuberance is being squandered. When they are unable to quarrel or kiss and make up, then their outlet for self-expression is being denied. Then even on days when children feel like jumping for joy, they may end up just 'mooching' around.

In Chapter 3 we learned how important physical play is for wellbeing and social inclusion and I can't imagine anyone reading this is in any doubt how valuable best friends are throughout life. I know Gill is talking about a few schools and about 'worst-case scenarios,' but I also believe that the balance has been lost and that there is not enough rambunctious (definition? - wildly boisterous) playtime in children's lives. Mooching feels like an activity for 'blue' days or for 'I don't know what to do' days, not for your average everyday school day.

And it really doesn't have to be this way. There are many movements, such as the Outdoor Play and Learning Programme (OPAL) (Lester et al 2011) that are changing school playgrounds and outdoor play provision in schools.

> Previously we had lots of sports equipment that could only be used in specific ways, and it always got broken or lost; now the scrap means that children can do endless things, more scope, and it doesn't matter about breakage as it can be replenished - there is always something new/different to play with.   Lester, Jones & Russell 2011, p.41

Some schools in the South West of England have taken on board similar ideas to South Gloucestershire Council's OPAL Programme. The idea of providing lots of scrap materials for playground playtimes frees children to play, and frees supervising adults from having to put limits on how resources can be used.

The Scrapstore Playpods (2013) programme is a scheme involving playworkers training staff in new skills to also support play with scrap materials in outdoor play areas. Feedback on the scheme suggests that children who have been engaged and active during playground playtimes behave differently after the play opportunities than when they have not had such scope for creativity and team work. Schools report that before they introduced the playpods materials, children:

After the programme started, children:

had fewer fights ☆ were more focussed after playtimes ☆ argued less
had smoother transition back into class
were calmer ☆ had less 'fall out' after breaks ☆ were more included

How would any school or Headteacher not want all of those great outcomes from the challenge and fun of play during their school day? As a parent, would you want your child getting the opportunity to develop all those social skills and maybe get physically fitter into the bargain? Yes please!

DO WE NEED A TOY TO MAKE A STORY?

Children feel differently about the need for 'things' to play with:

You don't always need toys to play; you can play with your imagination.

Eight-year-old girl

If you didn't have toys - you wouldn't be playing.

Nine-year-old boy *in* IPA Scotland 2011, p.29

In an IPA Scotland survey only 21% of the children asked thought that they needed toys in order to play (*ibid*). Not only do different children see the need for toys as of varying importance, but a child feels very different about resources on different days, in different moods and with different playmates.

You need toys for days when it's dark and stormy.   Ten-year-old girl, *ibid*

History and geography are no barriers to the universality of play resources. 'Children's play is supported by adults in all cultures by the manufacture of play equipment and toys' (Whitebread 2012, p.5). Archaeological digs in ancient cultures evidence support this claim. Early examples of play things include:

dice

gaming sticks

gaming boards

various forms of ball-play

miniature models made of pottery and metal, most probably used as toys

for children

drawings showing depictions of people playing and play objects such as

tops, dolls and rattles   *ibid* p.9

Play resources are many and varied, from boxes to blankets and pans to puddles. One difference in resources marketed as toys can be their limitation. Some toys do not lend themselves to play! Toys or specific play resources can also be expensive, and because of that become 'precious' and have 'rules' and restrictions on their use. *"It's not strong enough"; "It's not for big children"; "It's not meant to be used like that"* - all phrases guaranteed to inhibit play, which is a shame. Or maybe the rules and restrictions lead to resistance or rule-breaking from children, and that leads to we adults completely closing down the play.

Play indoors can benefit from the same idea as the Scrapstore Playpods (*see above*) - play materials that are not precious or expensive to replace make for relaxed adults and children who can improvise and create in endless ways. Such provision also removes the need to segregate children or resources by age or ability. Most play resources carry warnings for under-three year olds, and increasingly under-five year olds, on choking hazards associated with small pieces. Formal games, from snap to monopoly and five piece puzzles to thousand piece jigsaws may suggest which age it is suitable for. Otherwise the choice of which toys we provide for children is mostly about our perceptions of who likes what. This can be about a 'one size' cultural and social norm that may not 'fit all'.

My own experience has been that 13-year-old boys love playing with the doll's house and dressing up in the pink tutu and feather boa. A doll's house is the most symbolic of toys - it is a miniature representation of home and family. It is a space that represents the influences that form us, the constraints that contain us and the future independence we fear or long for. And the pink paraphernalia? Fun - pure and simple; or risk taking - *"I dare you!"*, or a question of identity; or a moment of regression to memories of dressing-up games and the freedom of being a five-year-old. Who knows? And who needs to know? That is the wonder of play.

Anytime, anyplace, anywhere

Play *will* happen. Sometimes my best toy is a rubber band, other times it is a phone or a serviette or a (jet propelled) office chair! Sometimes my play space is a department store, my car, the supermarket queue or the space between my ears. When I am an able player I can use anything or nothing, anywhere and nowhere. I often recognise when I am playing, but I'm sure I don't always realise that I am.

Seeing and believing when *others* are playing may need more attention and understanding on my part. When we get better at this we can support children's play with resources, whether they are resources we can see or whether it is their internal resourcefulness at play.

KEY POINTS

> *You are the most important resource*
>
> *Other children are usually a child's favourite resource*
>
> *Play does not need expensive toys or equipment*
>
> *Often play needs no resources at all - other than whatever is readily available in the environment when play breaks out*

Providing resources: *Where do we go from here?*

Although you are, and always will be, the *most* important resource, start to see the world around us as a resource and (nearly everything in it). Here is an idea to keep you busy.

Resources have to be safe but can be unconventional, cheap and even free (like Scrapstore playpods, see above). When I train school staff I always challenge them to fill a margarine or ice-cream tub (a clean one!) with a selection of everyday items, natural objects and free give-away toys or charity shop finds and the trainee who has the most exciting selection and spent the least money wins. Bearing the safety clause in mind (not broken, no jagged edges, no objects that are small if for children under five and so on) see what you can do. Then use your box of goodies to create your own world in a tray of sand, a shallow box or on a piece of material or card.

The play-full school would -

☺   Value play *without* resources as much as play *with*

☺   Recognise the ingenuity of children who use resources in innovative and alternative ways

☺   Create places where all children can play with resources that have been thought by some to be age or gender specific

☺   Value the most important resource of all - the staff

. . . .

If you want to know more, try reading

Some of the articles on the Toy Industries of Europe website, tietoy.org/publications, and find out lots about the development of the toy industry and take the opportunity to check out their reports on toy safety too. Take a trip down memory lane with their timeline of toys and find out about toys in other places and other times.

Lester, S., Jones, O. & Russell, W. (2011) Supporting School Improvement through Play. An Evaluation of South Gloucestershire's Outdoor Play and Learning Programme (OPAL). Play England. London: NCB. Available at: playengland. org.uk/media/340836/ supporting-school-improvement-through-play.pdf

If you want to understand more, try reading

Murphy, J. (2007) *Whatever Next* London: Macmillan Children's Books

If you want a 15 minute group or individual training, try watching

'The best kindergarten you have ever seen,' **Takaharu Tezuka**'s 2014 TED talk may be something to aspire to. Catch it on the TED website ted/talks, or on youtube.com

Conclusion

... and they all lived happily ever after

Once upon a time there was a world where everyone played. Dreamers dreamed, and problem-solvers fixed things, while thinkers thought up new questions. Artists created wonders for all to enjoy, and everyone laughed and everyone cried while sometimes time flew by and other times time stood still. In the world where everyone played, life was play and everyone played until they were all played out. Then they slept. And the next day when they awoke the world was new. So they all played again in order to understand and rejoice in the newness of it all.

The future for better play in better schools

Play: The boundary-challenging, reality defying, insanely optimistic, relentlessly experimental activity of children.   Kane 2005, p.3

Play is a landscape for living where colours are more vibrant, feelings are more intense and where anything is possible. Getting to play lots and lots makes it more likely a child will be optimistic, adaptable, creative, confident, sociable, popular and kind.

When you feel joyful you want to play. When you feel depressed it's hard to play but it helps you get better. You can play alone, in a pair or in groups. When you play you can run, jump, shout and jostle, or you can be completely silent and still. 'Play in all its rich variety is one of the highest achievements of the human species' (Whitebread 2012, p.3).

To Whitebread, play is an achievement: to educators and child-care workers, play achieves miracles. Play changes the brain. It changes the chemicals in the brain and it changes the structures in the brain. When we who work in schools work with this brain-changing phenomenon, we help each child to develop to their full potential.

Here comes the science bit - concentrate!   L'Oreal Elvive advert

> Knowledge of how the brain develops and learns will have a profound impact on education in the future. Understanding the brain mechanisms that underlie learning and memory, and the effects of genetics, the environment, emotion, and age on learning could transform educational strategies and enable us to design programs that optimise learning for people of all ages and of all needs.
>
> Blakemore 2010, p.746

The future depends on us using all the knowledge available to us to design and deliver relevant, appropriate and life-enhancing programmes in our schools. Reflecting on the theory you read in this book, you will better understand the needs of children; and using and developing the 'how to' skills, you will be better prepared to meet those needs.

When training for school staff, both in initial qualification and ongoing professional development, encompasses the learning from neuroscientists and ethnographers who help us to know what it means to be human, schools will be full of our passion for play.

Play looks to the future, and so must we. Aspirations are built on the 'hope in the not-yet' (Amin 2006, p.1010). The future, yet-to-be world where everyone plays would surely produce the future citizens that Sir Ken Robinson (2006) says everyone will want. People who:

see connections ☆ have bright ideas ☆ are innovative

communicate ☆ work well with others ☆ are problem-solvers

Robinson, among many others, advocates that we need a new kind of education that equips pupils to meet the new challenges of the 21st Century. He and others insist a new school ethos and curriculum must have creativity at its core. The challenges facing the world will need new ways of thinking, new ways of people relating to people and new priorities for how we all live together. We are going to need creativity, imaginative solutions, and as yet un-thought of possibilities in order to sustain life and wellbeing on earth. Playful workers, playful carers and playful researchers will create new ways of using world resources and of better sharing this increasingly shrinking and precious place in which we live.

Whatever the circumstances, play matters more than almost anything else to children. We deny them their right to play at our peril. At the end of the day, play *really* matters. It matters to society, to schools and to families; but most of all it matters to the child.

"I was trying to play so much. I told my mother later I was playing as much as I could because I had a feeling that if something happened and the fighting and shelling came back, I may die and I will never get another chance to play."

Ten-year-old girl in the Lebanese civil war

in Assal & Farrell, 1992, p.281

Maybe we don't all get to live happily ever after, but play can bring happiness into the darkest of places.

Play is the way that we learn, the way we make friends, the way we heal our souls and our minds. It makes strong bodies, flexible brains and joyful hearts. The resilience play develops matters more than all the knowledge and skills it cultivates.

Life is not about how fast you run or how high you climb but how well you bounce.   Komori, 2011

At the end of the day, and the end of this book, the call for *better play in schools* is about giving children the opportunities to do what comes naturally; because there will always be a very good reason why children need to play. Thank you for travelling with me through the amazing world of play. Your passion for allowing for play is another step towards that yet-to-be world, where everyone plays. But more important than that, your playfulness will help you to bounce, and will nurture the bounce-back-ability in everyone you work with and play with! I know play has done that for me, and I'm really glad to have shared it with you.

References

20ᵗʰ Century Fox (1988) *Big* (Motion Picture) Marshall, P. (Director) United States: 20ᵗʰ Century Fox

Adams, S. (2005) Practitioners and Play: Reflecting in a different way *in* Moyles, J. (Ed)
  The Excellence of Play Maidenhead: Open University Press

Ailwood, J. (2011) It's About Power: Researching play, pedagogy and participation in the early years
  of school *in* Rogers, S. (Ed) *Rethinking play and Pedagogy in Early Childhood Education: Concepts,
  contexts and cultures* Oxon: Routledge

Almond, D. (2013) *Desert Island Discs* Broadcast 10 March 2013

APA (American Psychological Association) (2014) apa.org

Amin, A. (2006) The Good City *Urban Studies*, Vol 43:5-6 pp.1009-1023

Anderson, C., Shibuya, A., Ihori, N., Swing, E., Bushman, B., Sakamoto, A. & Saleem, M. (2010) Violent
  Video Game Effects on Aggression, Empathy, and Prosocial Behavior in Eastern and Western
  countries *Psychological Bulletin,* Vol. 136, pp.151-173

Assal, A. and Farrell, E. (1992) Attempts to Make Meaning of Terror: Family, play, and school in time of
  civil war *Anthropology & Education Quarterly* Vol. 23:4 pp.275-290

Badenoch, B. (2008) *Being a Brain-wise Therapist: A practical guide to interpersonal neurobiology* NY: Norton

Bailey, D. S. & Bailey, D. R. (1993) *Therapeutic Approaches to the Care of the Mentally Ill* (Edition 3)
  Philadelphia: F.A. Davis Company

Ball, D., Gill, T. & Spiegel, B. (2008) *Managing Risk in Play Provision: Implementation Guide* Play England
  Nottingham: DCSF Publications

BBC (British Broadcasting Association) (1971) *The Morecambe and Wise Show*
  Season 6, Episode 7 The Christmas Show Broadcast 25 December 1971, 20.00 hrs

BBC (British Broadcasting Association) (2007) *The Catherine Tate Christmas Show* 25 December 2007
  Anderson, G. (Director)

Bekoff, M. (2011) *The Child's Right to Play: Let children be animals* Huffington Post The Blog. Posted: 08/13/11

Bekoff, M., & Allen, C. (1997) Intentional Communication and Social Play: How and why animals negotiate and agree to play in Bekoff, M & Byers, J. (Eds) *Animal Play: Evolutionary, comparative, and ecological perspectives* Cambridge NY: Cambridge University Press

Bekoff, M., & Allen, C. (2002) The Evolution of Social Play: Interdisciplinary analyses of cognitive processes in Bekoff, M., Allen, C. & Burghardt, G. (Eds) *The Cognitive Animal: Empirical and theoretical perspectives on animal cognition* Cambridge, Massachusetts: MIT Press

Bettner, B. & Lew, A. (1990) *Raising Kids Who Can* Newton, MA: Connexions Press

Blackard, S. (2012) *Say What You See for Parents and Teachers* Austin Texas: Language of Listening

Blastland, M. & Spiegelhalter, D. (2013) *The Norm Chronicles: Stories and numbers about danger* London: Profile Books Ltd.

Bodrova, E. & Leong, D. (2011) Revisiting Vygotskian Perspectives on Play and Pedagogy in Rogers, S. (Ed) *Rethinking Play and Pedagogy in Early Childhood Education: Concepts, Contexts and Cultures* Oxon: Routledge

Bombèr, L. (2007) *Inside I'm Hurting: Practical strategies for supporting children with attachment difficulties in school* London: Worth Publishing

Boseley, S. (2013) Ten Ways to Live Longer *The Guardian* 5 March 2013

Bratton, S., Landreth, G., Kellam, T. & Blackard, S. (2006) *Child Parent Relationship Therapy (CPRT) Treatment Manual* New York: Routledge

Bredikyte, M. (2012) *Adult Play Guidance and Children's Play Development* presentation at ICCP conference, Tallinn, 2012 iccp-play.org/documents/tallinn/bredikyte.pdf

Broadhead, P. (2004) *Early Years Play and Learning* London: Routledge

Bronson, P. & Merryman, A. (2009) *Nurture Shock: Why everything we think we know about raising our children is wrong* London: Ebury Press.

Brooker, L. (2011) Taking Play Seriously in Rogers, S. (Ed) *Rethinking Play and Pedagogy in Early Childhood Education: Concepts, contexts and cultures* Oxon: Routledge

Brown, S. (2009) *Play: How it shapes the brain, opens the imagination and invigorates the soul* New York: Avery

Bruce, T. (2005) Play, the Universe and Everything in Moyles, J. *The Excellence of Play* Maidenhead Berks: Open University Press

Bruner, J. (1974) *Beyond the Information Given: Studies in the psychology of knowing* London: Allen & Unwin

Carlson, F. (2011) *Big Body Play: Why boisterous, vigorous, and very physical play is essential to children's development and learning* Washington, DC: National Association for the Education of Young Children

Cattanach A (1993) *Play Therapy with Abused Children* London: Jessica Kingsley Press

Cohen, L. (2001) *Playful Parenting* NY: Ballentine Books

Cornelli Sanderson, R. (2010) *Towards a New Measure of Playfulness: The capacity to fully and freely engage in play* Dissertations paper 232 ecommons.luc. Edu?luc_diss/232

Cozolino, L. (2013) *The Social Neuroscience of Education: Optimizing attachment & learning in the classroom* New York: W.W. Norton

Cozolino, L. (2014) *Attachment-Based Teaching: Creating a tribal classroom* New York: W.W. Norton

Craig, C. (2007) *The Potential Dangers of a Systematic, Explicit Approach to Teaching Social and Emotional Skills (SEAL) Available at:* centreforconfidence.co.uk/docs/EI-SEAL_September_2007.pdf

Crenshaw, D. & Stewart, A. (2015) *Play Therapy: A comprehensive guide to theory and practice* New York: The Guilford Press

Davis, C. (1990) What is Empathy, and Can Empathy be Taught? *Physical Therapy.* Vol. 70:11 pp.707-715

DeBenedet, A. & Cohen, L. (2010) *The Art of Roughhousing: Good old-fashioned horseplay and why every kid needs it* Philadelphia: Quirk Books

Decety, J. (2010) To What Extent is the Experience of Empathy Mediated by Shared Neural Circuits? *Emotion Review* Vol. 2:3 pp.204-207 Sage Publications

Delaney, M. (2009) *Teaching the Unteachable: Practical ideas to give teachers hope and help when behaviour management strategies fail* London: Worth Publishing

De Lauretis, T. (1987) *Technologies of Gender: Essays on theory, film and fiction* London: Macmillan

Delors, J. (1996) *Learning, the Treasure Within: Report to Unesco of the International Commission on Education for the Twenty-First Century* Paris: Unesco Pub

Department for Education (DfE) (2014a) *Universal Infant Free School Meals: Departmental advice for local authorities, maintained schools, academies and free schools* London: DfE

Department for Education (DfE) (2014b) *Statutory Framework for the Early Years Foundation Stage: Setting the standards for learning, development and care for children from birth to five* Manchester: Department for Education

Desai, R., Maciejewski, P., Dausey, D., Caldarone, B. & Potenza, M. (2004) Health Correlates of Recreational Gambling in Older Adults *in American Journal of Psychiatry* Vol. 161:9 pp.1672-1679

Disney (1951) *Alice in Wonderland* (Motion Picture) Geronimi, C; Jackson, W. & Luske, H. (Directors) USA: Walt Disney Pictures

Disney (1995) *Toy Story* (Motion Picture) Lasseter, J. (Director) USA: Walt Disney Pictures Pixar Animation Studios

Disney (2003) *Pirates of the Caribbean* (Motion picture), Verbinski, G; Marshall, R; Ronning, J; Sandberg, E. (Directors) USA: Walt Disney Pictures

Disney (2010) *Like Stars on Earth: Every Child is Special* (Motion Picture) Kahn, A. & Gupte, A. (Directors) "Taare Zameen Par" (original title, 2007) USA: Walt Disney Company Home Entertainment

Doherty, J. (2007) Play for Children with Special Educational Needs *in* Brock, A., Dodds, S., Jarvis, P. & Olusoga, Y. (Eds) *Perspectives on Play: Learning for life* Harlow Essex: Pearson Education

Donaldson, J. (1999) *The Gruffalo* London: Macmillan Children's Books

Dr Suess (2003) *Oh, The Places You'll Go!* UK: Harper Collins

Dreikurs, R., Grunwald, B. & Pepper, F. (1971) *Maintaining Sanity in the Classroom: Illustrated teaching techniques* New York: Harper & Row

Edmiston, B. (2011) 'We are Hunters and Gatherers of Values': Dramatic play, early childhood pedagogy, and the formation of ethical identities *in* Rogers, S. (Ed) *Rethinking Play and Pedagogy in Early Childhood Education: Concepts, contexts and cultures* Oxon: Routledge

Elkind, D. (2007) *The Power of Play* Philadelphia: Da Capo Press

Else, P. & Sturrock, G. (1998) *The Playground as Therapeutic Space: Playwork as healing* Presented at 'Play in a Changing Society: Research, Design, Application' The IPA/USA Triennial National Conference 1998, Longmont, Colorado USA

English Teachers Network (1997) ETNI etni.org.il/bestteacherever.htm

Farb, N., Zindel, V., Segal, Z., Mayberg, H., Bean, J., McKeon, D., Fatima, Z. & Anderson, A. (2007) Attending to the Present: Mindfulness meditation reveals distinct neural modes of self-reference *Social, Cognitive and Affective Neuroscience* Vol. 2:4 pp.313-322

Feynman, R. (1985) *Surely You're Joking, Mr. Feynman! (Adventures of a Curious Character)* NY: W.W. Norton

Fisher, D. (1981) *Communication in Organizations* St. Paul, Minnesota: West Publishing Company

Frost, J. (2010) *A History of Children's Play and Play Environments: Toward a contemporary child-saving movement* NY: Routledge

Garbarino, J. (2000) *Lost Boys* New York: Anchor Books

Garvey, C. (1991) *Play* London: Fontana Press

Geddes, H. (2006) *Attachment in the Classroom: The links between children's early experience, emotional wellbeing and performance in school* London: Worth Publishing

Geldard, K. & Geldard, D. (1997) *Counselling Children* London: Sage

Gill, T. (2007) *No Fear: Growing up in a risk averse society* London: Calouste Gulbenkian Foundation

Gill, T. (2011) *Free Range Kids: Why children need simple pleasures and everyday freedom, and what we can do about it* Dairylea Simple Fun Report

Gill, T. (2012) *Schoolchildren Banned from Playing Hide-and-seek - and that's just for starters. Available at:* rethinkingchildhood.com/2012/02/16/school-ban/

Gladwell, M. (2008) *Outliers* Boston, Ma: Little, Brown & Company

Gleave, J. & Cole-Hamilton, I. (2012) *A World without Play: A literature review on the effects of a lack of play on children's lives* A report for the British Toy & Hobby Association with Play England.

Gordon, M. (2009) *Roots of Empathy: Changing the world child by child* NY: The Experiment

Gove, M. (2013) Michael Gove Proposes Longer School Day and Shorter Holidays *The Guardian* 18 April 2013

Gray, P. (2011) The Decline of Play and the Rise of Psychopathology in Children and Adolescents *American Journal of Play* Vol. 3:4 pp.443-463

Griffin, J. & Tyrrell, I. (2003) *Human Givens* Chalvington, East Sussex: HG Publishing

Gupta, A. (2011) Play and Pedagogy Framed within India's Historical, Socio-cultural, Pedagogical and Postcolonial Context *in* Rogers, S. (Ed) *Rethinking play and Pedagogy in Early Childhood Education: Concepts, contexts and cultures* Oxon: Routledge

Hae-Ryung Yeu (2011) Deconstructing the Metaphysics of Play Theories: Towards a pedagogy of play aesthetics *in* Rogers, S. (Ed) *Rethinking play and Pedagogy in Early Childhood Education: Concepts, contexts and cultures* Oxon: Routledge

Hammerstein, O. (1985) *Lyrics by Oscar Hammerstein 11* Milwaukee WI: Hal Leonard Books

Harris, D. (2012) *Brave Heads: How to lead a school without selling your Soul* Camarthen: Independent Thinking Press

Harvard Medical School (2013) *Understanding Depression: A Harvard Medical School Special Health Report* US: Harvard Health Publications

Health & Safety Executive (HSE) (2012) *Children's Play and Leisure - Promoting a balanced approach* Available at: hse.gov.uk/entertainment/childrens-play-july-2012.pdf

Holt-Lunstad, J., Smith T. & Layton, J. (2010) Social Relationships and Mortality Risk: A Meta-analytic Review *PLoS Med 7:7* (online)

Holland, P. (2003) *We Don't Play With Guns Here* Maidenhead: Open University Press

Howard, J. & McInnes, K. (2013) The Impact of Children's Perception of an Activity as Play Rather than not Play on Emotional Well-being *in Child: Care, Health and Development* Vol. 39:5, pp.737-742

Huffington Post (2012) *Best Education In The World: Finland, South Korea Top Country Rankings, U.S. Rated Average* Posted: 11/27/2012

Hughes, B. (2012) *Evolutionary Playwork* (Second Edn) London: Routledge

Hughes, F. (1999) *Children, Play, and Development* (Third Edn) Boston: Allyn and Bacon

Hyvonen, P. (2011) Play in the School Context? The perspectives of Finnish teachers *Australian Journal of Teacher Education*: Vol.36: 8 pp.65-83

IPA (Scotland) (2011) *"I'd play all day and night if I could": A Report on Children's Views on Their Right to Play* A consultation by The Children's Parliament on Behalf of The International Play Association (Scotland) Available at: ipascotland.org/wp-content/uploads/2014/09/Right-to-Play-Report-IPA-CP1.pdf

Jarvis, P. (2009) Building 'Social Hardiness' for Life: Rough and tumble play in the early years of primary school *in* Brock, A., Dodds, S., Jarvis, P. & Olusoga, Y. *Perspectives on Play: Learning for life* Harlow Essex: Pearson Education

Jarvis, P, & George, J. (2009) Play, Learning for Life: The vital role of play in human development *in* Brock, A., Dodds, S., Jarvis, P. & Olusoga, Y. *in Perspectives on Play: Learning for life* Harlow Essex: Pearson Education

Jarvis, P., Newman, S. & Swiniarski, L. (2014) On 'Becoming Social': The importance of collaborative free play in childhood *International Journal of Play* Vol. 3:1 pp.53-68 Routledge

Jones, E. & Reynolds, G. (2011) *The Play's the Thing* (2nd Edn)   NY: Teachers College Press

Jones, G. (2002) *Killing Monsters: Why children need fantasy, super heroes, and make believe violence* NY: Basic Books

Joseph, J. (1996) Warning *in* Jones, G. R. *The Nations Favourite Poems*   London: BBC Books

Kane, P. (2005) *The Play Ethic: A manifesto for a different way of living*   London: Pan Books

Kapasi, H. & Gleave, J. (2009) *Because It's Freedom; Children's views on their time to play* A Report for Play England   London: National Children's Bureau.

Karr-Morse, R. & Wiley, S. (1997) *Ghosts from the Nursery: Tracing the roots of violence* NY: Atlantic Monthly Press

Keeley, J. (2009) *Moving Towards Safe Uncertainty: The development of resilience and excitement in the future*   Available at: keeleycarlisle.co.uk/Movingtowardssafeuncertainty.pdf

Kellmer Pringle, M. (2000) *The Needs of Children*   London: Routledge

Kemp, G., Smith, M., DeKoven, B. & Segal, J. (2013) *Play, Creativity and Lifelong Learning* Available at: helpguide.org/life/creative_play_fun_games.htm

Kestly, T. & Badenoch, B. (2015) *The Interpersonal Neurobiology of Play: Brain-Building interventions for emotional well-being*   US: W.W.Norton

Kipling, R. (1939) *Sixty Poems*   London: Hodder & Stoughton

Kohl, H. (2009) *The Herb Kohl Reader*   New York: New Press

Komori, V. (2011) threemotivationalquotes.com/tag/vivian-komori/

Kuschner, D. (2012a) Play is Natural to Childhood but School is not: The problem of integrating play into the curriculum *International Journal of Play* Vol.1:3 pp.242-249

Landreth, G & Bratton, S. (2006) *Child Parent Relationship Therapy (CPRT)*   New York: Routledge

Langman, P. (2010) *Why Kids Kill: Inside the minds of school shooters*   New York: Palgrave Macmillan

Lathey, N. & Blake, T. (2013) *Small Talk: Simple ways to boost your child's speech and language development from birth*   London: Macmillan

Lehan, C., Morrison, J. & Stanley, J. (2004) *The Dignity of Risk*   London: NCB books

Lester, S. (2010) *Play and Ordinary Magic: The everydayness of play*   Playwork London Conference 2010   Available at: playworklondon.org.uk/upload/files/Playandordinarymagic3.pdf

Lester, S. (2011) *Moments of Nonsense and Signs of Hope: The everyday 'political' nature of children's play* IPA Workshop Play Wales Conference

Lester, S. (2012) *Vibrant Spaces: Re-configuring adults 'providing play'* Paper presented at: Providing Play: Applications for policy and practice from research, ICCP Conference Tallinn 2012

Lester, S. (2014) Play as Protest: Clandestine moments of disturbance and hope *in* Burke, C. & Jones, K. (Eds) *Education, Childhood and Anarchism: Talking Colin Ward*   London: Routledge

Lester, S. & Maudsley, M. (2007) *Play, Naturally: A review of children's natural play* Playwork Partnerships A Report for Play England London: National Children's Bureau

Lester, S. & Russell, W. (2008) *Play for a Change: Play, Policy and Practice* A review of contemporary perspectives Summary Report for play London, England: National Children's Bureau

Lester, S. & Russell, W. (2010) *Children's Right to Play: An examination of the importance of play in the lives of children worldwide* Working Papers in Children's Early Development, 57 The Hague: Bernard van Leer Foundation

Lieberman, J. N. (1977) *Playfulness: Its relationship to imagination and creativity* New York: Academic Press

Lonne, B., Harries, M., Featherstone, B., & Gray, M. (2015) *Working Ethically in Child Protection* London: Routledge

Lotto, B. & O'Toole, A. (2012) *Science is for everyone, kids included* A TED talk, Available at: ted.com/talks/beau_lotto_amy_o_toole_science_is_for_everyone_kids_included.html

Marshall, N. (2014) *The Teacher's Introduction to Attachment: Practical essentials for teachers, carers and school support staff* London: Jessica Kingsley Publishers

Mayall, B. (2000) The Sociology of Childhood in Relation to Children's Rights *The International Journal of Children's Rights* Vol.8: pp.243-259

Mental Health Foundation (1999) *Bright Futures: Promoting children and young people's mental health* London: Mental Health

Menuhin, Y. en.wikiquote.org/wiki/Yehudi_Menuhin accessed 11.01.2015

Milne, A. A. (1938) *Winnie the Pooh (twentieth edition)* London: Methuen & Co

Miskin Group (2014) miskin-group.org.uk/

Mitrega, M. & Najgebaur, B. (2011) *Childhood: Between Duties and Play* Wroclaw University Institute of Pedagogy Presentation at Wales IPA Conference 2011, Cardiff

Moberg, K. U. (2003) *The Oxytocin Factor: Tapping the hormone of calm, love, and healing* US: Da Capo Press

Morgan, N. (2005) *Blame My Brain: The amazing teenage brain revealed* London: Walker Books

Morpurgo, M. (2008) *Hansel and Gretel* London: Walker Books

Moyles, J. (1989) *Just Playing: Role and status of play in early childhood education* Buckingham: Open University Press

Moyles, J. (2005) Introduction *in* Moyles, J. (Ed) *The Excellence of Play* Maidenhead: Open University Press

Neal, D. & Chartrand, T. (2011) Embodied Emotion Perception: Amplifying and dampening facial feedback modulates emotion perception accuracy *Social Cognition and Personality Science* Vol.2:6 pp.673-678

Norton, J. (2012) Chasing the Light: Einstein's most famous thought experiment *in* Brown, J., Frappier, M. & Meynell, L. (Eds) *Thought Experiments in Science, Philosophy, and the Arts* (Routledge Studies in the Philosophy of Science) New York: Routledge

Orbach, S. (2013) *The Prozac Economy* Radio 4 9 April 2013 Producer: Kate Taylor. A Whistledown
production for BBC Radio 4

O'Sullivan, L. & Ryan, V. (2009) Therapeutic Limits from an Attachment Perspective
Clinical Child Psychology & Psychiatry 2009 Vol.14:2 pp.215-35

Panksepp, J. (1998) *Affective Neuroscience: The Foundations of human and animal emotions* USA: OUP

Paley, V. G. (1997) *The Girl with the Brown Crayon* Cambridge, Ma: Harvard University Press

Paley, V. G. (1992) *You Can't Say You Can't Play* Cambridge, Ma: Harvard University Press

Pellis, S. (2002) Keeping in Touch: Play fighting and social knowledge *in* Bekoff, M., Allen, C. &
Burghardt, G. (Eds) *The Cognitive Animal: Empirical and theoretical perspectives on animal
cognition* Massachusetts: MIT Press

Pellis, S. & Pellis, V. (2009) *The Playful Brain: Venturing to the limits of neuroscience* Oxford: One World

Perrault (2002) *Cinderella: A fairy tale* NY: North-South Books: New edition

Play England (2008) *Play in Schools and Integrated Settings: A position statement*
London: National Children's Bureau

Playlink playlink.org/about

Play Safety Forum (2008) *Managing Risk in Play Provision: A position statement* London: Play England

PTUK (Play Therapy UK) (2011) *An Introduction to Play Therapy* Available at playtherapy.org.uk/
Resources/Articles/ArticleMBIntro1.htm#First%20Principles

Play Wales (2003) *Play Deprivation: Facts and interpretations* playwales.org.uk

Proyer, R. (2013) The Well-Being of Playful Adults: Adult playfulness, subjective well-being, physical wellbeing, and the pursuit of enjoyable activities *European Journal of Humour Research* 1:1 pp.84-98
online open access europeanjournalofhumour.org

Riley, P. (2010) *Attachment Theory and the Teacher-Student Relationship* Oxford: Routledge

Robinson, K. (2013) *How to Escape Education's Death Valley* A TED talk
Available at: ted.com/playlists/125/tv_special_ted_talks_educatio.html

Robinson, K. (2006) *How Schools Kill Creativity* A TED talk
Available at: ted.com/talks/ken_robinson_says_schools_kill_creativity.html

Ropeik, D. (2010) *How Risky is it Really? Why our fears don't always match the facts* US: McGraw-Hill

Rosen, M. (1997) *We're Going on a Bear Hunt* London: Walker Books Ltd

Russ, S. & Niec, L. (2011) *Play in Clinical Practice: Evidence-based approaches* NY: The Guilford Press

Samples, B. (1976) *The Metaphoric Mind: A celebration of creative consciousness*
Reading, Massachusetts: Addison-Wesley Publishing Company

Sandseter, E. (2011) Children's Risky Play in Early Childhood Education and Care *ChildLinks*
Iss.3 pp.2-6 Dublin: Barnardos

Sawyer, S., Afifi, R., Bearinger, L., Blakemore, S-J, Dick, B., Ezeh, A. & Patton, G. (2012) Adolescence: A foundation for future health *The Lancet*, Vol.379:9826 pp.1630-1640

Scrapstore Playpods (2013) playpods.co.uk

Sendak, M. (2000) *Where The Wild Things Are* (New Edn) London: Red Fox

Shafir, R. (2010) Mindful Listening for Better Outcomes *in* Hick, S. & Bien, T. (Eds) *Mindfulness in the Therapeutic Relationship* (Reprint Edn) NY: Guilford Press

Siegel, D. (1999) *The Developing Mind: How relationships and the brain interact to shape who we are* New York: Guilford Press

Siegel, M. (1996) *Heinz Kohut and the Psychology of the Self* London: Routledge

Singer, D., Golinkoff, R & Hirsh-Pasek, K. (Eds) (2006) *Play = Learning: How play motivates and enhances children's cognitive and social-emotional growth* NY: Oxford University Press

Smith, D. (2012) *Sandtray Play and Storymaking* London: Jessica Kinsley Publishing

Smith, P. (2012) *Understanding School Bullying* London: Sage Publications

Steen, M. & Thomas, M. (Eds) (2016) *Mental Health Across the Lifespan: A handbook* Abingdon, Oxon: Routledge

Sturgess, J. (2009) Play as Child Chosen Activity *in* Cattanach, A., Stagnitti, K. & Cooper, R. *Play as Therapy: Assessment and therapeutic interventions* London: Jessica Kingsley Publishers

Sunderland, M. (2006) *The Science of Parenting* London: DK Publishing

Sunderland, M (2009) *Play, therapy and the developing brain; learning from neuroscience* BAPT Conference keynote, Birmingham, 27 June

Sutton-Smith, B. (1997) *The Ambiguity of Play* Cambridge, MA: Harvard University Press

Sutton-Smith, B. (2001) *The Ambiguity of Play* (New Edn) Cambridge, MA: Harvard University Press

Sutton-Smith, B. (2002) Recapitulation Redressed *in* Roopnarine, J. (Ed) *Conceptual, Social-Cognitive, and Contextual Issues in the Fields of Play* Vol.4 Westport: Ablex

Sweiry, D. & Willitts, M. (2012) *Attitudes to Age in Britain* 2010/11 Department for Work and Pensions In-house Research No 7. Sheffield: Department for Work and Pensions

Szalavitz, M. & Perry, B. (2010) *Born for Love* NY: Harper

The Children's Society (2013) *The Good Childhood Report 2013* London: The Children's Society

The Free Dictionary (2013) thefreedictionary.com/vital

Thomson, S. (2003) A Well Equipped Hamster Cage: The rationalisation of primary school Playtime *Education* 3-13: International Journal of Primary, Elementary and Early Years Education Vol. 31:2 pp.54-59

Thompson, S., Aked, J., Marks, N. & Cordon, C. (2008) *Five Ways to Well-being: The evidence* nef (the new economics foundation) Available at: neweconomics.org/publications/entry/five-ways-to-well-being-the-evidence

Tovey. H. (2007) *Playing Outdoors: Spaces and places, risk and challenge* Maidenhead, UK: Open University Press

Trawick-Smith, J. (1998) School-Based Play and Social Interaction *in* Fromberg, D & Bergen, D. (Eds) *Play from Birth to Twelve and Beyond* NY: Garland Publishing

Turkle, S. (2012) *Alone Together: Why we expect more from technology and less from each other* Philadelphia: Basic Books

Turkle, S. (2015) *Reclaiming Conversation* NY: Penguin Press

Twain, M. (1992) *Tom Sawyer and Huckleberry Finn* (Wordsworth Classics) Ware, Herts: Wordsworth Editions

Ulanov, A. (2001) *Finding Space: Winnicott, God and psychic reality* Westminster: John Knox Press, U.S

UNICEF (2013) *Child Well-being in Rich Countries: A comparative overview* Available at: unicef-irc.org/publications/pdf/rc11_eng.pdf

United Artists (1976) *Rocky* (Motion picture) Avildsen, J. (Director) US: United Artists

Van Dyke, J. (2012) Skeletons in the Closet: Death as the last taboo huffingtonpost.com/janice-van-dyck/death-taboo_b_828554.html

Van Fleet, R. (2000) *A Parent's Handbook of Filial Play Therapy* Boiling Springs PA: Play Therapy Press

Voce, A. (2007) Foreword to Lester, S. & Maudsley, M. *Play Naturally: A review of children's natural play* Play England

Vygotsky, L. (1978) *Mind in Society: The development of higher mental processes* (Trans. M. Cole) Cambridge, MA: Harvard University Press

Ward, C. (1978) *The Child in the City* London: Penguin Books

Watt, F. (2000) Is it Safe Enough to Learn? *in* Barwick, N. (Ed) *Clinical Counselling in Schools* London: Routledge

Weiner, B. (2010) The Development of an Attribution-Based Theory of Motivation: A history of ideas *Educational Psychologist* Vol.45:1 pp.28-36

Wellington, J., Bathmaker, A., Hunt, C., McCulloch, G., & Sikes, P. (Eds) (2005) *Succeeding with Your Doctorate* London: SAGE Publications Ltd

Welsh Assembly Government (2008) *School-Based Counselling Services in Wales* Cardiff: WAG

Wheway, R. (2011) Wales *Most Play Strategies are Wrong* IPA Conference, Cardiff, Wales

White, J., Draper, K. & Flynt, M. (2003) Kinder training: A school counselor and teacher consultation model integrating filial therapy and Adlerian theory *in* VanFleet, R. (Ed) *Casebook of Filial Therapy* Boiling Springs: Play Therapy Press

Whitebread, D. (2012) *The Importance of Play: A report on the value of children's play with a series of policy recommendations* Written for Toy Industries of Europe (TIE) Brussels

Wilson, R. (2001) A Sense of Place *EE News*, Vol.18: 2, pp.2-7.

Winnicott, D. (1974) *Playing and Reality* Middlesex: Pelican Books

Wood, E. (2012) The State of Play *International Journal of Play* Vol.1:1 pp.4-5

Woods, T. (2013) *BrainyQuote.com* brainyquote.com/quotes/authors/t/tiger_woods.html

Woolf, A. (2008) Better Play Times Training - Theory and practice in an EBD primary school *Emotional and Behavioural Difficulties* Vol.13:1 pp.1-14

Woolf, A. (2011) Everyone Playing in Class: A group play provision for enhancing the emotional well-being of children in school *British Journal of Special Education* Vol.38:4 pp.178-190

Woolf, A. (2013) Social and Emotional Aspects of Learning: Teaching and learning or playing and becoming? *Pastoral Care in Education* Vol.31:1 pp.28-42

Yarnal, C. & Qian, X. (2011) Older-Adult Playfulness: An innovative construct and measurement for healthy aging research *American Journal of Play* Vol.4:1 pp.52-79
Rochester, NY: The STRONG

Young Engineers UK young-engineers.co.uk

Young Minds (2014) youngminds.org.uk/about/whats_the_problem/mental_health_statistics

Zull, J. (2002) *The Art of Changing the Brain: Enriching the practice of teaching by exploring the biology of learning* Sterling: Stylus Publishing

Index